Andreas
Moritz

Ener-Chi  Wellness Press

Also by Andreas Moritz

• • •

Timeless Secrets of Health & Rejuvenation
(Formerly: The Key to Health and Rejuvenation)

The Amazing Liver & Gallbladder Flush
(Formerly: The Amazing Liver Cleanse)

Lifting the Veil of Duality
(Formerly: Freedom from Judgment)

Cancer Is Not A Disease

Art of Self-Healing
(available soon)

Sacred Santémony

Ener-Chi Art

It's Time to
Come Alive

***Start Using the Amazing Healing Powers
of Your Body, Mind and Spirit Today!***

Your Health is in Your Hands

For Reasons of Legality

The author of this book, Andreas Moritz, does not advocate the use of any particular form of health care but believes that the facts, figures, and knowledge presented herein should be available to every person concerned with improving his or her state of health. Although the author has attempted to give a profound understanding of the topics discussed and to ensure accuracy and completeness of any information that originates from any other source than his own, he and the publisher assume no responsibility for errors, inaccuracies, omissions, or any inconsistency herein. Any slights of people or organizations are unintentional. This book is not intended to replace the advice and treatment of a physician who specializes in the treatment of diseases. Any use of the information set forth herein is entirely at the reader's discretion. The author and publisher are not responsible for any adverse effects or consequences resulting from the use of any of the preparations or procedures described in this book. The statements made herein are for educational and theoretical purposes only and are mainly based upon Andreas Moritz's own opinion and theories. You should always consult with a health care practitioner before taking any dietary, nutritional, herbal or homeopathic supplement, or beginning or stopping any therapy. The author is not intending to provide any medical advice, or offer a substitute thereof, and make no warranty, expressed or implied, with respect to any product, device or therapy, whatsoever. Except as otherwise noted, no statement in this book has been reviewed or approved by the United States Food & Drug Administration or the Federal Trade Commission. Readers should use their own judgment or consult a holistic medical expert or their personal physicians for specific applications to their individual problems.

ISBN: 0-9765715-2-8

First edition, *It's Time to Wake Up*, 1998
Second edition, *It's Time to Come Alive* 2005/2006

Cover Artwork: Andreas Moritz

*As we leave behind the age of struggle and
ignorance we need to learn everything anew.*

*Only a new seed can yield a new crop.
And so, it is time now for a
new way of life.*

*It is time for Vibrant Health, Peace of Mind, and
Spiritual Wisdom.*

- Andreas Moritz -

Table of Contents:

Introduction   **xiii**

Chapter 1:

On the Road of Discovery   **1**

Maya – The World of Illusion   1

Lessons from the Past   3

Living the Law   4

The Turn of Destiny   6

The Ancient Message   8

Faith – A Healer?   8

Are We Spiritual by Nature?   9

What is the Body without its Mind?   10

Personality Shifts can Create "Miracles"   11

Chapter 2:

In Tune with Nature   **14**

Growing a New Limb   14

Instant Communication   15

Using the Power of Intent   16

The Amazing Memory Capacity of Water Molecules   17

Beings of Light   18

Invisible Messengers of Nature   18
There are no Secrets Under the Sun   20
Respecting the Sun   21
Only Fear is Dangerous   22
We are the World   23
The Mysterious "Odor Net"   26
Wisdom of the Plants   28
Do Plants have Feelings?   29
Losing Touch with Nature   31
The Plants' Willingness to Help   31
There is Purpose in all Life Forms   33

Chapter 3:

Well Begun is Half Done   **35**
Our Brain – A Universal Computer   35
A New Brain for a New Age   36
Wonders of the Brain   37
What Shapes Destiny   38
The Secret World of the Unborn Child   39
Rhythms of Happiness   41
Mixed Messages   42
The Workbook of Life   43
Surrender Your Past   44
Educated to be Ignorant   45
Consciousness – The Missing Link   46

Chapter 4:

It's All Within You   **49**
Escaping the Prison of Social Conditioning   49
You are What you Believe   51
Aging is a Choice   53
Who ages, Who doesn't?   54

Limitations Exist Only in the Mind   56

Opening the Heart   57

The Crime of Negative Thinking   58

You Can Make a Difference   60

No Thoughts are Secret   62

Ending the Mental Warfare   63

Doubting – the Cause of Failure   65

Material Wealth and Spiritual Wealth   66

Inner and Outer Abundance = 200% Life   67

Instant Results   68

Fatigue – The Beginning of a Vicious Cycle   69

Stress is caused by Fatigue   70

Chapter 5:

Healing the Cause   **72**

Emotions – Our Daily "Weather Report"   72

Repressing Emotions   73

The Physical Side of Emotions   74

Emotions and Body Types   76

Body Language   81

The Technique of Emotional Transformation   80

Emotional Welfare   85

Impatience Can Make You More Patient   86

Don't Try to Change Anyone   87

Conflicts are Opportunities for Growth   87

Depression – Anger Turned Inward   88

What Makes You Angry   90

"I Could" versus "I Should"   91

It's Okay to Say "No"   92

Get a Pet – It Can Make you Happy and Save your Life   94

Good Food – Good Mood   95

What Causes Mood Swings   95

The Mood Chemicals   97

Our Constitutional Disposition Towards Certain Moods   98

Two Important Things that Control Your Life   99

1. A Wholesome Diet   99

Sattva, Rajas and Tamas –Three Basic Forces of Life   100

The Sattvic Diet   101

The Rajasic Diet   102

The Tamasic Diet   103

2. The Power of Thought   103

A Change of Thoughts   103

Happiness – Your Key to Nature's Drug Store   105

Energy Follows Thought   106

Chapter 6:

The Principles and Technique of Primordial Healing   **108**

Part One: The Miracle of Conscious Breathing   108

Breath is All There is and Much More   108

How do I Start?   109

The Key to Success is "Letting go"   111

The Power of Attention   112

Part Two: Primordial Healing Sounds   113

You are What you Perceive   113

The World of Sounds   115

The Body – A Symphony Orchestra   117

Name and Form Relationship   117

Summary of the Technique of Primordial Healing   118

The Primordial Healing Sounds of the Seven Chakras   119

Primordial Siddhi Sounds   121

Chapter 7:

The Five Senses – Fountains of Youth   **123**

Healthy Senses for a Healthy Life   123

1. Inner and Outer Vision   124

The Importance of Liver Cleansing and Balanced Diet   124

Eye Exercises   126

A 1-7   126

B 1-7   127

Sunlight Eye-treatments   128

C 1-4   129

2. The World of Hearing   131

Hearing on all Levels   131

Sound Exercises   132

Vowel Power   132

Humming   133

Jaw Sounds   133

Throat Sounds   133

Stomach Sound   133

Sound Therapy   134

Music Therapy   135

Tuned to Heal   137

Ear Coning   139

3. Touch for Health   140

Marma Therapy   141

Body Techniques   142

4. Taste – An Intimate Source of Pleasure   143

Simple Rules for Healthy Eating   145

Better Taste   147

5. Sensing through Smell   148

Techniques for Improving your Sense of Smell   148

Chapter 8:

Spiritual Wisdom – Man's Final Lesson from Nature   **150**

Discovering the Love Frequency   150

Consciousness is the Key   152

Animals Know Something we Don't Know   154

Message from the Whales and Dolphins   155

Perhaps the Cows Are Holy After All   156
Learning the Hard Way   158
Respect for all Life   159
Earth knows Everything   161
The Healing Power of Mother Earth   161
The Planet is Alive   163
All Earth Changes Favor Life   164
The Shifting of Earth Poles   165
Entry into the New World   168
It's Time to Make a Choice   170
Owning the Wisdom of Nature   172
Conversing with Nature   173
Imagination Shapes Personal Reality   175

Chapter 9:

The Twelve Gateways to Heaven on Earth   **178**
1. The Gateway of Oneness   178
Opening the First Gateway   180
2. The Gateway of Solving All Problems   180
Opening the Second Gateway   183
3. The Gateway of Gaining Mastery over Time   184
Opening the Third Gateway   186
4. The Gateway of Abundance   187
Opening the Fourth Gateway   189
5. The Gateway of Success   190
Opening the Fifth Gateway   192
6. The Gateway of Non-Judgment   193
Opening the Sixth Gateway   195
7. The Gateway of the "Highest First"   196
Opening the Seventh Gateway   199
8. The Gateway of Silence   200
Opening the Eighth Gateway   203

9. The Gateway of Body Awareness   203
Opening the Ninth Gateway   205
10. The Gateway of Inner Guidance   206
Opening the Tenth Gateway   209
11. The Gateway of Spiritual Wisdom   209
Opening the Eleventh Gateway   212
12. The Gateway of Fulfilling Desires   213
Opening the Twelfth Gateway   218
Conclusion   220
A Simple Prayer   221

About The Author   222
Other Books, Products and Services by the Author   224
    Sacred Santémony   229
    Ener-Chi Art   230
    Ionized Stones   231
    Telephone Consultations   232

INTRODUCTION

There is nothing wrong with this world or its inhabitants. What is no longer necessary, though, is that we, the human race, are still caught up in the "three-dimensional dream" of ill health, problems and suffering. The dream prevents us from waking up to the enlightening discovery that we are everything but helpless victims of ill fate who are manipulated by forces greater than our own. What we need most at this stage in our human development is to wake up to the higher dimensional realities of our existence and to see, identify with and utilize our immensely powerful potential.

Life is mysteriously perfect, yet many of us still lack the conscious awareness to experience and understand its true workings. Most people in this world still believe that events, circumstances, accidents, illness, and relationships are more or less coincidental occurrences that have no deeper significance or connection to a larger purpose in life. Yet all the moments and events in a person's life are like the numerous and seemingly unrelated pieces of a giant jigsaw puzzle which when finally put together create a meaningful picture. When seen as isolated events, accidents, diseases or conflict situations seem to occur by chance and make little sense, but on a less expressed level of reality, where life is viewed from a wider perspective, they make perfect sense. The individual pieces of the puzzle are all very significant once they have found their destined place. Each one adds great importance to the whole picture. Unable to see the larger picture of life, isolated incidents appear deprived of their unique purpose, scattered at random and responsible for the confusion, instability and suffering we may be experiencing. This is a state when we may feel that life has no real meaning.

We all are still searching to become whole and fulfilled through whatever way seems appropriate; we thirst after happiness inside, yet we tend to look for it outside. Although not fully aware of the reasons, I have been searching spiritual wisdom since I was a child and I believed that the answers to my state of discontent could only be found outside me. After nearly 20 years of "trial and error", circumstances pressed me to look for the answers about life, the universe, and everything else within me.

My route to self-discovery was very bumpy at times. Yet when I look back at my life with the more heightened awareness of today, I can see clearly that the hardships and difficulties I had to endure turned out to be my greatest assets and invaluable blessings. They compelled me to create a manageable lifestyle that developed into a state of living grace. All that *really* happened to me was a change in awareness, which transformed my way of thinking and reshaped my destiny in a most rewarding way. I made the experiential discovery that we, and that includes our body, mind, soul, behavior, and extended self which is our environment – are mere products of our own awareness and its projections.

Our awareness expresses itself through thoughts, feelings, emotions, desires, likes, dislikes, intentions, which are the mental tools that shape our personal reality. Any shift in awareness will cause changes in the body, mind and spirit, and even in the environment. Through an unseen all-pervasive force, we create or co-create everything that happens to us. Our awareness is like the writer of a play; whatever it writes will be displayed in the theatre of life. Because our awareness is so basic to how we perceive and act in this world, its development deserves the most attention. We are here to write a new script that will help us identify with our spiritual nature and appreciate life for what it truly is. There is a sense of urgency in the air that says the time for individual and global transformation is now.

The entire presentation of this book is tailored towards awakening your awareness through profound insights that can transform it in any way you want, thereby turning it into the most powerful tool for fulfilling your desires and improving every aspect of your life. It also offers profound procedures for restoring wholeness of body, mind and soul. Furthermore, you will be able to recognize and transform the limiting and even harmful influences of many of your currently held beliefs, whether they relate to aging, emotions, relationships, environmental issues or death.

This book is both an offering of gratitude for having become more aware in my own life and an invitation to you to open your own doors to the world of abundance, love and spiritual wisdom. All that you are required to do is to be open and receptive and to accept the possibility that you may have to leave behind your old patterns of living and conditioning that have caused you pain and misfortune in life. This journey of self-discovery will take you to a place where nature rules and where the chains of your old beliefs, which may have imposed strong limitations on your body and mind, will break to pieces. This will leave you with the freedom to make your own unconditioned choices in life.

By discovering this new awareness of yourself, you will begin to perfect your ability to discern false assumptions and detrimental belief systems from those that enhance happiness and well-being. The old paradigms of living, which state "Life is suffering", "You cannot have everything" or "Aging is natural" will become obsolete once you tap into the *real you* – a field of all possibilities.

Experiences of struggle and strive can only take place when we get caught up in the second and third dimensional levels of reality which make up the illusion of time as well as the physical body and the material aspect of the world. Because most people have limited themselves to experience just this tiny fraction of reality, they felt subjected to its confines and hence created highly restrictive belief systems and rules of behavior. These (now crumbling and outdated) principles of living have dominated our worldviews for thousands of years and have contributed to chaos, destruction, and confusion everywhere. Man-made laws have, as it were, replaced the natural laws and become the self-fulfilling prophecies of modern life.

The main emphasis of the modern era has been on verifying every finding or discovery in a scientific way before accepting it as useful and practical, which was perhaps relevant on the more superficial levels of life but had little or no impact on improving the inner quality of life. This incomplete approach to living has led to the loss of excitement, adventure, mystery and fun and has made life mundane and even boring, as if it had no other meaning than following rules and regulations. Recently, the age of science-dominated life has entered a point of crisis where conflicting beliefs even within the scientific community are threatening its very foundation. Top physicists now speak of consciousness, a higher force, and even God when they refer to the origin of physical life. As we are moving into the new millennium, which will be under the *Aquarian* influence, the old paradigms and laws of living will no longer be sufficient to help us live a meaningful life. We all have the choice now to step into a new world order, which will be characterized by perfect health, abundance, love and spiritual wisdom. "It's Time to Come Alive" was conceived to awaken you to this new reality.

For thousands of years, man has been kept in darkness about his real nature and his unlimited potential. In most cases, his consciousness was so body-oriented that he was not even aware he had a mind. With the exception of a few enlightened people, man had no or only little conscious experience of the powerful influence the mind can have on the body, on destiny and on the world. Now humankind as a whole is going through a compulsory phase transition that will shift our awareness from being matter-oriented to being centered in our spiritual nature. Man will recognize himself as a spiritual being in a human body, whose most powerful tool is the mind. He will learn to use purely mental powers to handle his life's affairs, including his physical health and material needs. The insights and procedures given in this book can help make this transition the best experience in our lives. They are designed to awaken you to the new reality dawning on the human horizon. It is for you to find out what this reality is like.

Human potential is not limited, as we learned to believe; it is infinite. Like a prisoner who was confined to a prison cell for decades and is now released, it may take us a while to get used to the idea that we are truly free and unrestricted in our ability to shape our destiny and fulfill our deepest desires. We are released into the field of all possibilities, but to take advantage of it, we must wake up to this new reality and learn to trust in us first. This is really all it takes to enjoy the life we deserve.

CHAPTER 1
On the Road of Discovery

Maya – The World of Illusion

We generally see our body as being distinctly different than anything else that exists around us. Our planet and the billions of galaxies and stars that are floating about within the ever-expanding universe seem to be unrelated to our body, and most of us consider them to be just lifeless matter with hardly any or no relevance to our personal lives. But is this really true? Could it instead be possible that our eyes and other senses of perception project a picture of reality that overshadows our deeper connection with the universe?

Einstein, who was the pioneer of quantum physics, considered this idea to be the ultimate truth. He knew that all matter and energy are dual expressions of the same universal substrate that makes up all things, including us. Today's quantum physicists confirm what Einstein knew all along – the concrete world *appears* to be real but it is not. The Maya of illusion hides from us what is real by engaging our senses in a magic spell. The clouds in the sky only seem to make the sun "disappear." Even though the sun does not move away, we still use expressions such as "the sun has disappeared", or, "the sun hasn't been out today."

For practical purposes, such statements may be correct, but in reality, they conceal an even more significant aspect of the truth, which is our flawless connection to every part of creation. To rely only on our five senses to know the world and to act on that knowledge is comparable to building a house on sand; it is destined to collapse. A child watches the sun rise in the East and sees it disappear in the West. As it grows up and learns the basic lessons about our planetary system, the child may feel confused and bewildered with this information, or else it cannot grasp its logic at all. It has to accept that things are not always the way they seem. Only a clear intellectual understanding of the situation and a certain amount of distrust in his sense of sight can reconcile the two contradictory realities of the one event that is taking

1

place right in front of the child's eyes. The child's confusion will subside only when it has accepted and understood that the sun never rises or sets and that the earth rotates around the sun and not the other way round.

A further challenge may arise when the child learns that the earth is not as flat as it looks, but round, and that you may never reach the end of the world however far and long you travel. Only a few centuries back, humankind still believed that if you walked to the end of the horizon you would fall off the earth like from the edge of a cliff. Today we can only smile at such a notion of reality. Yet a person who will live even 30 or 50 years from now will smile at our perception of reality for it will no longer be relevant either.

Nearly all conflicts and struggles in man's historical past were based on beliefs that arose from misguided sensory perception. Even today, wars are being fought over "territorial rights" and "national boundaries" that only exist in the minds of the people. These rights and boundaries are mere artifacts of illusion. The earth is whole and it is not possible to divide her into segments. To most people, the right of owning a piece of land and cultivating it to make a living seems natural. By building a house on this land for shelter and protection, they may feel that ownership of this property is their personal birthright. In reality, however, they have only "leased" it from nature for the relatively short time of being here on Earth. The land has belonged to Earth for millions of years and a legal document will not be able to take it away from her. The conflicts arise not from using the land but from the false interpretation that we own it.

We furthermore believe that we are able to grow and provide our own foods but we forget that we could not even grow a blade of grass without the sun's and Earth's natural supplies of warmth, energy, air, water and nutrients. No life form can exist in isolation because everything, including human life, is intimately interwoven with every part of the Earth and the surrounding universe.

The sensory illusion, that the Earth and we are separate entities leads us to acquire more material things such as money and property than we do actually need. The amassment of wealth creates the illusion of safety. Yet, the sense of safety that is based on material wealth is a shaky one. It creates constant fear of losing one's possessions, which could happen at any time. We may even be willing to risk our lives to obtain or defend our possessions. Only when fire, tidal waves or a devastating earthquake destroys what we thought was ours, will a person perhaps begin to understand that we can never really own anything at all. True and lasting ownership of anything exists only in the conscious state of "oneness" with the living Earth, which is also the state of continual abundance and freedom from fear. In the past, certain civilizations as a whole have displayed such unity awareness. Their most precious secret was "the art of being in tune with nature" versus being against it. The wise men and women from our past have left behind traces of their greatness that can help us rediscover the essence of our being.

Lessons from the Past

For many years, the white human races have treated the Native Americans of North America, the Aborigines of Australia, and other tribal people around the world, as inferior races with "uncultured" beliefs or "uncivilized" ways of living. Several descriptive texts even refer to them as being "savages" or "barbarians." Nevertheless, more and more spiritually inclined people as well as scientists are now beginning to realize that there is a lot we can learn from their natural ways of living. The ancient cultures of the Incas, Mayas or the Vedic civilization had a far superior understanding of nature and creation than has been written in all the volumes of science and advanced technology.

Our understanding of Quantum Physics seems to have evolved enough to give reasonable explanations about how matter and energy share a common ground and source in a "unified field" of natural law as it has initially been conceived by Albert Einstein. Today's foremost scientists have developed the extremely complex mathematical formulas that attempt to prove these theories and they certainly deserve applause for their extraordinary contributions. They have led to the groundbreaking discovery that we and the rest of the universe are made of the same "stuff" and are fundamentally one giant living organism with different individual expressions or aspects. Yet these merely theoretical insights into the reality of life and the universe have failed to make such a state of unity and oneness with all of existence a

3

tangible and lasting experience for anyone. For the ordinary person it is irrelevant to know that quantum physics has discovered the common origin of all life. He would be more interested in actually living the wisdom contained in such a statement.

Textbook knowledge leaves wisdom behind. By contrast, the Native Americans spoke of a Great Spirit that guided their actions and helped them understand and see what their eyes and minds could not reveal. They considered the Great Spirit to be the Father of their souls to whom they would return at the time of physical death. For them the Earth was their real mother since all the nourishment they received came from her. They naturally obeyed the laws of the Father and the laws of the Mother without a need for other man-made laws. They did not require books to teach them about physics, biology, chemistry, or health. These ancient civilizations received their first-class education directly from their Father and their Mother.

Living the Law

The Native Americans, for example, felt inseparably one with the rivers and streams that gave nourishment to the earth and referred to them as the streams of their blood. They knew that their blood was essentially made from the "blood" (water) of Mother Earth (96% of our blood is water, which originally comes from the springs, rivers and lakes; the water in our blood transports thousands of nourishing chemicals and raw materials to the trillions of cells in our body). Her "blood" at times "fell" from the clouds, or it was "leaping up" from her womb, "sleeping" in her lakes or "raging" in the seas. They considered it madness to pollute their water as this would have polluted their own blood and cause disease.

Everything that happened outside their bodies, they also felt occurring within them. They could tell the onset of a thunderstorm long before it arrived. It was their belief that the storm was going to bless the soil of their land (lightning causes nitrogen to combine with oxygen, and when these compounds reach the surface of the earth with the rain, plants use them as fertilizers). For them the soil was not dead matter but alive, sustaining both humans and animals alike. They considered the soil holy. It never came into their minds to exploit or destroy the soil (millions of tiny living organisms can be found in just a teaspoon of soil and they convert the chemical elements of the soil into forms of nutrients that can be assimilated by the body). Later on, when the white people discovered their land and wanted to buy it from them, the Indians felt perplexed, for how could they be expected to sell something that was an integral part of them.

The food that Mother Earth provided for them was their very flesh. It was obvious to them that they became what they ate. When I ask patients of mine who suffer from Rheumatoid Arthritis, MS, heart disease, or cancer whether they have sought special advice regarding their diet, many of them have not even considered the possibility that food may have something to do with their disease. By contrast, the Native Americans understood that the flesh from the fruits of the trees and the crops from the fields kept their own flesh tender and strong. Their physical endurance and vitality, a direct result of a balanced and moderate diet consisting of purely natural and freshly grown foods, were extraordinary.

Mother Earth's breath was *their* breath. It kept their bodies healthy and strong but had to be clean (air carries 21% of life giving oxygen, nitrogen and other gases, including less than 1% carbon dioxide which serves as "breath" for plant life; an unbalanced composition of these fixed percentages caused by air pollution destroys cellular life). They considered trees and plants to be their lungs (only trees and plants provide us with vital oxygen). Spending most of their time outside was not only natural, but also vital for them; by contrast, the average person nowadays spends most of the day indoors.

The sun, moon, and all the stars in the heavens had deep meaning to them. They had a practically personal relationship with the starry world. They knew that the cycles of sun and moon affected their crops, their physical endurance and strength, and their very thoughts and feelings. The ancient Native Americans had no desire to subdue nature because nature was their invincible friend and protector. They never thought that death was the end of life; instead, they saw it as a new beginning.

The Indians had no reasons to be afraid. They showed little attachment to objects, possessions, and even their bodies because they knew who they were: immortal beings in the form of a mortal body. What strikes us the most regarding their way of expressing the eternal truths of life is their steady peacefulness and simplicity. Whenever they faced an unresolved problem, they left the noisy camp life, retreated to the top of a mountain and stayed there in silence until they had found a solution. Their profound patience gave them the confidence to know that there was always a right time and a right place for everything. They were quiet people and used their language wisely and prudently. Communication took place from mind to mind and heart to heart without the need for spoken words. Everyone was a brother or a sister, "of the same blood" and coming from the same source.

The Turn of Destiny

However, as more and more of their generations passed away, the deep inner connection to their unifying source became blurred and the experience of oneness with their Father and their Mother gradually diminished. They increasingly violated the eternal laws of nature which had ensured the support by the great elements of earth, water, fire, air and ether for centuries. In due time their free spirit and peaceful nature succumbed to fear, anger, lustfulness and gluttony.

Greed and conflicts arose and brought unhappiness and suffering to their people. The Earth served no longer as the sole provider of all their needs and they had to look for other means to sustain their lives. Since the climate was no longer under their conscious control, the killing of animals became necessary due to harsh weather and subsequent scarcity of grown foods. All those things that the Earthly Mother gave them so abundantly before were now no longer sufficiently available.

Sickness, too, became an increasingly common experience as they cut off their ties from the laws of nature. Their descriptions of diseases were simple and straightforward, yet highly accurate, and they match today's chronic diseases: "Man's breath becomes short and stifled, full of pain and evil-smelling like the breath of unclean beasts (our asthma and bronchitis). His blood becomes thick and evil smelling, like the water of the swamps; it clots and blackens like the night of death (our blood and heart diseases). His bones become hard and knotted; it melts away within and breaking asunder, as a stone falling down upon a rock (our rheumatoid arthritis and osteoporosis). Their flesh waxes fat and watery; it rots and putrefies, with scabs and boils that is an abomination (our obesity, edema, cancer, acne and other skin disorders). His bowels become full with abominable filthiness, with oozing streams of decay; and multitudes of worms have their habitation there (our constipation; accumulation of toxic waste; worms, and parasite infections). His eyes grow dim, till dark night enshrouds them (our glaucoma and cataract leading to blindness), and his ears become stopped, like the silence of the grave (deafness)." Breath, blood, bone, flesh, bowels, eyes, and ears, all gifts of the Earthly Mother, were gradually taken away from them.

One of the greatest Red Indian sages was Chief Seattle. His words contain a timeless message – a message that may even be more appropriate today than it was at his time.

Teach your children
what we have taught our children –
that the earth is our mother.
Whatever befalls the earth
befalls the sons and daughters of the earth.
If men spit upon the ground,
they spit upon themselves.

This we know.
The earth does not belong to us;
we belong to the earth.
This we know.
All things are connected
Like the blood, which unites one family.
All things are connected.

Whatever befalls the earth
befalls the sons and daughters of the earth.
We did not weave the web of life;
we are merely a strand in it.
Whatever we do to the web,
we do to ourselves.

Enemies from both the white and red races increased in number and gave the final death sentence to a civilization that had already destroyed itself through the loss of oneness with the natural laws given to them by the Great Spirit and the Earthly Mother.

The Ancient Message

All the great civilizations that inhabited our planet are long gone and mostly forgotten. They only left behind a few scattered pieces of the physical evidence of their existence. Monuments, sculptures, and ancient scriptures such as the 6,000 years old Vedic textbooks remind us of their superior knowledge and spiritual advancement. However, we have ridiculed some of their "strange" cults or what we consider religious practices because we do not understand their true meaning.

Besides, times have changed. We live in the present and not in the past of our ancestors; although it might very well be that we actually *were* these ancestors in previous lifetimes. Today we face different challenges and we have to meet them with different means. Yet there seems to be one important message that comes to us from our historical past and that is: "Follow the natural laws of life, for if you don't, you will fall too, like we did."

The Native Americans and other "fallen" great civilizations paid their price for deviating from the path of natural law and so do we. Stress, sickness and lack of true abundance in life may be the indications that we have forgotten or never learnt *how* to live. While negative events increasingly dominate our lives, *bliss* or even *simple happiness* is an experience confined to a few rare moments here and there. What is going wrong in our lives and in our world, or better, what is it that we are not doing right? Deep inside ourselves, we know the answer because we are all pre-programmed to be healthy, wealthy and wise. All we really need is someone to confirm what we already know and to trust that what he saying to us is true.

Faith – A Healer?

What seemed impossible even a few years ago, conventional medicine now attempts to prove: faith, prayer, and spirituality may improve physical health. For nearly 100 years, doctors and scientists have tried to rid medical science of all remnants of mysticism. Some scientists are beginning to look at just what is helping patients when they resort to spirituality. Already over 200 studies relate improvement of physical health to faith, spirituality or religion. They have certainly aroused interest in both the general population and medical circles.

A 1995 study conducted at Darthmouth-Hitchcock Medical Center, USA, found that among 232 heart surgery patients those who said they drew comfort and strength from religious faith had the highest survival rate. Those who didn't, had a three times higher death rate than those who did. When the members with religious conviction were also receiving social support as part of their churchgoing, then their advantage was 14 times higher compared with those who felt isolated or lacked faith.

Other long-term studies showed that churchgoers have lower blood pressure, are less depressed and anxious, have a four times lower rate of suicide, recover faster after hip surgery, and are generally more healthy than non-churchgoers. The studies took into account smoking, and other socio-economic factors that could have an influence on health. In one study, smokers who regarded religion as very important to them were only 14 percent as likely to have abnormal blood pressure as smokers who did not value religion in their lives.

Are We Spiritual by Nature?

The new trend comes at a time when according to the latest opinion polls 82% of Americans believe in the healing power of personal prayer. Before long, scientists will equate this healing power with the placebo response – a healing response in the body that is triggered by one's belief in a particular drug or treatment. The faith in someone who can accomplish anything, even cure a cancer, is the intuitive knowledge that HE or SHE would be there when you are in need. This is called unerring faith. To pray means putting one's attention on and moving that infinite power, love or God energy in a desired direction. The *limbic system*, which is common to all primates, plays a major role in emotions, sexual pleasure, deeply felt memories, and as research has shown even in spiritual experiences. The ability to have such experiences has a neuro-anatomical basis, according to Rhawn Joseph,

9

a neuroscientist at the Palo Alto VA Medical Center in California. So are we spiritual by nature?

By identifying with more than just your body or the physical reality, you enter the unbounded world of consciousness within yourself. Everyone who will stay on the planet for the next 10-15 years will make this profound shift. Many of us are already going through this transformational process. Since the unbounded cannot be divided or even appear as an event in space or time, it is everywhere, meaning in us as well. By becoming aware of yourself and the spirit of nature, you become automatically spiritual. Our body cannot function without being connected to that supreme intelligence that controls it at every moment. Some people give it a personal touch and call it God and thus it becomes a religious experience, others feel deeply connected to nature and simply feel like "coming home." Deep down within ourselves we are all spiritual by nature, whether we are willing to acknowledge it or not. Life is simply not possible without contact to our non-physical origin. Spirit, regardless of what we name it, is our essential nature and the body is the tool to make us aware of it.

For as long we live, we are likely to believe in ourselves to some degree. Otherwise, we would end our lives. Diseases and difficulties are merely the signals indicating that we are not properly connected with or don't trust in that spirit or *super intelligence* within. Being out of "touch" with our higher self, the body's DNA begins to write false programs that may lead to physical deficiencies and further confusion about our true identity. This is the beginning of a crisis in life, which may manifest in the form of an accident or a disease.

What is the Body without its Mind?

It may be necessary at this stage in our growth process to accept the understanding that the body is not capable of conducting any activity or producing any hormonal drug without a command or instruction from our body-mind. It is quite irrelevant whether the instructions come from a brain cell or any other cell in the body. The total genetic information, which is contained in the nucleus of every single cell in the body, is deeply rooted in our own inner consciousness – the sea of pure intelligence. This intelligence keeps the body in perfect health and can also repair any damage that may have occurred.

If we encounter fear, doubt or distrust or fear, however, the otherwise clear instructions from our body-mind become distorted which will render that intelligence incapable of conducting its healing work. This means that the healing response will remain absent. If we cannot recover from an illness, that is, when it turns chronic, we prevent our inner intelligence from continually expressing itself through the numerable parts of the body in a balanced and organized manner. We can liken the state of sickness in the body to an army that has lost its leader; the soldiers run in panic in all directions as there is nobody to direct them what to do.

The saying "a healthy mind in a healthy body" rings true in our ears when we look at the relationship of body and mind. To have a healthy body it is essential to have a healthy mind. A healthy mind is one that connects with the inner intelligence or higher self. Anyone can achieve such a state of mind. The only limitations that occur in a person's body are the ones that exist in his mind. The body, being the epiphenomenon of the mind, will unerringly carry out the mind's instructions, whatever they may be. The quality of the instructions determines the quality of our life, and in particular, the health of our body as well as the degree of abundance and spiritual wisdom we can enjoy. If you feel that something needs to shift in your life, you may have to change the directions you pass on to your body-mind.

Personality Shifts can Create "Miracles"

The mind/body relationship is shared by every human being, regardless of the health problem or emotional difficulties he may experience. You may have heard of "personality disorder", a condition when a person accommodates up to a dozen different personalities in his physical body. Researchers and medical professionals are still puzzled by such occurrences. Women who have three distinct personalities with different memories, feelings, and even language accents, are found to have three different menstrual periods in one month. Some of the afflicted persons may even change the color of their eyes as they make the shift from one personality to another.

11

Several years ago, a team of doctors in the United States studied the personality disorder of a young boy who was known to have twelve identifiable personalities. While experiencing one particular personality, the boy develops strong allergic reactions after drinking orange juice. In this state, his immune system regards orange juice as an allergen or "invader." When the orange molecules contact the immune cells in his mouth cavity and intestinal tract, they begin to mass-produce antibodies to counteract the orange juice as if it were harmful bacteria. The abnormal reaction causes mouth swelling, skin eruptions, burning eyes, an asthma attack, migraine or diarrhea. After shifting to another personality, his immune system considers the same orange molecules to be "friendly." Without any trace of sensitivity to orange juice, all the previous symptoms of the allergy will have disappeared.

It would be intriguing to find out which aspect of the boy's personality triggers the allergy and which one turns it off again. However, even without knowing the cause of the allergy we can say that a change in his thoughts, feelings, emotions, memories, likes dislikes etc., which make up his personality, alters his body's behavior so drastically that ingesting a few harmless orange molecules can lead to the destruction of his entire body.

A number of people with personality disorders suffer from insulin-dependent diabetes. Since their pancreatic cells (Islets of Langerhans) are no longer capable of producing enough of this vital hormone, the patients may require injections of insulin to keep the sugar level balanced. Conventional medicine assumes that with this form of diabetes (Type I) a large number of the afflicted pancreas cells are non-functional or quasi dead. However, after a sudden change of personality, these people no longer suffer from diabetes; insulin levels are normal, and pancreatic cells are resurrected back to life.

One might consider this periodically occurring "resurrection" of cells to be a "programmed miracle", but it may be a far less mysterious phenomenon than that. The pancreas cells, at one moment in a deep slumber and without a sign of life, the next moment are awakened by a kind of alarm clock or wake-up call. The sudden awakening to another personality or entity, which has a different mind with different feelings, emotions and memories, redefines the functioning of the entire body. That particular aspect of intelligence, which makes the pancreas cells tick, is active and awake when the corresponding state of mind is active and alive.

The phenomenon of personality disorders reveals a very simple but very important law of the body-mind. By avoiding a certain unresolved issue such as deferring a long due apology to a good friend or not talking to our partner about a problem that bothers us, we create a blockage in our mind that in due time begins to manifest also in our body, in our relationships and even in our environment. We cannot negate this intimate connection between body and mind, but we can use it as a tool to create a life that is perfect for our world and us. If only we could stop doubting that our mind is capable of creating anything at all, our lives would be full of miracles. Those with personality disorders, although they may not be aware of this, remind us that mind indeed rules over matter.

Note: As confirmed by my personal experiences with people who have multiple personalities, I believe that they are afflicted by soul entities that have not moved on to the "other side" when their physical bodies died. Roaming the astral planes of existence, they seek to express themselves and their desires, frustrations and rage through a physical body, just as they used to when they were still alive (in human form). Through my healing system of Sacred Santémony, I have been able to remove these entities from the host, which resulted in the return of the original mono-personality. Most, if not all, bi-polar or schizophrenic personalities simply suffer from an invasion by one or several such entities, and their symptoms of mental disease vanish along with these entities. For more information on Sacred Santémony, please see the back of the book or visit my web site.

CHAPTER 2
In Tune with Nature

Growing a New Limb

Personality disorders and many other diseases (psychosomatic) demonstrate that our mind controls our body, whether this occurs in a negative sense or constructively. We may have to give up our attachment to the idea that we are helpless against disease or physical handicaps. Even more striking than the above examples is the case of Jim, a man living in the United States, who grew a new limb after an accident destroyed one of his legs.

Doing repair work on a roof, Jim accidentally touched a high-powered voltage cable and died. One of his legs "burned out" leaving just the bones and a few scattered nerves. Nevertheless, as his body fell from the roof his chest touched the ground in such a way that his heart received an "electric shock" (similar to heart-reviving practices in hospitals). After he had regained his consciousness, he decided against all the odds and the arguments of his doctors not to have his leg amputated but instead to keep it and grow it back to normal.

Within just one year, Jim had grown an identical leg, something unheard of in human history. Although thought to be a physiological impossibility, his trusting mind nevertheless directed the necessary carbon, nitrogen, hydrogen, and oxygen atoms etc., to reassemble and form new cells of flesh and skin, and all this under medical surveillance. The destruction of his physical leg had not damaged the intelligence of his mind, his trust in a higher power and the readiness of his body to rebuild his leg. Because Jim refused to believe that he had lost his leg forever, the DNA or genetic intelligence that is responsible for every single process in the body was able to direct the body's immune system, digestive system, nervous system, circulatory system and body cells etc., to grow an identical limb. This incredible feat was possible because the cells of the body can "think" and know how to store information in a similar way as we do.

14

Instant Communication

Hundreds of studies in the field of genetic research have shown that every (healthy) living cell constantly communicates with its surrounding cells. Its means of communication is similar to our satellite transmissions, except the cells use energy in the form of light. Light can store and transmit information. This extremely fast communication network works separately from all existing biochemical or physical networks including the circulatory system, endocrine system, nervous system and immune system.

This makes the entire body literally a body of light, a concept that so far has existed only in esoteric scriptures, which describe the body as being made of light and radiating light into the environment. The idea that human beings, animals, and plants have a glow or energy field around them has been documented by religious paintings and scriptures for hundreds of years and has been described as *the aura* by numerous mystics of the past. Only after the Russian couple, the Kirlians, invented a photographic technique to take pictures of these light fields around living objects such as leaves or fingertips, began the idea of an aura surrounding every living thing move from the "uncertain" metaphysical realm into the "tangible" world of scientific investigation. Since then, cameras have become available for anyone to photograph other people's auras, in all their various color formations.

Some people whose sense of sight or psychic vision is more refined than average, are able to see these light fields emanating from the living world. In reality, though, there is nothing that is not alive, including so-called lifeless matter. Similar light fields also exist around molecules, atoms and their subatomic particles, regardless whether they appear to be the components of stones, metals or the human body. Atoms consist mainly of empty space and a tiny nucleus of protons and neutrons which in turn can be imagined as compressed points of energy, sometimes appearing as particles, sometimes as waves. The protons and neutrons consist of even smaller particles or waves of energy known as gluons and quarks. They change their pattern of substance at a rate of 10^{-23} times per second!

The unimaginable speed of constant transformation of subatomic particles keeps the cells in the body dynamic, vibrant and alive. The genetic information (DNA) contained in the nucleus of the cells ensures that the repeatedly changing pattern of their subatomic substance remains identical, thus guaranteeing the health and vitality of the whole body.

The physicist Max Planck calculated that at a scale of 10^{-33} cm, time and space merge and matter ceases to exist. This is the realm of consciousness, the unified field of all matter and energy. It is beyond space and time, self-luminous, and the core of all life forms. It is the true home of an atom, of a molecule, of a cell, of an organ, of the body, of our planet, of a galaxy and of the universe. If consciousness becomes tainted or overshadowed by fear, anger, depression, or the body is exposed to toxic air, harmful foods or drinks, microwaves, viruses or microbes etc., there is strong interference in the pattern of subatomic transformations that will manifest in the body as disease. The first step to reverse this process and repair any damage that may have occurred on the physical level must take place in your consciousness. Once you made the right intent, all factors required for complete healing will come along like a spider's web that is pulled by one of its threads.

Using the Power of Intent

Through daily meditation, a pure and healthy diet and a balanced lifestyle, Jim had gained access to the source of matter and energy. He was able to reassemble all the necessary atoms to construct a new limb according to the body's genetic blueprint or DNA. Although the atoms that occupied the space of his leg before the accident were scattered and displaced by the strong electric currents, his body of consciousness remained intact. Because Jim's consciousness did not identify with the loss of his leg or become angry or depressed over it, he was free to formulate an intent that took him all the way to fully restoring his leg. His DNA therefore had no choice but to follow suit and do the actual repair work.

As he was increasingly able to strengthen the connection with his consciousness of Higher Self and trust that his decision to keep the burnt leg was a right one, the correct number and types of atoms required to form new, healthy cells began to occupy the same space again. Stupid, inert, or lifeless atoms could not do such a thing. Atoms, however small they may be, are intelligent "beings" that can store large amounts of information. Their "memories" allow them to bond with other atoms to add a greater purpose to their existence. Similar to body cells, they communicate with each other through the same medium of light, bonding to form molecules. Molecules keep a memory of all the individual purposes of their atoms. In Jim's case, they knew of his intent to grow a new limb.

The Amazing Memory Capacity of Water Molecules

French research has demonstrated the remarkable ability of water molecules to remember their contact with a soluble agent even after it has been diluted to the point that no molecules of the original substance remain. Homeopathic Medicine is based on this principle. Over 85 studies to date have proved that homeopathic remedies work, despite their lack of any ingredients.

There is an increasing body of scientific research to show that we have only just begun to understand the qualities of water. It seems that water, although it looks "plain" to us, is one of the most complex substances that exist. Just take a look at the amazing water crystal photographs that the Japanese scientist Masaru Emoto has taken of different sources of water (book by Masaru Emoto: "The Hidden Messages in Water." Since most of our body consists of water, understanding its structure and functions can help us understand more about ourselves. Water molecules know how to assemble and reassemble themselves in various types of clusters, including five-sided shapes known as pentameters, with a speed of millions of times each second. This mutability implies that water may have an enormous capacity for storing information, greater than a giant computer.

Another intelligent property of water is its ability to fold linked amino acids into protein chains. Without this feature, life would not be possible at all. Water also stabilizes the DNA helix; if water molecules were to forget how to do that, our body would be in complete turmoil and unable to sustain itself. Hydrogen atoms have different memories from oxygen atoms but they both remember that through proper bonding they can make water molecules. They also know about their ability to bond with other molecules. It is the intelligent networking of billions of atoms that eventually forms clusters of molecules and makes proteins, the building blocks of our cells, tissues, organs and body.

Beings of Light

The "thinking" cell with its apt abilities to make decisions and repair damage within itself has to co-ordinate over a trillion chemical reactions per second. It has to communicate its continual needs for nutrients, water, and oxygen to its neighboring cells and to the larger organs and systems that are responsible for meeting all the cell's demands. As necessary, the body informs the host or consciousness, that it is time to eat when nutrients become scarce. We experience this as the sensation of hunger. In a similar way, the body signals thirst when it runs short of water. It urges you to search for fresh air when oxygen supply is low and tells you to look for the means to cool it down when it becomes overheated. When your body feels cold, it wants you to seek warm shelter. It tells you to go to sleep when it is tired and to exercise when it feels stiff etc.

This "Internet" system works so well because there are "light beings" in the smallest units of life (the quarks, atoms, molecules, cells etc.) as there are "light beings" in the larger units of life (the organs, the body, the Earth, clusters of stars, the universe). All that exists in the universe "is." Moreover, whatever "is" is made of light which can store an almost infinite amount of information and communicate it anywhere at any time. By becoming aware of this essential aspect of ourselves and of everything else in the physical world, we tap into a new reality of life that promises us freedom from limitation.

Invisible Messengers of Nature

When you look at a tree you are not only looking at a collection of material particles but also at a Being of light that is responsible for the organized and systematic growth of the tree. This Being lives in total harmony with the existing laws of nature and environmental conditions. The tree being is able to communicate all its needs to the soil, the air and the water. It knows how to call and attract other forms of life, such as insects, birds or bacteria to help its own growth process and to pass on information to other trees.

Looking at a tree is a two-way process. Your entire being, including your thoughts, feelings, and emotions and the corresponding chemical components produced by your brain, are literally "read" by the tree you are looking at. There are trillions of particles of light bouncing back and forth between your eyes and the tree at a frequency of millions of times per second. The light particles pick up the tree's inherent information, particular frequency and essence of light and deliver all that to your body by entering your eyes, your aura and other parts. When the various colors of light emanating from the tree enter your eyes, they pass through the hypothalamus, which is the brain's brain, and the pineal gland. There they receive specific chemical codes that help the body communicate the essential characteristics of the tree to all the cells of your body. Your body cells respond to this information by beaming their impressions of the tree back to the tree. You may feel that the tree is strong and healthy or even say: "What a beautiful and wise-looking tree!" All this happens within the fraction of a second.

Trees, animals, insects and humans are all part of a giant organism in which every piece of information is shared and exchanged if needed. This networking takes place on the level of existence where light energy is the common factor. If you want to cut a tree because it is obstructing your view, it will know of your intent almost at the same time you think of it. In a similar way, we radiate the very essence of what we are, what we think and what we do into our near and far environment. We are literally surrounded by numerous invisible messengers that let our surrounding know who we are, how we are and what we are doing.

We all are being "read" by the Earth and especially by the sun. Incredible as this may sound, deep within us we know it is true. To discover our essence and the essence of everything else that exists we need to trust what we feel inside rather than wait for the scientists or the learned experts to tell us what we ought to believe or not to believe. This spark of understanding needs to become a powerful beam of spiritual wisdom in order to dissolve all the limited thinking that keeps us from recognizing who we are.

There is a human aspect of us just as there is a universal aspect of us. The two aspects of self must be bridged before we can find our true purpose in life. This, however, cannot be accomplished through intellectual analysis of the world and us but by trusting that feeling of deep inner knowing. Once we trust this feeling, the intellectual satisfaction of understanding our purpose in life will come along automatically. For the time being, I suggest that you accept the possibility that there is a sentient universe that knows everything about you. The more you will feel this to be true the more you will recognize yourself to be an important power to help raise planetary vibrations and usher in a new era of peace, love and enlightenment for mankind and all other life forms in the universe.

There are no Secrets Under the Sun

We may have to get used to the idea that there can be no secrets under the sun. We know that all visible objects reflect light. This permits us to see these objects with all their various colors, shapes, forms and textures. What most of us are not aware of, however, is what takes place behind the scenes: As the sun's rays hit an object such as our body, the light particles absorb all the information contained within the body and transmit it back to the sun.

This two-way process occurs continually. The sun stays in touch with everything that takes place on Earth. This also occurs during the night when the moon and the stars transmit the information back to the sun. According to whatever is happening on Earth, the sun changes its activity and feeds back corresponding responses to all of Earth's inhabitants in a unique way. It receives clear notice of the collective effect of the thoughts, behavior and physical condition of all humankind, as well as of the developing stages of plants, animals, insects etc. It executes the natural law "as you sow so shall you reap" with immediate effect. As the sun's rays touch our skin, it reads our vibrations of who we are and is thereby able to "fuel" our existence. The sun regulates our energy intake and creates the right environment for each of us to evolve. It ensures that the entire planet is a livable place.

Whatever we do to harm ourselves, in word or action, directly or indirectly, is transmitted to the sun and will trigger the appropriate "corrective" measures. The sun is concerned with life as a whole like a president who has to serve all the people in his country. Occasionally, he is forced to send some people to prison to protect others. Similarly, the sun returns to us only what we have given out. It serves as an "incorruptible guarantor of justice," which is motivated by the force of love to sustain planetary life as a whole.

Growth is always oriented towards sunlight whereas decay and death are geared away from it. For this reason, people who wish to hide something go into dark places where the sun does not reach, hence the term "underground movement"; or else they use dark sunglasses so that the sun cannot enter their eyes and read their soul. When you carry fear of life and of Earth, the solar rays completely understand your state of consciousness, and they reinforce and amplify these fears until you are able to consciously experience fear, pass through it and feel free enough to love. When you begin to love and honor life and Earth, the sun will change its messages towards you, rewarding you with renewed energy, information, and greater opportunities. This is an automatic process.

Respecting the Sun

The sun undergoes changes all the time, a phenomenon that has puzzled scientists repeatedly. It changes because the world, which receives its light, is changing. The sun knows how to correct imbalances on our planet and in our solar system. We may need to remind ourselves that without the sun, Earth would be a lump of ice. We would have no fuel because there would be no fossils to produce any fuel. There would be no food, no oxygen and no water. The earth could not rotate around its axis or experience seasonal changes. The sun uses the force of gravity to keep the earth in its proper position. The sun's activities can even cause the shifting of the earth's poles, which is occurring now. The sun is our sole source of life and it is in the interests of the sun and the rest of the universe to keep it that way. To see the sun as being harmful to life on Earth reflects ignorance of the vast intelligence contained in sunlight. The sun is capable of creating and organizing an infinite number of processes to ensure the continued evolution of our planet Earth.

There are people, some of whom are respected scientists, who out of deep concern for man's safety, try to persuade large portions of the population to keep away from the sun. We are told we need to protect ourselves against sunlight because it may cause skin cancer or destroy life. If a respectable person says the sun is harmful, we tend to believe it. If we read it in a newspaper or magazine, we trust that it must come from an authentic source. If someone delivered you a published a hand-written letter to claim the same thing, you might at best ignore it. We let ourselves be so controlled by external sources of information that we can no longer trust ourselves to know what is right or wrong. In truth, 95 percent of what we know today we learn from other sources rather than trust our intuition of what we know to be right for us. We are in a bit of trouble now because, collectively, we no longer trust and honor nature, the sun, the Earth and ourselves.

Only Fear is Dangerous

The sun responds to each one of us in a specific way. If you are terrified of the sun, you may absorb a massive dose of rays from the sun that can cause you skin cancer even while walking from your house to your garage. This in no way is meant as an act of punishment, we are rather given the opportunity to learn from the effect we create through our thoughts and actions and to discover how we attract the results of our own fearful projections.

Studies show that the rate of skin cancer increased after sunscreens were introduced to the masses. If the sun were dangerous to our eyes and skin, we would have been equipped with the proper protection right from the beginning of human life on earth. The Aborigines of Australia where the sun supposedly is more harmful than in Europe do not use sunscreens and do not get skin cancer. People living in high altitudes and near the equator have the lowest skin cancer rates. On the other hand, those who work mostly indoors or use UV-blocking sunglasses and suntan screens have the highest incidence of skin cancer. Animals do not wear sunglasses; they don't not suffer from skin cancer either. Plants, too, do not seem to agree with this theory.

22

We have a very intimate relationship with the sun. Its activities and rays change according to the consciousness of each one of us. Light is a manifestation of intelligence and intelligence knows exactly what it is doing. The sun is a massive source of light and thus an enormously intelligent form of existence. We cannot expect this to be verified by a scientist whose training allows him only to observe and verify objective events. However, the world is not objective at all; it is subjective in every sense of the word. Even scientists see the world through different eyes; hence so many different theories on the same subject. Words are uttered by conscious beings, which makes knowledge to be a projection of subjectivity. Since knowledge is different in different states of consciousness, each person perceives the world in a different way. Therefore, we all live in a world of subjectivity. We can change our world by changing ourselves. This requires letting go of the fear-generating idea that you are a nobody in respect to the world, the universe or God.

We *are* the World

In the core of our being, we are one with the world, the universe, God or by whatever name we call the omnipresence of Being. Separation exists only as a belief system which we have acquired collectively over a period of thousands of years. In truth, we are all that there is. True mind is not localized; I am not closer to my body than I am to the universe.

The particles or rays of light (photons) that beam down on me from the sun, which is billions of light years away, enter my body within the flash of a moment. This is possible because my body and the sun are part of the same enormous field of existence. As Albert Einstein said in 1920, "there is no atom, there is only field." Nothing exists outside that field, everything *is* the field. We also are made of the same stuff. What we call matter is essentially "non-matter", even if our physical senses don't agree with that. The sun is my body and the stars are my body, too. I cannot live without them, they are as necessary to my body's functioning as my heart and my lungs. If someone removed the moon, Mars, Saturn, or Venus from our planetary system, our bodies would quickly disintegrate and die. We see our bodies as distinctly different

23

from the environment, yet this is only so because the veil of sensory illusion conceals the consciousness that underlies all physical manifestations.

Stephen Hawking, one of the world's most renowned physicists stated once: "The universe is, with no beginning and ending of time and no edges in space." If we were situated in the middle of a large bubble we would recognize neither its beginning nor or its end, simply because the bubble doesn't have a starting or an end point. Linear time, which gives rise to the two-dimensional world, would simply be non-existent. This notion of timelessness, however, would tumble if we started drawing a line from one point of the bubble to another. The experience of time and space, life and death, matter etc. is an illusion which we have created in order to act out *Karma* and thereby increase the frequency of universal Being or Spirit. We see limitations where limitations don't exist. Spirit is the non-physical aspect of the universe, which is in all of space and all of time, i.e. past, present and future. We also are in all of space and all of time. We are one with eternal Being or Spirit. *We are Spirit.* This may be the ultimate science of life, but it is purely subjective science.

A scientist who is also essentially nothing but pure subjectivity, may decide to study something else such as the behavior of a subatomic particle but in reality he only studies another viewpoint of the same field. By trying to be objective, he disconnects himself from the object he wants to examine, thinking they are two incompatible things. Such an approach leads to incomplete knowledge, i.e. more ignorance, and to possibly harmful consequences. Among them are the warnings that the sun can be dangerous to your health or that ozone holes further the destruction of our planet. Apart from spreading ignorance faster than knowledge, purely objective science takes all the fun out of life.

People are made of subjectivity, they have feelings and a soul that does not act or work like a computerized machine or robot. Eighty percent of the people who fall ill get sick from a stressful experience and seventy percent die from it. This may be an objective finding but stress reactions are purely subjective experiences. One person responds to a stressful situation by having a heart attack, which is an "I can't cope" experience, another feels positively challenged by the same problem and thrives on it. Similarly, out of ten people who suffer the same cancer and share the same age and risk factors of disease, five may die, three improve and two have a spontaneous remission. There is no objective answer to the question why the same deadly cancer does not kill all of them.

Objective science is incomplete because it does not account for the subjective experiences people may have when they interact with one another, with nature or with the sun. Scientists know, for example, that sun spot cycles influence our weather patterns. However, this represents only a tiny fraction of the truth. To know what the sun is really there for, one has to know oneself and to love and honor life, the sun and the universe.

Knowledge of any kind is only correct and fundamentally useful when we know ourselves. Once we fuse objective science with its subjective source, i.e. spiritual science, we will have a truly universal science rather than just a human science. This will open us to possibilities previously believed impossible, including sustained space travel, neutralization of nuclear waste, and controlling gravity. The marriage between physical matter, including human biology, Spirit within matter, and the relationship and co-ordination of these two, is what will make this world a paradise. The real power and understanding lies in the spiritual, not in the physical or mental. The Native Americans identified with the *Great Spirit* within them and thus had direct access to the power and wisdom that is contained in the spirits of the moon, the sun, the stars, the Earth and all of nature. They adored the sun as a god, something that is found in many ancient cultures, and they cherished their personal relationship with the sun, a practice that sounds so meaningless to us in our purely "objective" world.

The sun is our support system and we can rely on it in every way. Nevertheless, it appears we need to prove to the sun that we are sincere and really value life. We have to do our bit, which is to have a pure and uncluttered consciousness, to clean up our bodies and the mess we have created in our environment. As the sun's energies are drastically increasing now, negative thoughts are greatly energized and amplified as well; they literally can turn to poison, thereby causing havoc in the body. For this reason, today there are so many more psychosomatic, i.e. stress-related diseases than there were 50 – 60 years ago. By contrast, everything that supports life and promotes happiness is also becoming tremendously empowered now. In other words, at a time when disease

25

can strike so easily we are also given the insights and energies to create a new way of life that will allow us to have only constructive thoughts and healthy bodies.

What we require now more than ever before is openness, honesty and a trusting relationship with the sun, the moon, the stars, the Earth and our fellow human beings. This actually is easier done than it sounds. By deciding for yourself that this is what you want, you set the ball rolling in the right direction. The communication links with our surroundings and fellow human beings are already established. All we need to do is to identify with the essence of our subjective nature, which is unlimited love, and the whole world will get to feel and know about it.

The Mysterious "Odor Net"

There are many different ways to relate to the "outside" world, and each of them utilizes different elements of nature. A tree, for example, can convey messages to other trees by releasing hormone-like compounds called "pheromones" into the air. When a fire breaks out at one end of a forest, within seconds the entire forest is informed of the imminent danger. Research has shown that trees have a built-in biochemical alarm system that helps them trigger special chemical responses that are used to ward off environmental threats.

Both animals and humans use similar pheromones to communicate with each other in a biochemical way. All of us leave our individual biochemical "finger prints" on everything and everyone we come into contact with. This creates an incredibly complex network of invisible threads consisting of chemical odors. A recent study showed that people leave their unique genetic markers all over the place, such as on pens, keys and coffee mugs etc. These invisible "fingerprints" can be traced to an individual. The researchers found that we can pick up other people's DNA through our hands simply by touching a doorknob or somebody's hairbrush. Pheromones, too, have their specific genetic markers.

By means of the pheromones, fish find their way back to their spawning grounds after years of being out in the seven seas. Cats that have been moved hundreds of miles from their homes, unerringly find their way back home. A calf that has been separated from its mother will unerringly find her in a large herd of cattle. A mother whose newly born child has been removed from her soon after birth will recognize her child thirty years later when confronted with the now adult. This recognition is not based on the vague memories that the mother may have about her baby's features. The pheromones of the baby are permanently locked in the olfactory nerve center of the mother's brain and will match the same pheromones that her child is producing and dispersing even thirty years later. Through the sense of smell, she can instantly identify her child out of ten other persons. This is what has formerly been described as "motherly instinct."

We use sayings such as "I can smell danger" without being aware of the literal truth in them. We all have smelled the pheromones of fear, anger, sorrow and pleasure. The more we produce them, the more we spread and inhale them again. Pheromones attach to everything and everyone around us. If you are angry, you will inhale more of these angry hormones and become even angrier. If you feel happy, you spread happy pheromones and you may make other people feel happy, too. By ingesting their happy molecules as well, your personal happiness increases even further. On the other hand, sad people depress their environment simply by spreading sad pheromones. This happens because molecules can store information, both negative and positive.

We also imprint our feelings and emotions on objects like chairs, cars and houses. You may walk into an ordinary looking house yet it feels like home. The people living in this house are happy people; they have left numerous chemical "deposits" of good feelings in every nook and cranny. By contrast, if you enter a beautiful, well-decorated house whose owners are quarrelsome, unhappy and tense you may wish to take a U-turn. You can virtually smell the tension in the air by inhaling these mental pollutants produced by the hosts. Both visits can change your biochemistry and with it your mood.

You may have briefly met someone who "has deeply touched you" or "moved your heart." The caring, honest words he spoke to you or the loving kindness of his eyes turned into "friendly" pheromones, which in turn attached themselves to your skin or entered your blood via the lungs. This pleasant stimulation of your sense of touch may have triggered the release of "pleasure hormones" into your blood stream and your heart felt a comforting warmth, love or joy. It may even have started to pound or "move" with excitement.

Even money is influenced by pheromones. During its journey through many pockets and hands, some of the money may become marked by good intention, whereas other parts of it may pick up the chemicals of ill-minded intention. Money can feel "dirty" when you hold it in your hands and you may then feel you want to spend it or pass it on as quickly as possible. There is also the kind of money that makes you feel happy and you may want to save it for a while. Certain coins or notes have collected various types of feelings and emotions, positive ones and negative ones. As we touch the money, we ingest some of the pheromones produced by the previous owners and even link into the imprints of their thoughts and feelings.

An old truth claims that money cannot bring you happiness unless it has been earned through honest means. This is not just myth or psychological blackmail to make us become more honest; it is one of the most profound insights into life and its workings, showing us that the quality of our thoughts and feelings and intentions determines how we live our life. This is what mankind as a whole is about to discover, something that plants knew all along.

Wisdom of the Plants

The first scientist who accidentally stumbled over "plant consciousness" is the polygraph expert Cleve Backster. Polygraphs monitor electrical changes on a person's skin corresponding to emotional states and thoughts. The instrument that measures these changes is called a galvanometer, commonly known as a "lie detector." When hooked to a person's skin, which is a conductor of electricity, you can derive information about his emotional state. Skin resistance drops when he is anxious or feels tense and stressed. On the other hand, when he is rested and relaxed as during meditation or while listening to gentle music or the sounds of the sea, his skin resistance may increase by up to 300 percent. Such a dramatic increase indicates a significant reduction of stress, anxiety and emotional imbalance. Obviously, if a person tells a lie during a criminal interrogation, his fear levels are high; they will be recorded and used as central points for further investigation.

In Backster's accidental experiment, however, the "interrogated" subject was a philodendron plant at his office. After he playfully hooked his galvanometer to his indoor plant, he dunked some of its leaves into the cup of (not very hot) coffee he happened to hold in his hand. Since he didn't get any response, he decided to burn some of its leaves with a match. From the moment he had made this decision, the galvanometer went wild.

This finding was followed by thousands of experiments with plants and their ability to monitor and respond to human thoughts and feelings. In one such experiment a researcher destroyed one of two plants. The surviving plant, which was hooked to a galvanometer, had the task to "identify" the researcher among six other persons. It did so correctly. Plants seem to know when other life forms are threatened or destroyed by people and they remember the person involved. In another interesting study, a researcher placed jam into a cup of yoghurt. The preservatives contained in the jam killed some of the yoghurt bacilli and, amazingly, the nearby plant accurately recorded their death. Plants seem to have a higher sense of right or wrong than we do; they might even be useful as reliable "eyewitnesses" in murder cases!

Plants are also known to show various typical responses to music. During experiments that exposed plants to hard rock, they reacted with panic and shivering, and some of them eventually died. When they "listened" to classical music, they responded with gentle movements, harmoniously swinging back and forth. The most dramatic effects, however, were observed when Indian Sitar music was played to a creeper. After a while, the creeper wrapped itself around the musical instrument, obviously enchanted.

Do Plants have Feelings?

I remember an incident nearly 30 years ago when I put a few tulips into a vase and placed it in front of the portrait of a saint that I kept in my room. Like sunflowers, tulips have the tendency to turn their flowers towards the sunlight, which sustains them. In this case, however, within a day all the tulips had turned away from the window and bowed down to the saint's feet in the portrait as if they derived great pleasure from it. Some of them even managed to touch the portrait and stayed there until they withered away. Can anyone say that flowers have no feelings? I also noticed that whenever I repeated this experiment with tulips and other flowers, especially roses, the flowers lasted often twice and three times as long as they normally would. Did they have a reason for wanting to live longer?

In recent years, micro-nutritionists became interested in conducting research on the changed nutritional potency of plants after they had been treated with "positive human attention." There are already several studies that show higher percentages of protein, carbohydrates, vitamins, minerals and trace elements in edible plants and vegetables that received personal care. Carefully conducted double blind control studies revealed that the plants that received the most attention by the horticulturists were also the most potent ones. When the attending person mentally asked the plants to grow stronger and put his attention on them for longer periods of time, they not only increased their potency more significantly but they also grew faster and bigger. When these plants and vegetables were consumed by human experimental subjects, there was a dramatic increase of their bodies' efficiency that could not be accounted for by simply receiving more nutrients.

Chinese medicine attributes this rise of vitality to the *Chi* or *Life Force*. The energy field or aura of an organically grown and "well-treated" carrot can radiate as far as 25cm (10 inches), whereas the aura of a chemically fertilized carrot is merely 1cm (1/3 inch) wide. Food that is rich in vital energy is revitalizing the system, whereas food that is depleted of most of its vital energy puts a heavy strain on the digestive system. It is not so important to understand exactly what makes a plant more vital and potent, but it is very useful to know that vegetables and plants, which are treated in the above manner, can work like medicine. Perhaps it is for this reason that the ancient doctors declared food to be the best medicine. Current research, which includes highly sensitive blood tests, indicates that there is a very close link between the functioning of organs and the quality of the food consumed.

Losing Touch with Nature

Our relationship to the vegetable kingdom has become very sterile, in many cases it is non-existent. Most of us never get to see a fruit or vegetable ripen or grow. We don't have much influence any more on the degree of vitality they can obtain. Instead of getting human attention, they are handled by cold and hard machines that convey no feelings. Most plants are "fed" with chemicals and insecticides that makes them look good but feel bad, drastically reducing their aroma, potency and nutritional value. They feel mistreated and abused. By exploiting our soil, we sabotage the purpose of their existence, which is to transfer their vitality and perfection to humans, animals and insects.

For political and economic reasons, we overproduce and throw half of the produce away. This abuse of nature effectively cuts our ties with her resources. Food processing, pasteurization and further degradation of originally vital foods through preservatives, artificial flavoring, stabilizers etc., deplete the life-giving enzymes, natural healthy bacteria and nutritional values and convert the former food into "no-food" or junk food. Food processing companies, whose main interest lies in capitalizing on one or several food items, have effectively annulled our body's original "contract" with nature. What makes matters worse: *we* have allowed them to cut our ties with nature.

The Plants' Willingness to Help

Nature's supreme interest lies in creating perfect health of the consumer whether the consumer is a bacterium, an animal or a human being. To make this relationship effective, however, it must be mutual. Plants require the high frequency vibrations generated by an intact and harmonious environment to be able to grow to the level of perfection needed to maintain or restore the health and vitality of the consumer.

All the ancient civilizations were aware of the secrets of plant life. Almost everyone knew how to communicate with flowers and plants, better than most people communicate with their pets. One living example of such abilities is Dr. Balraj Maharshi, a famous Indian herbalist and Ayurvedic physician who knows the medicinal value of over 6,000 plants, herbs and fruits. Their therapeutic values have been repeatedly tested and verified in hundreds of experiments. What is amazing in this case, however, is that Dr. Balraj Maharshi did not study their effects and properties through books. Instead, he learned everything about the plants from the plants themselves.

While walking the Himalayan forests in search of medicinal plants, he used to hear "whispers" coming from the plants which contained clear instructions how they were to be used, for what kind of ailment and in which dosage. Some plants even knew of the plight of humanity and offered their help in relieving sickness and suffering. Some of the plants let him know exactly when they were ready to be picked, whereas others informed him that they were not yet mature and potent enough to be used as an effective remedy. Medicinal plants are also more likely to release their healing properties when they are magnetized through positive human attention; a negative attitude can negate the plant's healing energies, a positive attitude enhance them. An injured and unconscious body can also benefit from the plants, provided subconscious programming is positive, thus facilitating the placebo response.

Nature is capable of helping us to solve our problems but as a human race we have managed to divorce this primary life support system. The vital energy that Mother Nature provides in the form of food, air, water, light etc., seems no longer vital enough to keep us healthy and strong. This is the time to welcome the deep concern of plants to help humanity in obtaining unified awareness.

Research shows that plants can register ecological disasters that occur hundreds of miles away. A tree feels "the pain" of a neighboring tree that is being chopped down. As mentioned before, plants can register the negative vibrations that occur when microscopic life forms such as bacteria get destroyed unnecessarily. Plants are extremely sensitive, if not psychic. They can differentiate between purposeful death and useless death, something humans still need to learn. It is important to recognize that a plant or a piece of fruit or vegetable shows "happy" reactions when it is picked to serve as nourishment for a human being or an animal but feels "distraught" when it is wasted or abused through methods of gene manipulation.

Plants are well aware of the purpose of their existence. Since a plant does not have the choice of violating the laws of nature, it is perhaps more aware of its origin than we are of ours. Where there is purpose there is also intelligence. Plants have great purpose, which makes them very intelligent beings, a quality that is not only reserved for human beings. Without the plants we could not survive on this planet. They not only produce vital oxygen for us but they are also at the bottom of the food chain, meaning that animals and humans depend on them to live and survive.

The ability to discern a "good" intention from a "bad" one is not likely to be expected from a plant, yet polygraphs can reveal at least some of their feeling responses. The sensitivity displayed by trees, plants, or animals may give us a sense of how the entire living Earth must feel when nuclear test bombs explode in her womb; when forests thousands of years old are burnt down to produce secondary grade foods in form of meat; when imprisoned cattle and chicken spend their entire existence deprived of even one ray of natural sunlight to satisfy the carnivorous desire of man; or when soil, air and water are polluted with deadly chemicals.

There is Purpose in all Life Forms

Quantum physics informs us that nothing in the entire universe lives in isolation and that everything influences everything else. Every particle has an anti-particle. If one subatomic particle spins in one direction, its anti-particle spins in the opposite direction even if it is located at the other end of the universe. In the flash of a moment, they may have exchanged positions. Everything that exists in this physical universe is alive because its atoms and subatomic particles are alive.

At the scale of 10^{-33} cm, matter simply ceases to exist. That's where the so-called particles recognize themselves as the field, which is everywhere, an infinite sea of energy, intelligence, and life force. This intimate connection with the universal source makes even a grain of sand a living being with a specific purpose, not less important than a river or a forest. Many grains of sand make a beach. The shore is needed to contain the sea. The sea is vital for the ecological balance of the planet etc. Thus, the grain of sand is of vital importance for the continued existence of the entire planet.

Every bit of the planet is purposeful like each link of a chain. If we are unable to recognize the purpose of a mosquito, a bat or a pebble on the ground we miss out on the experience of wholeness. Our planet is a conscious, intelligent organism, just like our body with its trillions of individual cells. We all share the same atoms which yesterday may have helped to constitute the planet Mars, today compose the food we eat and tomorrow turn into the blood that flows through our veins.

Each star in the skies is essentially a higher dimensional Being which, however, cannot be perceived by our physical eyes since they can perceive only two or three-dimensional images. The higher dimensional aspects of each planet, galaxy or clusters of galaxies all know their individual and collective purpose. They do not operate like machines but rather behave like obedient servants to all life forms in the universe. They know that they are the expressions of a Supreme Being that has infinite love and intelligence. It is time that we, too, begin to understand and realize our purpose. In the same way as plants use their full potential and know their purpose, we are also meant to use our full potential and know our purpose in life. Everything we ever need in life is within us; so all we need to do is to start living more consciously. To discover our true potential and to use it fully, we first have to understand what we are capable of doing.

CHAPTER 3
Well Begun is Half Done

Our Brain – A Universal Computer

Learning is one of the most powerful tools we have to shape our reality. We are able to learn new things only because our brain, unlike that of an animal, has preprogrammed neural equipment that allows it to create ideas and images from what we see, language from what we hear and thoughts from what we experience. Another way to say this is that although we have many built-in capacities for learning, how and what we learn is up to us.

It is through the input from our surroundings that we are able to program the brain; otherwise, nothing resembling the human mind would develop. Without that immense infusion of new experiences, we would scarcely have a trace of intellect. Animals, by contrast, have hardwired instinctive wisdom, but limited capacities to learn new things.

Almost all human brains have the same hardwire for learning an incredible number of things, yet these capacities are used to a varied extent by different people. This accounts for their variance in skills, knowledge, and goals. For example, if two languages are spoken in a home, the child can learn to speak them both. If exposed to a third language it can even learn three. One girl was exposed to seven foreign languages while she grew up; by the time she was eight she spoke eight languages fluently. Experimental evidence suggests that the more we learn in a spontaneous, effortless way, particularly during the early stages of life, the more our brain is capable of increasing the numbers of microscopic nerve fibers. These in turn serve to reinforce learning.

For a baby, the number of new objects, colors, shapes, sounds, impressions, odors etc., increases very rapidly each day. They stimulate the construction of an increasingly complex network of eventually as many as a quadrillion connections between the billions of nerve cells in the brain. This makes it possible for a person to perceive and process a vast amount of external and internal information.

35

An adult's brain is usually exposed to a billion bits of information per second. They are channeled to the brain through the five senses of perception. This enables our brain to "measure" the temperature of the air when it touches our skin and even to read its composition of various atoms. The brain also knows the frequencies and inherent properties of the various colors that objects reflect and direct towards our eyes. It processes, interprets and responds to the different sound waves that hit our eardrums; and it categorizes the smells of the earth, the sea, or food so that we may recognize their identities in the future. Our brain registers the vast number of chemical reactions that occur in our body at every moment and takes note of all the phenomena that we are not able to register consciously. This makes our brain a universal computer, unmatched by any other computer.

A New Brain for a New Age

A network of nerves in the brain stem serves as a sort of traffic control center that permits only a few hundred of these millions of messages, at most, to enter our conscious mind. The rest is filtered out as "not useful" or "not relevant." In practical terms, we are able to access only a tiny fraction of the "real" world. We cannot even begin to comprehend what the *real* world looks like, sounds like or feels like. If we only could use more of the brain's inherent capacity than is currently available to most people, that is between one and five percent, we would perceive the world differently. Apart from experiencing it as purely three-dimensional (material), we would also perceive its fourth dimensional reality (higher consciousness, where thoughts become instantly materialized). This would present the world in a completely new light to us.

Unknown to the scientific community, the human DNA, which holds the genetic blueprint of the body within the nucleus of every cell, was stripped of its original 12-stranded structure about 500,000 years ago. This is the time period we believe to be the beginning of human civilization. In truth though, this was only the beginning of the latest phase of civilization, which is characterized by using just a double-stranded DNA. Other variations of human life before this period had an active DNA of twelve strands. The degraded state of our DNA was the main reason for keeping us imprisoned within the boundaries of a materialistic and dualistic perspective of the world.

Within the coming years and decades, however, the human DNA will once again be upgraded to twelve strands or more. Already a few years ago, a tidal wave of light-encoded rays (as photons) began to infuse the earth and create a potential third DNA in the masses, one that will first manifest in the form of a magnetic strand. Genetic scientists are already perplexed about the changes occurring in our DNA. The new light infusion will awaken many brain cells that have been lying dormant until now. This process will continue until we begin to use the full potential of our physical body and brain rather than a mere fraction of it, as we have done so far. Eventually, all of humankind will have established the physiological basis for consciously living in the higher dimensions of our own existence. This will mark the time when the problems humanity currently faces, including starvation, poverty, pollution, physical diseases, crime, terrorism and conflicts, will begin to vanish from the surface of the earth.

Wonders of the Brain

Even with its current limited capacity, our brain is nevertheless able to conduct an inconceivable number of complex activities. In comparison to an adult's life, a baby's internal world seems to be a lot simpler. Yet in time, while it is exposed to more and more stimulation from the external world, the baby's brain adjusts its performance to compute as much of the external information as possible. Within the first year, the size of its brain has tripled. Even with that capacity, the child's brain could hold information that would fill millions of volumes.

Some children exhibit extraordinary skills such as playing difficult musical compositions on the piano at a very young age. It is hard to imagine what must be going on in a child's little brain when all its fingers are flying over the keys as if they were doing this on their own. Is it not astonishing that the human brain can sense and co-ordinate the quick movements of ten fingers, striking the right keys at the right time with the right force to match the musical notes running through the artist's mind? If the musician makes a mistake, the brain is right there to intervene and to let him search for the correct note.

At the same time, the brain has to control an extraordinary amount of additional functions and responses in the body that directly and indirectly support the artist in his performance. They include: intake of adequate amounts of oxygen and the removal of harmful carbon dioxide; digestion and metabolism of food; generation of muscular energy; listening to the music; sensing the atmosphere in the audience; sitting straight and pressing the piano pedals; perhaps reading the music in front of him; producing an astronomical number of chemicals in the brain that sustain the performance and give pleasure and satisfaction to the performer. It is an extraordinary feat of the musician's brain to co-ordinate these extremely complex processes with each other and keep them running *all at the same time*! This, however, is merely a fraction of what the brain is capable of accomplishing.

What Shapes Destiny

Childhood turns out to be one of the most crucial factors in determining the features of personality, but also the difficulties in a person's life. Once the hardwire of the brain has been structured at an early age, these permanent personality features may stay with us until the brain stops functioning altogether. Positive personality characteristics include self-acceptance and self-worth, spontaneity, capacity for warm interpersonal relationships, tolerance, ability to love and to forgive, maturity, creative spirit, good humor, liveliness, and emotional stability. It is unlikely that someone will have significant emotional or psychological problems later in life if these or similar qualities are developed in childhood. A supportive environment with loving parents, teachers and friends helps to create "positive wiring" in the child's brain during the period of growing up, which will make him cope better with the challenges of adult life.

By contrast, if a child is influenced by rigid rules imposed by close relatives and social systems, he is likely to adopt rigid patterns of behavior when becoming an adult. Distrusting parents, egotism by the people around him, frequent insults, punishment, abuse, all may cause an "inadequate" performance in school sufficient to create a "negative hardwiring" in his brain. All this can shape a personality that is easily thrown off balance when similar instances occur later in life. Recently, a 15-year boy committed suicide because he felt he could not live up to the standards of his parents' expectations. In a suicide note, he apologized to them for not having produced good enough marks in school and wished that, if they were to adopt another child "the new one would bring home better grades." Such low self-esteem can only be the result of many expectations, disappointments, and rejections. Before a child attempts to take his life, he must feel completely lost and "empty" inside.

Christos was a young married man in his early thirties who came to visit me because of his severe digestive problems. When I asked him what his diet was like, he said: "I don't like eating and I rarely think about food but when I eat I gobble it down as fast as I can, usually whilst standing." I inquired from him whether during his upbringing he had any negative experiences with food or eating. He reluctantly told me that his mother used to literally throw the food at him if he did not like it or did not eat everything that was on his plate. This developed into an aversion towards food, which stayed with him until recently. By sitting down at mealtimes and consciously eating his food, Christos gradually managed to separate the emotional abuse by his mother from the nourishing qualities of food. This corrected the mistake in the hardwiring of the brain and soon his digestive system began to receive the go-ahead signal to digest food properly again.

The Secret World of the Unborn Child

Childhood experiences are not the only factors that can determine our destiny. A child's life does not begin with its birth. Because we cannot see the infant before he is born (except through Ultrasound machines), it does not mean that he has no links to the outside worlds. Although the unborn child lives in a world of his own, he is still most profoundly influenced by everything that happens around him, especially the thoughts, feeling and actions of his parents. Research has shown that a fetus can lead an active emotional life from the sixth month on, if not earlier. He is able to feel and can even see, hear, taste, experience and learn while in the womb. The feelings that he has during his stay in his mother's womb depend largely on how he deals with the messages that he receives mostly from the mother, but also from the father and the environment.

An anxiety-ridden mother, who is constantly worried about making mistakes or who suffers from other forms of emotional imbalance, can leave a deep scar on the personality of the developing fetus. Likewise, a self-assured and confident mother instills in him a deep sense of content and security. These or similar initial emotional imprints shape a person's attitudes and expectations and can ultimately create a personality that acts them out either as shyness, anxiety and aggression, or self-confidence, optimism and happiness. Contrary to common understanding but discovered by recent research, the father's feelings towards his wife and the unborn child play one of the most important roles in determining the success of a pregnancy. There is strong evidence that a father who bonds with his child while he is still in the womb can make a big emotional difference to his well-being. A newborn baby can recognize his father's voice in the first one or two hours after birth and respond to it emotionally, provided the father had been talking to the child during the pregnancy. The soothing, familiar tone of his voice, for example, is able to stop the child from crying, indicating that he feels protected and safe.

It is common knowledge that a mother's dietary habits can influence the growing fetus, too. Smoking cigarettes and drinking alcohol have proved to cause irreversible damage to a growing fetus. A series of precise experiments have demonstrated that the thoughts, feelings, and emotions of parents (particularly of a mother) can assert an even greater influence on the unborn child.

There is much speculation about exactly when the unborn child begins to recognize and respond to these external stimuli, but this seems secondary. What is more important is that human life begins in the womb and is shaped by all its experiences during the gestation period (the nine months in the womb). Studies have shown that the heartbeat of an unborn child quickened every time his mother thought of smoking a cigarette. Without lighting up or picking up a cigarette, the mother's thought caused an instant adrenaline response by the fetus in anticipation of a dreaded oxygen decline in his and his mother's blood. This stress response made his heart beat faster. The mother's desire to smoke may also be linked to a sense of uncertainty, nervousness and fear within her. While she translates these emotions into the corresponding chemical compounds in her brain, the same emotional responses are triggered also in the fetus. This situation can eventually predispose the unborn child towards deep-seated nervousness and anxiety later in life.

Rhythms of Happiness

Maternal emotions of anxiety have repeatedly been shown to cause exaggerated fetal activity. Researchers were able to demonstrate that the most active fetuses would one day become the most anxious youngsters. They would become abnormally shy and shield themselves away from teachers, from schoolmates, from forming friendships and from all human contact. It is most likely that the youngsters will remain inhibited and shy even in their thirties and through to old age unless they find a way to correct the initial emotional imbalance from fetus-hood.

The rhythms and tone of its mother's voice also influence the unborn child. The fetus moves his body rhythm to harmonize with his mother's unique rhythms of speech. He also responds to sounds and melody from another source than his mother's. Agitated unborn children calm down when they listen to calming music such as Vivaldi. Beethoven, on the other hand makes them kick and move around more, as do sounds made by yelling parents. Pregnant musicians have even "taught" their fetuses intricate musical pieces. From a certain age, the children were able to play the music by heart without ever having heard it before, except whilst they were in the mother's womb. Other children were found to repeat words or phrases which the mother had used only during pregnancy. One child grew up speaking a foreign language that the mother had used during her pregnancy while working in a foreign country but had stopped using after giving birth.

The maternal heartbeat is one of the most powerful means to keep the growing fetus happy and attuned to the outside world. The steady pace of her heartbeat reassures him that all is well. He can "read" the mother's emotional states through the changing rhythms of her heart. During the gestation period, the fetus senses the comforting maternal heartbeat as his main source of life, safety, and love. The emotional value attached to heartbeat was confirmed by a study that used a tape-recorded human heartbeat being played to a nursery filled with newborn babies. To the astonishment of the researchers, the babies who were exposed to the sounds of heartbeat ate more, weighed more, slept more, breathed better, cried less and were less sick than those who were deprived of the rhythmic sound of a heart. Of course, in natural settings, babies would never be separated from their mothers after birth and therefore would continue feeling their mother's heartbeat.

"Cot death" is a phenomenon that occurs almost only among babies who have been kept apart from their mothers after birth (another major risk factor is cigarette smoke in the babies' environment). Such babies feel abandoned by their mothers and are unable to sustain their vital functions without feeling and hearing her heartbeat. Most babies survive this dramatic measure of separation from the mother but may be left with emotional scars that show up as low self-esteem, weakness and anxiety later in life. By contrast, the babies who stay with their mothers most of the time feel wanted and loved right from the first moments of life. They are much less likely to have a reason for feeling insecure when they grow older. Their personalities will be friendly, confident, optimistic and extrovert.

Mixed Messages

A fetus may be strongly influenced by stressful events that occur in the mother's life. The resulting release of stress hormones can trigger similar emotional responses in the fetus as those felt by the mother. However, if she feels unconditional love for her baby and believes that nothing else is as important to her as her growing child, then the baby will feel safe and protected. A major German study on 2,000 pregnant women concluded that the children of mothers who looked forwards to having a baby, were much healthier, both mentally and physically, at birth and afterwards, than those born to mothers who did not really want a child. Another study conducted at the University of Salzburg in Austria procured even more stunning results. Psychological tests revealed that the mothers who wanted their unborn children both consciously and unconsciously, had the easiest pregnancies, the most uncomplicated births, and the healthiest offspring – physically and emotionally. The group of mothers who had a negative attitude to their unborn children had the most serious medical complications during pregnancy, and bore the highest rate of premature, low-weight and emotionally disturbed infants.

Many pregnant women give mixed messages to their babies. They often would like to have a child but do not want to give up their career. These unborn children are often apathetic and lethargic after they are born. A woman's relationship with her husband or partner is the second most influential factor in determining infant outcome. A recent study that involved over 1,300 children and their families showed that women who feel they are locked in a stormy marriage have a *237 percent higher risk* of giving birth to a psychologically or physically abnormal child. Children who feel loved while in the womb have every good reason to give, trust and love when they are living in the outer world. They generally develop a deep bond with their parents and have no or little tendency to become affiliated or involved with problematic personalities during their lives.

The Workbook of Life

Every moment in a child's life, whether it occurs before or after its birth, plays a very important role in shaping his personality. Each instance contributes to either a happy or an unhappy life in the future. The brain can be programmed in either way. Yet it is not in the child's direct capacity to protect himself against parental abuse or to create a wonderful home full of love and support. The first 16 – 20 years of human life are generally subject to "karmic contracts and requirements," which are only known to the soul before it is born in human form. After it has incarnated, all memory about deciding what lessons it needs to learn and which surroundings would be the most suitable to accomplish this, have vanished. It is for this reason that so many young people feel imprisoned until they have reached age 18 or 20. They don't realize that they have voluntarily placed themselves into the limiting, often adverse surroundings and circumstances, only to work off their karmic "debts" or obligations and thereby uplift their personal vibrations and those of their surrounding. Before the soul incarnates in human form it is aware of its highly developed status and power. It is our task here on Earth to consciously link up with this aspect of our soul and to use its immense wisdom and power while in matter. Each time we go through difficulties in life, we get closer to this goal.

After a certain age when the psychology and physiology of a person has matured enough to be able to live in a reasonably self-sufficient way, the soul becomes more free to consciously decide the course of its new life. The "book of *Karma*", which the soul has brought into this life from the previous ones, is then ready to be understood and the real life teachings can begin. All the previous "positive and negative" programming of the brain and personality during gestation and the first phases of life (from birth to 20), can now be used by the soul as a private "tutor." Every resistance, problem and opportunity in life can be a profound lesson in the "Workbook of Life." Human awareness is then able to rise above the challenges of life and harness the total capacity of its brain. Thus, it can reach the highest state of human development – unity consciousness.

To know that "I Am in Everything" and "Everything is in Me" is the humble experience of unity consciousness similar to the essence of a golden ring, a golden chain or a golden figure which forever remains the same gold despite its appearance in different shapes. The human brain is capable of producing such sophisticated hardwiring that it can perceive consciousness and matter, which are the two most extreme opposites of life, as expressions of the same thing – the Self. You are that Self; everyone is that Self. Like a huge spider web, we are all connected through this infinite field of vibrant existence. Your brain is the tool to know and live this final truth of life.

Surrender Your Past

The Neurologist Richard M. Restak stated once: "Since the brain is different and immeasurably more complicated than anything else in the known universe, we may have to change some of our most ardently held ideas before we are able to fathom the brain's mysterious structure." The same applies to every other area of life. As humankind is moving towards the end of the twentieth century, old-fashioned ideas and belief systems are fast becoming obsolete. Deeply rooted convictions and ideologies that seemed to be valid until recently are increasingly perceived as dated dogmas from our historic past. The political, social, and economic systems that have ruled humanity through the many years of "cold war" don't seem to be so practical any more. Our current systems of administration, too, show signs of rapid disintegration.

What we still believe to be important and necessary today may be irrelevant tomorrow. Old paradigms of living die fast now and new ones are emerging in every field of life. Religions, political systems, economic principles, scientific understanding etc., are quickly moving from one "truth" to the next. If one particular system lasted for ten years just two decades ago, it now may take less than a year for it to become outdated.

Some of our old ideas and belief systems, however, are solidly wired into our brain and many people are still controlled by rigid rules or self-fulfilling prophecies. Fragmented knowledge can only bear fragmented results. Therefore, these misconceptions of reality have contributed to the multiple problems that humankind is facing at the moment, individually and collectively. We still use most of the old ideas of living that have been conceived by people from our historic past, who we deem wiser or more knowledgeable than we are today. Most of today's worldviews are influenced by the thoughts of other thinkers. The lack of trust in our own creativity and sense of right or wrong may be at the root of the current crisis of world existence, such as global energy crisis, terrorism and natural calamities. Most people who blow themselves up to kill others for what they consider a holy cause, were taught to believe that this would save them a place in heaven. If they were taught that they would go to hell instead, there would be no suicide bombers. Alternatively, if they trusted their own hearts, they would go out of their ways to help and support those who they would otherwise try to destroy.

Educated to be Ignorant

Our modern system of education which is mostly left-brain oriented, often stifles the student's spirit of love, creativity, spontaneity and intuition. This current approach of learning may have greatly

45

contributed to the unrest, disorientation and confusion experienced among so many young people today. Knowledge is structured in consciousness. Without developing consciousness, the benefits that arise from the acquisition of knowledge are trivial. Instead of teaching the young people to unfold their infinite creative potential, they are stuffed with information that has little or no relevance to their lives. By the time they have reached adulthood and are ready to find a job, most of the learnt information has slipped from their minds and will never be used again.

The purely academic approach to learning judges a student's intelligence by his ability to memorize information. This turns the student into a machine, although sometimes a very efficient one. Kids who have "played" with computers for a year or so have often mastered complex programs and created new ones simply by using their intuition, imagination and resourcefulness. By contrast, those who are *forced* to learn the same programs are likely to have great difficulties with them and rarely become efficient programmers.

The more a student is encouraged to use his left-brain which supports the analytical, rational, logical mind, the less he is able to enliven his right brain which could unfold his creative, artistic and intuitive faculties. An educational system that addresses both aspects of the brain could turn any student into a truly resourceful, self-sufficient, and responsible human being who knows from within himself what is right or wrong. The modern standard system of education makes the students conform to a restrictive social system that is governed by "cold" figures, rules and money, with only little or no room for human values. Yet life is *all* about human values.

Consciousness – The Missing Link

Education, as it is presented by today's schools, colleges and universities, causes a division within the student, separating his heart from his mind. Intellectual abilities are favored over those that develop his heart or the creative spirit within him. A purely academic approach to education turns economics into a battlefield where career oriented people fight for superiority over others. Modern competitiveness has led to the current loss of humanness in society. The consequences of such an education are immeasurable.

All problems of life, whether individual, social, national or international are directly linked to one crucial flaw in our educational system – the lack of development of the student's consciousness. This is the missing link that could make modern education complete and fulfilling. Instead of expanding the student's mind through meditation, visualization, intuitive training or other techniques of self-development, it is overloaded with a lot of information that has little or no relevance to his life. This suffocates a young person's creative spirit and stresses him to the point of depression, anxiety and even severe mental and physical disturbances that can propel them to take such "emergency exits" as recreational drugs, alcohol and violence.

Young people are released from school with a paper in their hands that can determine the rest of their lives. The dependency of a person's destiny on his ability to pass exams is a frightening prospect, particularly when learning by heart has nothing to do with a person's intelligence. I personally never did well in school. Being forced to repeat a grade and just barely making it through the others, I experienced the 14 years of my German school education as a living "nightmare," both during the day and the night. My fear of failing exams never left me, even during the eight weeks of summer vacation. Apart from the basic skills of writing, reading and counting, I cannot remember anything else that I had learnt. Yet today I believe I am at the height of my creative skills, covering many more fields than I had been presented with during 14 years of education.

The great minds and successful people of our historic past like Plato, Einstein, Michelangelo etc., received their insights, skills, and creative power from within themselves and not through an acquired ability to repeat what others had said or created before. Today's system of education prevents the student from using his own infinite potential by emphasizing mainly mechanical approaches of repetitive thinking and learning. Such approaches ignore the important issues of life. For one thing, they may give us the (false) impression that we cannot fulfill our desires other than through struggle of some kind. Most people in the world seem to have made the collective agreement that in order to earn a reasonable living one has to work hard. The strong competitiveness among people and businesses in our modern societies reinforce this belief system.

Many claim that suffering is necessary or that once you have reached a certain age you are no longer fit enough to earn a living. Ignorance about ourselves and the nature of reality is so ingrained in collective consciousness that we no longer object to such actually quite nonsensical statements as: "Sickness is a natural part of life", "to err is human" or "everyone must age and grow old." We even seem to have gathered enough proof to substantiate our beliefs. Wars, famines, statistics on old age, heart disease, cancer and AIDS leave no doubt in our minds that this is how life is supposed to be and there is not much we can do to change that. All these experiences support the validity of our original belief systems, which are based on the old paradigm of understanding human life. However, the time has come to surrender our past and let go of these limitations, because they do not really exist, except in our mind.

CHAPTER 4
It's All Within You

Escaping the Prison of Social Conditioning

The new paradigm which views life in a different way than it has ever been seen before claims: "You are what you believe!" Your brain can allow only that information to enter your mind, which supports or reinforces your currently held beliefs. That's why it is unrealistic to say that *I only believe what I can see with my own eyes*. In actuality you can only see what you believe exists out there. To state this differently, if you see someone levitate in front of your eyes and your beliefs do not accept such a possibility, you will find all the reasoning to prove that the act of levitation was a trick performance. Your perception of the world is but a concept formed by your own beliefs and your present understanding or knowledge of this world. Whatever does not fit into your belief system, you will consider unreal or fictitious.

Physics' law of the "Observer - Observed Relationship" may place destiny back into your hands. The law states that by observing the movements of a microscopic particle or by looking at a flower, a child, or food, you will change the observed object in one way or another. This fact makes every "objective" scientific experiment dependable on the subject or the observer and may even render it unreliable. Since the state of mind of the observer is highly changeable, it can significantly influence the process of observation and substantially alter the outcome of the experiment. By way of insisting that what you believe is the truth, you have already manipulated the outcome of your observation in as much as it will fulfill and reinforce your original ideas or beliefs. Every experience takes place in consciousness. Everything that is "outside" is, therefore, just a transformed state of consciousness. We see our own consciousness in different modes, colors, shapes etc. In other words, what I believe I am is identical to *my* perception of the world. Each consciousness creates and lives its own world of reality.

49

An acquaintance of mine told me recently about her friend who has developed multiple sclerosis (MS), a debilitating disease that affects the nervous system. She said that his condition was worsening day by day and wanted to know whether I could give him any advice. She also mentioned that none of the therapies tried so far produced any improvement. Having worked with quite a few MS patients, I asked her whether he had any negative belief systems in his life. She said that for many years he had collected every scientific theory and supportive evidence that could be found anywhere in the world to prove the imminent destruction of our planet. His main words to describe the world's situation were "It is too late," meaning that the ecological damage has gone beyond possible repair.

I explained that when a person projects his negative attitude or outlook of life on the outer world, he will try to find all the valid reasons for supporting and reinforcing his beliefs, which will consolidate his original conviction. In this case, the man's body, too, had accurately responded to his destructive "instructions." As a soldier obeys the command of his superior, so does the body translate each signal that comes from his mind into concrete chemical responses, even if it means harming or destroying oneself.

MS belongs to a category of disorders that are known as autoimmune diseases. According to the doctors' beliefs, the body attacks its own biological defense system. Destruction of one's immunity renders the body susceptible to any type of disease-causing agents. However, disease never strikes indiscriminately. If we hold deep resentment towards someone, for example, we may literally be eaten up by it; we label it as cancer.[1] The immobilizing effect of MS is the body's response to feeling helpless and victimized. In the above case, the man is unconsciously committing suicide because he is terrified by his fear of global annihilation. Without being aware of it, he prefers to die before the planet does. Unless he finds a way of drastically altering his self-destructive belief system, he may not find any other "remedy" for changing his negative programming than the death experience itself. Eventually, when physical death occurs, he will discover that he, being consciousness, is beyond death and destruction

---

[1] To understand what cancer is and why it occurs, please see *Cancer is Not A Disease It's A Survival Mechanism* by the author.

and so is the planet. This is one of the greatest lessons we are meant to learn and master, ideally while we are still in a human body.

You are What you Believe

In 1988, when the well known French allergist Jacques Benveniste published his research paper on the memory properties of water, it aroused much opposition in the world of scientific investigation. Soon after, two "fraud busters" were sent to Benveniste's laboratory with the intent to prove that his experiment was invalid. To be brief, the "opposition team" produced the exact opposite result: Water molecules have no capacity for memory. Now the question arises, who was right?

The answer is that there is no truth other than what you believe is true. You continuously create your own reality every moment of your life. Society is a synthesis of individuals and their ideas, beliefs, ideals, preconceived notions, desires, likes, dislikes etc. When approximately one per cent of the population begins to support a new idea or a new trend in the areas of fashion, politics, economics or computer science then suddenly the entire society begins to adopt the new innovations, too. That is how a few can influence the whole. The result is that a large portion of the population agrees upon the ideas of reality that are created by a few.

As you look back in human history, all the major cultural, political, and social reforms were inspired by a few leading thinkers of society. Even revolutions and wars were often incited by individuals (Hitler, Mao, Saddam Hussein etc.) and quickly spread to larger parts of the world. *Your* personal way of seeing reality can be crucial for the entire society. When a few monkeys living on a Japanese island learned to wash their potatoes in seawater to clean them and give them a better taste, all the other monkeys on the island and the neighboring islands began to adopt this new technique to make potatoes more edible. There were no obvious links of physical communication between the various groups of monkeys, yet on a consciousness level the monkeys were perfectly able to communicate this new way of treating potatoes to the monkeys living hundreds of miles away.

Most of what we know today we have learned in the past. We receive our information (and misinformation) mainly through the channels of education, media, and traditional beliefs. Usually we conform to one or more of the dogmas presented to us and we often use such phrases as: "That's life!" or "I can't change the world."

Fruit flies behave in a similar way if they grow up in a closed glass jar. When one day you take off the lid of the jar you may be surprised to discover that the flies have no inclination to escape, in fact they have no good reason why they should escape. The fruit flies have in a way committed themselves to live in their prison of glass until they die. It is their conviction that the world is a closed glass jar because that's all they know about the world. However, if enough "pioneers" were adventurous enough to go through the fictitious prison gate, more and more flies would do the same and eventually find an infinite world lying at their very doorstep, ready to be explored. In our own ways we, too, have committed ourselves to living in a "prison", but our prison walls are made of old and seemingly unshakeable belief systems that we have accepted to be valid and true for centuries and decades.

A classical experiment with more evolved creatures than fruit flies can demonstrate this principle even more clearly. A team of researchers kept a group of kittens in a room that had nothing but vertical stripes painted all over. Once grown, the kittens were released from their vertical confinement, but they were unable to see or recognize any horizontal objects and consequently bumped into them. Beds and tables were not part of their belief system.

Another group of kittens grew up in a room with only horizontal stripes and after they were released into the normal world they bumped into all vertical objects like pillars or chair legs. All they were allowed to learn while growing up was one out of many thousands of basic perceptual realities. Their brains had made only those connections that supported the perception of one visual stimulus; they were oblivious of the rest of the physical world.

As a part of the experiment, a third group of kittens was blindfolded right from birth. After they became wise old cats, so-to-speak, their blindfolds were taken off. But their eyes, even though fully intact, could not see anything at all and remained blind for the rest of their lives. For these cats, the reality of the world was without colors, shapes or forms. Since they never learnt to know the world through the visual sense, their idea of it was radically different from that of the other groups of cats. Our experience of the world is also merely a projection of what we believe it to be. In truth, we are what we believe. Just as the kittens, we are confronted with a certain view of reality that other people have upheld and adopted before we did.

Aging is a Choice

One of the best examples of how we create our reality is aging. Biological aging, which should not be confused with chronological aging, is a natural phenomenon that will affect every person at some stage in life; at least this is what we have been led to believe. Since everyone repeatedly tells us the same story, we begin to accept the "reality" (of aging) and reinforce it through our personal experiences. So it must be true! But this does not explain why some people age much faster than others and why some do not seem to age at all.

It would be intriguing to find out what really determines our life span? Some of us may live up to 100 years or more without feeling old whereas others might die from "old age" 50 years earlier. The ancient Indian sage Shankara who displayed extraordinary wisdom from the age of eight saw the process of aging as being deeply rooted in a person's own belief system. He said: "The only reason why people age and die is because they see other people age and die." We all have more or less different viewpoints or opinions about the world as such. This may lead to varied perceptions of reality. What is the "truth" for one person may not be relevant at all for another person. Yet with regard to the ideas of aging and illness, we seem to agree with each other for we rarely step out of the main paradigm altogether.

To avoid looking for the real cause of decline with age, we prefer to believe in an invisible force that somehow and gradually programs our life to deteriorate according to a numbering system (from years 1 – 100…). It seems too farfetched for us to accept the idea that we may be causing the aging process ourselves. Do we perhaps give ourselves the (unconscious) permission to age because this lets us off the hook to take responsibility for our own life and that of other people?

Who Ages, Who Doesn't?

The mind/body connection is at work as long as we live. This is also true in the case of aging. If you believe that your biological age is sixty today because you have passed that many birthdays and that you are soon ready for your pension, then you are likely to be in the process of adjusting your biological age to your psychological one. This means that your biological organism may soon be as old as you believe it should be. When you become aware of the regular automatic "servicing" that renews your body (each year 98 percent of the atoms of your body are turned over) and you are not afraid of aging either, you will find it difficult to age in the negative sense of the word.

People in poor relationships or living in social isolation, those who create stress and worries in their lives, whose lifestyle (overeating, alcohol, tobacco, drugs etc.) is unnatural, or who have no purpose in life, age fast. Those who put themselves first in everything are also known to be prone to accelerated aging. People who suddenly lose their purpose in life are known to age and die very quickly.

By contrast, individuals who care about their health, who often think how they can be of help to others and the world, and who are in a secure and loving relationship, are known to halt the aging process and maintain their youthfulness. According to research on Transcendental Meditation, those who meditate regularly at least twice a day for 15 – 20 minutes, can reduce their biological age by 12 – 15 years within five years. Similar results have been demonstrated among those practicing other forms of relaxation as well as yoga, Tai Chi, Chi Kung etc.

Locusts, too, have a physical body, yet they can live forever if nobody kills them. Their secret is that they change their bodies once a day. We, too, replace our proteins, which are the building blocks of our cells, within 2-10 days. Why should we age, when our "replacements" are as good as the old ones? Locusts do not suffer from stress in their lives, nor do they smoke, watch television, and eat more than they need or count their years of age. What about red wood trees? They can live from 6,000 – 10,000 years. Trees have no reason to believe that aging is a necessary part of their life.

We believe, however, that it must be different with us humans. It's true; we are not trees or locusts. Yet there is no rational, scientific reason to show that aging is a *natural* part of human evolution. Even the science of aging has not yet come up with a consistent theory that could explain *why* we age. Aging should not be confused with death. Nobody dies from old age but from other reasons such as accidents or illness. Aging is usually equated with a loss of vigor, physical strength and mental abilities. Accordingly, everyone who grows in age should be suffering from such or similar debilities. Yet this defies the reality of thousands of old people around the world who remain in good health throughout their lives.

Most people who live very long lives come from the Himalayas, the state of Georgia in the former Soviet Union, The Hunza mountains, Japan, the high Andes and other regions of the world where our idea of aging has not yet penetrated. One of *our* "rules" of aging suggests that that it is normal to experience a deterioration of your eyesight after the age of forty or forty-five. Yet societies who live in such isolated regions of the world as the Abkhazian Mountains of Southern Russia have completely contrary experiences. They are certainly not less human than we are. Abkhazians have their senses of vision and hearing in perfect condition at almost any age. People a hundred and more years old are seen swimming in ice-cold streams and riding on horseback. The elders (70, 80 or more years old) from certain tribes in Northern Mexico can run up to 60 miles a day without any sign of fatigue or exhaustion; they even show lower heart rates after their marathons than before.

These people rarely die from a disease. When their time has come they know it, and without making much of a fuss they experience the end of their lives with a profound sense of peace, accomplishment and fulfillment. Because their social systems honor old age more than any other "achievement" does, they don't regard death as a form of punishment. For these people, advanced age is synonymous to maturity, wisdom, a wealth of experience and a good reason to become older faster.

For many women in Western societies, menopause represents a mid-life crisis. In some societies of the Far East menopause is very rare and some women are still fertile at age 70. On the other hand, if it occurs early it must not necessarily indicate a physical imbalance or progressed state of aging. Menopause can signal a new phase of living, when maturity, wisdom and love get a chance to reach unprecedented heights. If a woman is convinced that menopause is bad for her or if she is afraid of the mid-life changes, she may indeed experience it as one of the most difficult periods of her life.

Limitations Exist Only in the Mind

As a golden rule, beliefs, which restrict us in some way or contain negative characteristics, are man-made dogmas or ideas that have no absolute truth in them. By accepting them into our lives we conceal our true nature, which is without any limitations. To live free and independent lives we don't need a belief system at all. The perfect and invincible power of natural law that organizes the entire universe with perfect precision is already inscribed in the hardwiring of our brain. Although, most of us, being a part of the societal set-up, have taken in plenty of limiting and destructive forms of information right from the beginning of life, our pre-programmed neural equipment for youthfulness and perfect health nevertheless remains an integral part of our physiology. We don't need to *study* the laws of nature to harness their power; every part of us is already controlled by natural law. The ability to live spontaneously according to the laws of nature has been given to us right from the beginning of life.

To permit ourselves to be guided by natural law we only have to stop reinforcing our adopted and artificially derived "truths." They only serve to disconnect us from our life support system. A garden in need of precious water can only grow and flourish when the pipes of the irrigation system are clear. If they are clogged, the flowers, fruits and vegetables will wither, age and die. By opening our channels of perception and keeping our body vital and healthy, we can re-establish a *universal belief system* in our consciousness that will nourish ourselves in every respect. The universal belief system says that there are no limitations, restrictions or shortcomings for a person whose mind and heart stays open to receive inner and outer abundance. This new paradigm, which says that everything is possible, is part of a cosmic plan that is already in the process of being implemented.

Opening the Heart

World War I was a turning point in human history. It initiated an era of war, famines, and conflict. Konrad Adenauer, the first German Chancellor after World War II, said once: "Before 1914.... There was real peace, quiet, and security on this earth - a time when we didn't know fear..." One year before the outbreak of World War I, the US Secretary of State Bryan made the observation that conditions promising world peace were never more favorable. Soon after that over 100 million people lost their lives in wars, large and small. Widespread famines added hundreds of millions more casualties to this number.

Even today, 12 million children die each year before their first birthday; 800 million more are underfed and 400 million live constantly on the brink of starvation. On the other hand, the industrial revolution and the advancement of science and technology have given us abundance in food, comfort and material affluence. There are two worlds coexisting on our planet. One world has more than it needs but suffers from over- stimulation, stress, and psychological wasting; the other world ails from poverty, inadequate shelter and physical malnutrition.

Violent crime and chronic illnesses, including heart disease, cancer, and AIDS, are further signs of an unbalanced modern society. As individuals, we tend not to take responsibility for any of these global trends and events. Our response is based on our predominantly analytical and mechanical way of thinking, which calculates the chances of us exerting a positive influence on the world's population as 1 in 6,500,000,000. Such calculations are based on the old paradigm of understanding human nature. What could one person do to change the trends of time, not to speak about the fast pace of destruction of our so heavily polluted and greatly disturbed world ecology? Our historic past seems to support the notion that any attempts to make the world a better place for us and future generations are most likely going to fail.

Yet the past is gone and a new era is dawning. There is a simultaneous "awakening" of significantly large numbers of people who are beginning to recognize their power and ability to transform the world into a place worth living for. This awakening process is the beginning of "heart-based" life, in recognition of our deep interconnectedness with everyone and everything that exists on the planet. Collectively, we are in the process of realizing that there cannot be lasting happiness for anyone unless poverty, starvation, stressed living conditions and destruction of our environment are completely rooted out everywhere.

Our generation is unique in the sense that we are the first one to make the transition from a very difficult and dark period to an era of unprecedented freedom, abundance and joy for everyone everywhere. Only those who have experienced the dark can appreciate and enjoy the light. Humankind has been on the brink of total annihilation at the time when the superpowers competed in constructing huge nuclear arsenals of mass destruction. Today the fear of total destruction has subsided and we are now moving towards the light of peace and opportunity. Our hearts are opened through calamities like the ones caused by the Rwanda conflict and global child abuse. Large conferences such as the World Food Summit in 1996 in Rome have placed world starvation on top of the international agenda for Third World aid programs.

When our brains work in co-ordination with our hearts, even problems of global magnitude will begin to subside. As a human race, we will be able to achieve a very high degree of technological skill and experimentation that will be beneficial to all and have no detrimental side effects. There will be no need for conflict, hardship and lack of any kind. It is up to every one of us to make this a living reality for all humankind, in both the developed and the underdeveloped world. This makes it even more important now than ever before that we don't add fuel to the current flare-up of conflict and disasters in the world because everything we do or think today is magnified thousands of times.

The Crime of Negative Thinking

To some extent, we all contribute to the current state of unbalanced world affairs by passively participating in the generation of negativity, violence and wars. Whenever we listen to the news coverage about a new war, the capture of a mass murderer, the robbery of the local grocery store or the kidnapping of an innocent child, we may feel the immediate urge to pass judgment. We may catch ourselves directing anger against the "aggressor" who has started the new war and take sides with the innocent victims, out of sympathy or sense of righteousness. We may feel outraged or personally threatened when the house of our good neighbor is burgled, knowing that ours could be next.

Although it seems to be the right thing to do, the very moment we are drawn to pass even the slightest judgment or take sides, we actually help to prepare the ground for renewed conflict, crime, and violence. It is time now to realize that our thoughts, both positive and negative, are powerful events in the non-physical realm that can have great bearing on others and on society as a whole. Because energy follows thought, all the thoughts generated by the billions of people in the world day after day have a much greater influence on world events than their original causes do.

Our personal attitudes, beliefs, emotions, and thoughts carry their inherent messages straight towards the addressed person(s) or situation(s) and link us up with a universal network of reciprocal influence. What *you* think and feel does make a difference. Any form of fear, anger, or greed that you may have inside you will jam this communication system and lead to a build-up of negative and destructive energies, which we may call collective stress. Once the build-up of stress and tension in the collective consciousness of a city, a nation or the entire world's population has reached saturation point, it explodes into collective calamities that affect entire societies.

Crime is not a universal or natural phenomenon. It stands in direct relation to the concentration of stress and disharmony that exists in the minds and hearts of the people living in a particular area of society. For this reason crime rates often differ from city to city and from country to country. It is the degree of dissatisfaction and unhappiness in the people that determines the intensity and frequency of incoherent, aggressive and criminal behavior by a few individuals. The few are only an outlet for the collective stress in society. During the 1996 G-7 Summit, the American president put the fight against terrorism on top of the agenda. Yet with all the powers the government has to track down terrorists, terrorist acts have increased and have become a greater threat than ever before.

The main approach of governments to combat terrorism is still based on deterrent measures and punishment, both remnants of the Middle Ages and none of them successful. Terrorist groups are able to

59

exist and survive because of the massive amount of attention and negative energy they receive from the public. This enormous concentration of negative energy in a few "outlaws" turns them into ruthless and completely irrational murderers.

Every person who hears about new bombs exploding in Israel, Spain, Saudi Arabia, or London is likely to denounce those who planted them. This generates a massive amount of anger, fear and hatred throughout world consciousness. World publicity plays a major role in spreading crime and terrorism today. An international ban on spreading negative news would be the first and most sensible way to undermine terrorism and many other forms of crime. This would substantially reduce global stress and tension, a prerequisite for more coherent thoughts and feelings among all members of society, including criminals.

You *Can* Make a Difference

Russian scientists have linked earthquakes to the incoherent brain waves of the people living in an earthquake zone. Corrective measures by nature or by a nation are only necessary when there is something that needs to be corrected. To improve society, we must put our own house in order first. If a minimum of 1 – 2% of us resist the temptation to participate passively or actively in the spreading of negative world events the rest of society will gradually begin to change as well. This is about the easiest and most profound contribution each one of us can make towards creating a more peaceful world. We can help clean up the mess that we have created for our world not necessarily by *doing* something but by stopping ourselves from participating in "world gossip." The more of us become committed to desist from recycling negative thoughts and events, the faster the world media will reduce their coverage of negative news, not only because there will be less to report.

If by any chance you have linked into the spiritual websites of the Internet, you will know that world trends are much better and encouraging than presented by the mass media. Since nearly all the media focus their attention on negativity and misfortune, the man in the street has no choice but to believe that this is all there is. Yet for every calamity that gets reported there is something wonderful that does not. For every act of greed, crime or violence that is reported in the press, there are an untold number of acts of generosity and compassion. You could fill the mass media with positive and uplifting events many times over. They are at least as important as the negative ones. The reason why they rarely get reported is because *we*, the media consumers, prefer to "consume" negative news instead.

By resisting absorbing negative news, we are making the world a better place. This does by no means mean to become passive or to stick our heads in the sand. Such denial does not help the world either. Knowing that the world needs help is good enough to motivate us to make the necessary changes in this direction.

However, we often feel so helpless when governments make obvious mistakes and harm the interests of the population. The mismanagement of public funds, fraud and miscalculations by a government are but reflections of negative collective consciousness. The efficiency of a government is determined by the collective energetic impact of all the thoughts, emotions, feelings and desires produced by the entire population day after day. The government only mirrors back to the people what they think about themselves, their country and their fellow countrymen. As atmospheric tension builds up and is released by a thunderstorm, so are the powers of crisis unleashed in a nation when its collective stress has reached a climax. The degree of release is proportional to the degree of tension, fear, and frustration that is accumulating in every individual on a daily basis. Once the point of saturation has been reached, only a little spark may be needed to trigger a massive explosion. A typical example for this could be Albania where a seemingly insignificant mistake made by the government was enough to ignite huge collective rage and overthrow the government.

However, if collective stress builds up again, the new government administration will have to face the same problems as the previous government. All initial hope in the newly elected president or Prime Minister slowly fades away as he finds himself helpless in face of a disruptive and unsupportive collective consciousness. However, when the population becomes more coherent and positive at large, the government will reflect this improvement through a renewed ability to help overcome economic, social, and political problems. That's when

61

the government is applauded and praised for its success. In either case, the government is always governed by the collective consciousness of the nation.

The same law applies to treating illness. To help a sick person we have to see a symptom of disease in relation to its underlying cause. Medical intervention, which tends to mask the symptom of a disease and attempts to alleviate it or make it disappear, may be insufficient to truly restore the health of a sick person. It is most likely that the problem will re-emerge perhaps in another part of the body, but this time it will be more persistent than before. Crime, terrorism, and wars, are only the symptoms of an underlying disease process that has affected the entire society. For societal healing to be effective and complete, it must take place on the same level where conflicts are generated, in the minds and hearts of the people. "Sick" thoughts are known to cause illness and suffering. Thought and feelings of love generate health and bestow vitality and happiness. *Your* quality of thought may just make the difference when it comes to resolving a conflict in your own home, your society or anywhere else in the world.

No Thoughts are Secret

Whenever you participate in other people's negative thinking, you become negative yourself. On the other hand, if you are able to look beyond the mask of negativity you will discover a deeper meaning in whatever happens. In both cases way, you link into a universal grid of information that runs parallel to the conventional ones. Imagine that all the people in the world are connected with each other through (invisible) threads that are capable of transmitting electromagnetic messages to any person or group of people they are thinking of. This is exactly what happens when we think, except it works more eloquently than that. Your mere observation of or participation in negative thoughts of other people energizes or magnetizes the existing negativity even further. This is how a person may unintentionally contribute to a further escalation of destructive tendencies in his family, community or the world.

Our ability to influence each other in a positive or negative way is greatly amplified when we link up through electronic or electromagnetic means of communication, of which television and computers are the most prominent. News items can be transmitted around the world within an hour. If the guerrilla organization of a particular country takes innocent people hostage you may have one group of people that approves of the act and another group that condemns it. World opinion becomes divided every time a news item flashes on the television screen.

This creates various thought forms in the minds of the people. Millions of people around the world "shoot" the aggressors in their minds, with "bullets" of anger and judgment. The various time zones in the world make certain that this form of violence in front of the television set is a 24-hour phenomenon. Wars are not only waged on the battlefields, they are also fought in the minds of the people who watch them on television in the privacy of their own homes. Each time you take sides or feel emotionally distressed while watching such unfortunate scenes, you become an active participant in the conflict. If your thoughts or feelings are directed against one particular party it makes that party even more reactive and aggressive than before. This means that you directly link into the global network of thought communication and together with the involved parties and other viewers add fuel to the conflict.

Ending the Mental Warfare

By contrast, if you are able to have genuine feelings and thoughts of compassion and love for both the victims and the aggressors, without judgment one way or the other, then your linkup to the network of thought forms will significantly help to improve or resolve the conflict altogether. We are the immediate participants in everything we observe or witness. When millions of observers link into the energy grid of the thought forms generated for instance during a world championship event, violent feelings such as rage and aggression begin to infiltrate collective consciousness. This may lead to increased unrest in the streets, a rise in crime and terrorism. Anything bad will become a little worse and anything good will deteriorate, including our personal well-being.

The next time you choose to watch a violent event on television, or when you see a violent war or action movie, ask your partner or friend to muscle-test you according to the system of Kinesiology. Your muscular strength will diminish if your interpretation of what you see is scary or unpleasant. Become aware how quickly your energy is "sapped." Negative thought forms create physical congestion and toxins, which in turn inhibit the vital energy flow in the body. One part of the body experiences an excessive build-up of energy that becomes destructive and may make you feel ill, and another part subsequently suffers from lack of energy, which causes weakness or fatigue.

Universal thought communication is open to all sorts of information. The mass media serve only one aspect of this system. They feed the news of events right into your brain and into your feeling center – the heart. The power of your thoughts is intimately connected with your ability to convert them into hard-core chemicals, which may either be pleasure hormones or stress hormones. Your own power of thought, however, is no less potent than the one that is delivered into your home.

Our curiosity about wanting to know what is "going on in the world" may often be stronger than our will to resist such information, but it has its price. By linking into the network of destructive energies, you may become vulnerable to all kinds of harmful influences from within and without; they have the power to slow your mental, physical and spiritual vibrations. But if you decide to focus on creativity, progress, and positive information instead, you have a much greater chance to remain at peace with yourself; this helps raise your vibrations to a degree that you become a constant source of happiness and love for your family and your society.

Currently, this network of communication is still mainly used for spreading destructive information and energies, but positive changes are imminent. Many people in the world have already begun to change their way of thinking. Since our world with all its good and not so good sides is but the product of human thought, the trend towards generating peace and harmony among the people forms the basis for creating an ideal world. Thoughts are waves of varied wavelengths that contain specific messages or information. Their flawless connection to their source, which is our Higher Self, provides them with the power to bring their intents to fruition. As a human race we are on the verge of becoming aware of our true potential and we are also in the process of empowering ourselves, which is needed to make our Earth a more hospitable place and to change the course of destiny for all humankind. However, it is important now that we stop doubting our capabilities.

Doubting – the Cause of Failure

Your thoughts appear to be weak only if they are severed from their powerful source. This happens when you attach to them such "doubting instructions" as, for example: "There is nothing I can do to improve anyone anyway, so why should I even try?" You may initially feel very inspired to make major changes in your life or to contribute towards improving your society until your doubting intellect begins to interfere and rob you of all your inspiration and enthusiasm. By assuming that you are too "small" to influence the "large" or too insignificant to make a major contribution you admit to failure or self-defeat, which will certainly nullify your original intention. In truth, the only insignificant thing in our life is our limited thinking. Yet, there is nothing greater than our infinite potential. The only obstacle that prevents us from using it is the doubt in our own power.

This hesitancy or doubt cannot be removed by intellectually understanding your doubts. When you follow the simple instructions contained in this book, particularly the "Twelve Gateways to Create Heaven on Earth" of Chapter 14, you will learn how to grow into the awareness of unity and interconnectedness. As a result, your doubt-free desires will result in dramatic improvements both within and around you.

We are, in fact, just a breath away from fulfilling our desires spontaneously and without any effort. But because we tend to judge our present abilities on the basis of our past experiences, it may take us a little while before we can fully accept the idea that all we need to fulfill our desires is to clearly intend or formulate what we wish for. This applies to all life-supporting desires, regardless of whether they relate to health, abundance or spiritual success.

Material Wealth and Spiritual Wealth

If you have good and loving thoughts for someone, you are not only sending uplifting and harmonizing messages to him but also to yourself. This helps repair any short circuits that may exist in the universal grid of communication. When the main water pipe of a town becomes obstructed, all the homes are left without this life-giving nutrient. In a similar way, a congested universal communication system prevents constructive energy from penetrating the collective consciousness of society and interrupts the flow of universal energy to you and your environment. It is up to each one of us to maintain or strengthen our links with nature and our fellow human beings. By sincerely wishing them greater material and spiritual wealth, we automatically open our doors to receive the same or more. Because of our intent to give something from our heart, we are automatically connected to the circuit of love, wealth and happiness. This allows us to draw from the very same source and become more loving, generous and happy ourselves. In other words, what you wish unto yourself, first wish unto others.

Connecting our ties with this universal circulatory system results in greater strength and reduced physical, emotional and psychological difficulties in life. But wherever there is congestion, energy will begin to stagnate. Like in a blocked river, stagnating energy can cause immense pressure and become destructive. The originally life-supportive energy of the river may become so powerful, in the negative sense of the word, that it bursts the wall of the dam and destroys everything that lies ahead of it. Mass violation of natural law by millions of people has disturbed the ecological balance and forced us to build dams to derive electricity and improve water supply. Rivers, together with the sea, serve as the planet's energy circuit, and once interrupted, build up very powerful destructive energies.

Likewise, the amassing of material wealth without circulating it for the benefit of humanity, makes a person unhappy and destructive. Egotistic behavior indicates inner poverty and loneliness. To fill this painful vacuum, we may try to amass everything we can get hold of, including power, food, relationships, money and possessions. The fear of never having enough is real poverty and it will persist even when we have collected an abundance of material wealth. Material wealth adds only very little to the inner wealth of love, freedom and fearlessness that occurs spontaneously when we are *in* the flow.

The happiness of a person who is connected to the flow of inner abundance cannot be shattered by the lack of material possessions. A river finds solace and peace in the knowledge that new water is coming in all the time. There is no need to hold on to the old water because there is no fear of losing it. Material wealth can give us great pleasure as long as we are not afraid of having to give it up for some reason. The fear of losing one's wealth is as a sign of attachment. In order to learn letting go of that fear we may actually need to lose what we so feel attached to. You certainly wouldn't want to hang on to your old run-down car or clothes forever unless you were afraid of not being able to afford new ones.

For life to progress and expand, the old has to make space for the new. Only fear stops the river of life and abundance from flowing. Fear is like a dam that may burst one day and cause great destruction. Truly abundant people do not need to run after money, because money "runs" after them. It is always there when they need it. "Worry" is not a part of their vocabulary as they are always linked to the universal supply system. They feel joyfully creative and have an awareness of being wealthy, both spiritually and materially. Life is incomplete when one or the other is missing, both of them are essential parts of life.

Inner and Outer Abundance = 200% Life

To renounce material possessions and devote one's life exclusively to spiritual matters is neither a sign of wisdom nor a sign of courage. Although temporarily retreating from the mundane matters of modern living is almost a necessity today, giving up all other responsibilities in life in order to obtain enlightenment serves only half our purpose on Earth. Our very purpose here is to reach higher states of consciousness *in the midst* of a material world. For life to be complete, both aspects of self need to be appreciated fully, that is 100% spiritual and 100% material. Life can only become fulfilling when we see the material world in a spiritual light. As we begin to fathom the deeply spiritual aspects of our self, we will also recognize them in the material world around us.

67

Our three-dimensional existence (body and surroundings) will only make sense to us when we know who we are – a higher-dimensional being living in a three-dimensional world. Entire generations have devoted their life and breath to spirituality to such an extent that physical needs were no longer taken care of adequately. Starvation, extreme poverty, disease, and lacking sustainability were the sad results of neglecting the material reality of life.

By contrast, our advanced so-called civilized world has almost exclusively emphasized that we can find true happiness in life only by enhancing our physical comfort and material wealth. Everything we do seems to revolve around what job we have and how much money we make. If we got both, then we could acquire a car, a house, a new TV, the latest fashion clothes etc. It is ironic, through, that with all that outer affluence we have reached the limits of inner poverty and starvation. Stress, drug abuse, crime, and general disillusionment with life as well as the fearful, isolated and lonely existence so common for so many people today indicate a sick and poor civilization.

Man is a social animal and cannot live in isolation for very long. Yet loneliness is not necessarily removed by being with other people, even though our society is keen to promote the idea that finding the right partner to spend your life with is a guarantee for true happiness. We can search for many partners and still not find happiness in life. Being with one another is not merely based on physical proximity or contact. To allow for the unfolding of our personal inner and outer abundance, the universal grid of energy and communication, which is omnipresent and connects *all* life forms with one another, needs to be without impediments. Every thought impulse of yours counts because of its power to influence the whole system.

Instant Results

Since all people are tied together on the level of consciousness, a strong, vital and healthy person is a major force for creating a healthy collective consciousness and removing friction in the global energy circuitry. At the same time, this person may also become a powerful magnet for drawing positive and harmonizing energies towards him. Because the sun energies are on the increase now, they will further amplify the intensity of positive trends in society. It is in our own best interests to make choices that are in favor of improving life. Our rewards for involving ourselves with mainly life-supporting news, events, and situations will be an instant increase in happiness, energy and vitality.

The more people make such choices, the fewer of us all will suffer the consequences of unconsciously reinforcing conflict situations in the world and in our own lives. Once you have made such a commitment to yourself, you will almost immediately notice a big burden being taken off your shoulders. The world will have a much greater chance of improving when together we link into the global network of positive information. Your participation *will* make a difference both for the planet and yourself. If you link in today, you will notice a difference tomorrow.

Fatigue – The Beginning of a Vicious Cycle

A disruption of the energy circuit in our lives can be caused by many factors which all fall under the umbrella of violating the laws of nature. The result is fatigue, which is a form of energy depletion. Sleep and rest, on the other hand, are responsible for restoring energy and rejuvenating body and mind.

Let's assume that due to a social engagement or late arrival from the airport you come home early in the morning at around 3 a.m. You feel exhausted but due to an early appointment at your office you can only afford to sleep for 3 ½ hours. You drag yourself out of bed after a second merciless reminder from the alarm clock. Still feeling tired and physically drained, your mind anticipates trouble at work because you do not feel up to facing any of the challenging situations that usually arise. You may be saying to yourself that you are not yourself today.

At work, you seem to be out of touch with everything that otherwise would give you the motivation and enthusiasm to be creative and to achieve the goals you have set for yourself. Lacking in serenity, you may become restless and impatient if things do not move fast or smoothly enough. Suddenly you may find yourself criticizing one of your co-workers and you begin to shout at him. He is upset with you and tension arises.

Consequently, your colleague begins to talk to other people in the office to gather support and sympathy. Now the working atmosphere is divided or even hostile. Nobody takes any notice how tired you are. At the end of the day you feel even more drained and irritable than in the morning. As you return home, instead of finding some time to relax and unwind, your children are quarrelling and arguing with each other. You simply cannot tolerate any more noise and you angrily tell them to shut up. Your partner insists on discussing a financial problem with you but you tell him to leave you alone. He is upset with you and more tension fills the atmosphere.

Stress is Caused by Fatigue

The story could go on and on. The unresolved issues at work and at home won't let you go to sleep the second night and you are even more tired during the following day. More problems come up and you start blaming everyone else for making mistakes and for not being considerate enough. Slowly your personality makes a shift from being a kind, tolerant and efficient person to being cynical, impatient and unreliable. What has happened? Your life has changed overnight because your body, mind and spirit have lost their balance. Lack of sleep with subsequent loss of its rejuvenating and energizing effects has severed your energy supply. The laws of nature can no longer support your thoughts, feelings and actions adequately. Fatigue creates a short circuit in your network of energy and makes you highly susceptible to what we call stress.

Today, an estimated 92% of new patients complain of problems relating to tiredness. Most people use words such as "drained", "exhausted" or "worn out" to describe their condition. There is indeed no physical or emotional problem that is not accompanied or caused by fatigue. Inefficiency of an organ in the body is a sign of fatigue. Restlessness, impatience, nervousness, and tension in the mind are also caused by fatigue. Sayings like "I am tired of waiting, I am tired of so-and-so," or "I am too tired to argue" are unconscious but accurate descriptions of underlying fatigue. When people say that they are too tired to live, they really mean it. Their life force is cut off and they don't have even an ounce of energy left to continue living. Chronic fatigue is a strong signal indicating the need for healing.

True healing always begins with repairing this damaged or broken energy circuit and there are many ways to accomplish that. The following few chapters describe what disrupts the flow of the life force, what causes fatigue and what *you* can do to restore balance and vitality on all levels of life, i.e. body, mind, spirit and behavior.

CHAPTER 5
Healing the Cause

Emotions – Our Daily "Weather Report"

Emotions are signals of comfort or discomfort that our body sends us at every moment of our conscious existence. They contain specific vibrations that serve as a kind of weather report, telling us how we feel about ourselves, about others and about what is okay in our lives and what is not. Emotions are like the reflections from a mirror that reveal to us everything we need to know to go on in life. Our body is that mirror. A dirty mirror reflects only part of us or makes us look distorted. If we are emotionally stuck and unable to understand what is happening to us, it is because we are not open to listening to, understanding and following the messages that our body is trying to convey to us.

All emotional problems indicate a lack in awareness. If we are not completely "aware", we are out of touch with ourselves and hence are incapable of making positive changes in our life. Many people are so disconnected from their feelings that they do not even know *what* they feel. Practicing mindfulness brings our attention back to where we are and to who we are. By staying *with* our emotions as long as they last, we can unleash the tremendous creative powers that lie dormant within us. Emotions are not there to be judged or suppressed; they are there to be understood. As we learn to observe them, we will begin to understand their true meaning. Instead of unconsciously *reacting* to a difficult situation or a person, we will be able to consciously *act*, out of our own free will.

Emotions want to be acknowledged because they are the only way our body can tell us how we really feel about others and ourselves. They can alert us to the mistakes we may have made and even encourage us to correct them. As we begin to express our emotions more consciously, they begin to lose their grip or power over us. We can do that by asking ourselves the following questions: *"How do I feel right now? What is my body trying to tell me? Where in my body do I feel angry, frustrated or sad? What do I wish to gain from being with this person or listening to that particular conversation?"*

Talking to oneself in this way is not a sign of madness, in truth we are doing this all the time. The more conscious we become about our natural and spontaneous internal dialogue, the more we can learn from our body. The body speaks to us through the language of emotions, which is a far superior guidance than all the knowledge or information we can obtain from outer sources. Learning to decipher this language is the key to opening the door to perfect health, abundance and spiritual wisdom in life. By ignoring our internal messages we get stuck in the vicious circle of action and reaction, with little hope for change or improvement in life; such a situation is created by repressing emotions.

Repressing Emotions

In one form or another, we all have repressed our emotions. During childhood, many of us learnt that it is not okay to express negative emotions. However, if we expressed them nevertheless, we felt judged or told off by others. We try to avoid any uncomfortable feelings because we would like to see ourselves as being always kind and loving, friendly, generous, honest and happy. If for any reason we become angry, frustrated, and jealous or depressed, we understandably don't like it and prefer to push these emotions away or repress them.

Yet this doesn't seem to work. If we try to avoid certain issues because they make us feel uncomfortable, they are even more likely to stick to us. In due time such "mental deposits" shape a personality that we may not like very much and through guilt we begin to deny ourselves the love and care that we deserve. Subsequently we learn to *pretend* to be all the things we would like to be. Deep inside, however, we feel increasingly dissatisfied, unhappy and uncomfortable. At times, we are not able to contain ourselves any more and release some of the bottled-up emotions. Without being in conscious control, we may burst into bouts of anger in situations that would normally not justify such intense reactions.

When we calm down again, we begin to see more clearly but instead of feeling relieved, we may feel drained physically and emotionally. What makes matters worse is that we begin to feel guilty about having

73

hurt other people's feelings, especially those close to us. If we have the courage and humility to ask for forgiveness, we can release this burden of guilt, but if we are too ashamed to bare our soul to others, we repress the guilty feelings as well.

The Physical Side of Emotions

When I first came across the ancient wisdom of Ayurvedic medicine in 1981, I had no idea how profoundly it would change my life. It gave me a new perspective that made everything in life more meaningful and important. The Ayurvedic sages, from their unbiased perspective of unity consciousness, clearly saw that all problems begin with a "mistake of the intellect." They claimed that by not knowing who we are, we could not see where we are going or what we are doing. Instead of referring to our unbounded Self or bliss consciousness to know the world and ourselves, we refer to the various roles we play in life, which can create an identity for our small self or ego. At one moment, I may play a doctor in my office. When I am at home, I play a husband. At other times, I may play the roles of a father, a friend, a cook, a traveler, a teacher, a student etc. Most of our life is centered on the various roles we play, but we no longer know the person who is playing them. This creates fear because we lose contact with our own source of love, power and stability. The following are the most likely physical responses that will result from the experience of fear and other types of emotional upset.

Fear: Fear is a form of negative awareness that can take the shape of a negative emotion. All negative emotions are rooted in fear. Although they occur on the level of our mind, they have profound effects on the body as well. Fear affects every cell in the body and particularly the kidneys and the adrenal glands. The adrenals respond by secreting *adrenaline* and other stress hormones into the blood stream, which drastically alters the functioning of every cell, muscle and organ in the body. If fear is strong enough, it can practically paralyze a person. Fear normally results in frustration, and frustration causes anger.

Anger: We only become angry if we have already "compiled" a sufficient amount of fear and frustration. Through a "provocative" situation, the accumulated anger may become released. Even a minor annoyance can be the trigger for a powerful emotional explosion. We may feel the anger rising up in our body until it bursts out in the form of mental or, as is in some cases, physical violence. During such moments of anger, some sensitive people report that they feel pain in the liver, which is caused by a retention of toxins. As a measure of protection, the liver releases large amounts of fats that subsequently clog up the blood vessels and cause coronary heart disease. Bottled up aggression or anger can virtually burn up the heart; the lesions that develop around the coronary arteries look very much like burns.

Anger also changes the flora of the gallbladder, bile ducts and small intestine. Everyone who becomes angry easily has large numbers of gallstones in his liver and gallbladder, which causes irritation and inflammation of the mucous lining in the intestines and the stomach.[2] Gastritis and stomach ulcers, for example, are some of the most typical psychosomatic diseases to be directly associated with stress and anger. Constant anger drives up blood pressure and weakens the immune system, which predisposes a person to all sorts of infections. Anger also triggers the release of *noradrenalin*, a normally very useful hormone that becomes enormously damaging under the influence of heavy stress. If the body is not given an outlet for releasing the tension, each bit of repressed anger becomes the reason for a new outburst, more powerful than the previous one.

Insecurity: If you feel insecure in your life, your bladder may begin to contract and urination become difficult or even painful. Bladder constriction may lead to frequent urination, especially during the night and be accompanied by strong burning sensations. Bladder infection has become a common ailment among women who feel insecure and unprotected in their lives. Being defensive is a typical sign of feeling insecure.

---

[2] Gallstones in the liver and gallbladder can be removed through a simple, painless cleansing procedure which is described in the book "The Amazing Liver & Gallbladder Flush."

Nervousness: Nervousness creates toxins, which can lead to the manifestation of irritable bowels. Nervous people often suffer from diarrhea, constipation, or inflammation of the colon lining.

Hurt: If you feel unloved or carry feelings of deep hurt, you will notice a sense of heaviness in your heart. A deep unresolved hurt is likely to manifest as a heart condition. Sadness and grief, which can cause respiratory problems, often accompany hurt; the lungs feel too tired to even breathe normally and easily.

Hate: Hate is a form of severe attachment. Low self-worth and the inability to forgive may manifest as intensified anger, which severely affects the liver and gallbladder and subsequently the entire digestive process. Hate produces highly toxic substances in most of the body cells; once released into the blood stream, the toxins poison the entire body and cause irrational and even violent behavior.

Sense of failure: Those who feel a sense of failure in life or think that they are not "good enough," often develop intestinal problems leading to mal-absorption of nutrients. The small intestines are no longer "good enough" to nourish the body. This can cause the development of toxic gases, abdominal bloating and an undernourished physiology.

Greed and other negative emotions: Greed, attachment, and possessiveness all lead to heart and spleen disorders. This in turn affects the immune system and diminishes energy distribution in the body. Lack of inner satisfaction or fulfillment creates stomach problems. Fear of future events can send shudders through your kidney cells and if you feel unsupported your adrenal glands become anxious, too. Both fear and anxiety alter the flora of the large intestine. This leads to a build-up of harmful bacteria and toxic gases, and in some cases to alternating constipation and diarrhea.

Emotions and Body Types

Ayurveda categorizes all emotions according to the three bodily humors or *doshas – Vata, Pitta* and *Kapha.* These three energies maintain and control all mental and physical processes. If they become unbalanced, physical and emotional disorders result. The variability of the three *doshas* determines our constitutional body type, our susceptibility to certain diseases, the body's general status of immunity, our responses to treatment and our personality traits. [3]

The characteristics of Vata, Pitta and Kapha types can be summarized as follows:

The *Vata* Type

o Light, thin physique, narrow body frame; bent or irregularly shaped nose
o Moves and performs activity quickly
o Tendency towards dry, rough, cold, and dark skin
o Aversion to cold weather
o Irregular hunger and digestion
o Light, interrupted sleep, insomnia
o Enthusiasm, vivaciousness, imagination, perceptiveness, spiritually inclined
o Excitability, changing moods, unpredictable
o Quick to grasp information, but also quick to forget
o Tendency towards worry, anxiety, restlessness
o Tendency towards bloating and constipation
o Tires easily, tendency to overexertion and hyperactivity
o Mental and physical energy comes in bursts
o Low tolerance to pain, noise, bright light

The *Pitta* Type

o Medium build, well-shaped, athletically toned
o Medium strength and endurance
o Sharp hunger and thirst, strong digestion
o Tendency towards anger and irritability when under stress

---

[3] To know your exact body type and the methods to keep it balanced refer to "Timeless Secrets of Health and Rejuvenation."

- Can be arrogant, self-cantered
- Adaptable, intelligent, bright
- Tendency towards reddish skin and hair, moles, freckles, skin problems
- If out of balance, prematurely bald and/or grey
- Pointed, reddish nose
- Piercing, sometimes bloodshot eyes
- Aversion to sun, hot weather
- Prefers cool foods and beverages
- Enterprising character, likes challenges, good organizer
- Sharp intellect
- Good, precise, articulate speaker
- Can't skip meals
- Medium memory
- Successful leader

The *Kapha* Type

- Compact, strong and heavier build
- Well developed and lubricated joints
- Great physical strength and endurance
- Hair may be black, blond, dark brown, thick, wavy, oily
- Stable and reliable personality
- Steady energy; slow and graceful in action
- Tranquil, relaxed personality, slow to anger
- Cool, smooth, pale, often oily skin
- Hidden veins and tendons
- Slow to grasp new information, slow to forget
- Heavy, prolonged sleep
- Tendency to excessive weight, obesity
- Slow digestion, mild hunger
- Excessive need for sleep
- Calm, affectionate, placid, tolerant, forgiving, nurturing, maternal
- Tendency to be possessive, stubborn, attached, narrow-minded

If you can identify more with one set of characteristics than with another, you are most likely to be of that body type. The following three sections give you the opportunity to discover some of the basic emotional characteristics that accompany your body type. The advantage of knowing your body-type is that you can take the necessary measures to return to a balanced state, emotionally and physically. A Vata type, for example, lives in a "Vata-colored" world and by learning what keeps Vata balanced, he can focus more on Vata-balancing foods, exercises, routines or situations. This will affect his emotional life in a very constructive and positive way.

Vata-emotions

Balanced *Vata* types display characteristics that are inspiring and uplifting to others. By nature, their personalities are enthusiastic, vivacious, imaginative, vibrant, and lively. They feel excited about new things and they express it through talking. It is fun to be around them and boredom is not part of their vocabulary.

However, when out of balance, *Vata* types tend to be changeable regarding their moods, and irregular concerning their activities, meals, habits and daily routine. At one moment they may feel on top of the world, but moody and unhappy at the next. Under pressure, they tend to become impulsive, nervous, and anxious. Fear is the dominating factor that compels them to become hyperactive and overexcited. This eventually leads to exhaustion, constant fatigue and a form of depression that is characterized by "inner emptiness." They always find a reason to worry about something or someone.

Vata, which is composed of the elements of space and air, is the most important of the three *doshas*. Being responsible for all internal movements such as circulation, elimination and communication, *Vata* is the first to go out of balance. Any obstruction in the flow of nutrients, oxygen or hormones through the complex network of channels in the body can create debility and weakness. No longer able to properly sustain itself, the body responds with fear, which triggers a stress response (fight or flight). Hence the *Vata's* experience of physical nervousness.

79

Pitta-emotions

Balanced Pitta types make good leaders and eloquent speakers. Many leaders of society are Pitta. They are reliable and trustworthy. Brave in spirit, they love adventures and strive for new challenges. Pittas are often admired for their strong self-confidence. They are friendly, loving and dynamic by nature. You can see the glow in their faces when they are happy and content.

When out of balance, however, *Pitta* types become critical of others and of themselves. Their competitive streak becomes overemphasized and they feel that they have to succeed under any circumstance. *Pittas* can turn into workaholics, become demanding and sarcastic and are often unable to tolerate failure or criticism. Under stress, *Pittas* become angry, irritable and impatient.

Kapha-emotions

Balanced Kapha types are serene, calm, and peaceful. Their forgiving and affectionate nature makes them liked by everyone. You will hardly ever see a balanced Kapha upset, nervous or angry. However, when unbalanced, the Kapha type becomes insecure and distressed, particularly when he puts on too much weight. Under stress, he tends to withdraw rather than fight. When feeling unwanted, the Kapha plays the victim. His sense of insecurity is expressed in his unnatural emphasis on possessing, storing and saving things, including money. Kapha types turn quiet, depressed and hopeless when things don't work out for them.

Rigid behavior is another expression of their hidden fears. They are often overly attached to their possessions and relationships. You can also identify an unbalanced *Kapha* by his greediness and tendency to postpone dates or arrangements. *Kaphas* may develop a large body to counterbalance their lack of inner trust. They also have a tendency to keep things as they are, which may turn them into rigid and stubborn personalities.

All repressed emotions create an imbalance of Vata, which in turn disturbs Pitta and Kapha. The first effect of repressed emotions is the suppression of AGNI, which is the body's digestive fire and auto-immune response. A strong AGNI is the key to perfect health of body, mind and spirit, which makes emotional balance a prerequisite for health and happiness in life.

Body Language

The body speaks to us through the *language of emotions*. It uses this language to attract our attention, to communicate with us and to inform us about its state of well-being or discomfort. The word emotion is derived from motion or movement. If something moves us on a mental level we express or "e-mote" it on a physical level as well. Do you know someone who feels that he carries a heavy burden of problems and responsibilities on his shoulders? If you do, you may notice that he moves his body in a way that reflects his depressed feelings. His head is lowered, his eyes are downcast, his back becomes rounded and his shoulders slouch forwards. He hardly seems to be able to breathe. *Vata* types are the most likely to respond to overwhelming difficulties in this way.

Similarly, sad people have sad-looking eyes and a skin that has lost luster and glow; they even *look* heavy. *Kapha*s show this kind of response more clearly than other body types. *Pitta*s who are very angry, bring their blood to a "boil." Their bodies experience an actual rise in temperature and blood rushes into their face. They turn red when enraged and their face turns into a grotesque mask.

A happy person on the other hand can be recognized by his very relaxed face muscles and a gentle but not exaggerated smile. It is known that each muscle in the face corresponds to a particular organ or system. As a muscle tightens due to stress or tension, the corresponding organ does the same. This creates further tension in the body and the mind.

On the other hand, if you move your facial muscles to produce a smile, you not only improve the functions of the corresponding organs but you also create the emotion of happiness. This was proven in an experiment during the eighties, when subjects were told to imitate certain facial expressions such as the ones produced during sadness, anger and happiness. When imitating the facial expressions of anger, they began to feel irritable and angry. Creating a sad face made them feel rejected or lonely, whereas posing a happy face made them cheerful. Every little activity in the body is registered by the brain and triggers the release of neurotransmitters. The "happy" face releases happy neurotransmitters that influence the body positively. Try to laugh or smile at yourself when you look in the mirror in the morning and notice what difference this makes to your day.

At first the medical community was surprised when a terminally ill cancer patient cured himself through the emotion of laughter by watching funny videos for three months. While lying in his hospital bed, this patient who suffered from lung cancer, overheard his doctor's remark that he had only a few more days to live. He then decided to check out of the hospital and spend the "rest of his life" having fun, not knowing that this would actually save his life.

After several weeks of constant laughter, the patient returned to his doctors who could not find a trace of his lung cancer. Inspired by this finding, he worked out a practical theory that could explain the sudden and complete remission of his lung cancer and he subsequently became a dean of medicine at UCLA Medical School in California, USA. This episode has led to further serious investigations into the therapeutic effects of laughter, which now is a verifiable technique to help promote the cure of major diseases. As a result, patients throughout American hospitals are encouraged to watch funny movies.

The body shapes itself around all the emotional data it receives but emotions are also generated by every move of the body. Simply by changing the body posture from downcast to upright, lifting up the head and pulling the shoulders back, a person can actually change his emotions from being depressed to being cheerful and hopeful again.

The natural world can teach us a lot about how to deal with negative emotions. For example, if a wild cat feels frustrated over having missed its prey, it rids itself of that emotion by crying out, jumping up in the air and licking itself until it falls asleep. Upon waking, there is no trace of failure left and the cat is ready for a new hunting experience. Had the cat not removed the frustration through a series of physical movements, the previous failure would have impaired her future ability to catch prey.

We also can negate the stress that has accumulated in us during moments of frustration, anger or disappointment by consciously moving our body into a different posture or mode of activity. For this reason, regular practice of exercises that increase Chi (vital energy) such as Chi-Lel Chi Kung[4], Tai Chi and Yoga can have a tremendous healing impact on body and mind. Ayurveda suggests that you eliminate tension by giving yourself a massage every day, just as cats do. This relaxes all the muscles in the body and removes repressed emotions.

Negative emotions generally indicate that we are on a path that no longer serves us and we need to make major changes in our life. They serve as our guides and direct us towards a greater sense of well-being and wisdom. We can learn everything about ourselves from these internal "teachers", provided we listen to them. I would like to recommend a few simple awareness techniques that can help transform negative emotions into useful and positive experiences.

The Technique of Emotional Transformation

Ayurveda recommends neither *repressing* nor *expressing* emotions. Both create unwanted side effects. Someone will always get hurt. It would be far better for everyone involved if you could learn from your emotions and understand their true origin and meaning. This can be difficult, however, if you are in the middle of an emotional upset. The first step to learn from and deal with your emotions is to distance yourself from them and observe them as they come and go. This happens automatically if you go through the entire emotional release consciously. Although this might bring up fear, by working through the fear, the cause of the emotional upset becomes released. Simply have your attention on everything that happens when you get angry, for example. Watch yourself becoming upset and be aware of your reactions to other people's remarks or actions. From this observation you can learn about the nature of anger. This also enables you to let go of the anger, to release it. Verbalize your experiences, write them down or simply talk to yourself during the process.

To free yourself from negative emotions first bring them into your awareness and second observe and experience them from the moment they begin right to when they end. This in itself is a powerful technique to remove the painful "sting" that accompanies

---

[4] See "Body Techniques" in "Touch for Health" of chapter 7.

every negative emotion. The only mistake we can make is to ignore an emotion or to push it down. If we have done this in the past, the following procedure can be used to release any repressed emotions from the body:

1. Close your eyes and gently put your mind's attention on your breath. If your mind is preoccupied with thoughts, this is fine, but allow your attention to be on the breathing, too. Do this for at least 1-2 minutes.

2. Let your mind wander to that area of your body that feels most tense and, like before, be aware of your breathing. Notice how the tense area prevents your breath from flowing easily. Stay with it until the tension eases.

3. Now allow your attention to move sequentially to the following areas of your body, while still being aware of your breathing. Begin this exercise by turning your attention on the lips, …breathing; then on the nose, …breathing; etc. Continue in the same way until you have reached the "whole body" at the end of the list. Wait for 1-2 minutes before opening your eyes again.

1. Lips
2. Nose
3. Eyes
4. Ears
5. Forehead
6. Head
7. Neck
8. Chest
9. Abdomen
10. Hips
11. Lower back
12. Upper back
13. Shoulders
14. Forearms
15. Lower arms
16. Hands
17. Fingers
18. Upper legs
19. Both knees
20. Lower legs

21. Ankles
22. Toes
23. Whole body

You may need to practice the sequence a few times before it becomes effortless. It doesn't matter much if you miss out on one or two parts. Wherever your attention goes, energy follows. With regular practice, this simple method helps to relax and enliven all the larger and minor muscle groups in the body (most emotional experiences are impressed on the memory of muscle tissues).

This awareness technique, linked with breathing, can release the trapped and repressed emotions and help you overcome both past and current tension and emotional stress. I recommend that you practice this technique twice daily, ideally after Conscious Breathing (see next section), and/or during or after a crisis.

Another very effective technique to deal with acute, negative emotions is to take a cold shower. As simple as it sounds, the shock-effect of cold showers permits our awareness to leave the body for a split second, enough to create a distance to an existing problem. Cold showers also strip our emotional body of anger, resentment, and fear. Anytime you feel stressed and tense, take a cold shower and you will feel much better afterwards.

The *Emotional Freedom Technique* (EFT), from www.emofree.com, is another excellent method to remove emotional and physical blocks.

Emotional Welfare

You can effectively deal with emotional difficulties from both angles: the body and mind. Once you have distanced yourself from an emotion or begun to witness it through the above technique, it is much easier to see why the emotion has arisen in the first place. Emotions are useful messengers that help us understand others and ourselves in a better way.

Impatience Can Make You More Patient

If you feel restless because an important letter you expect has not arrived yet or you are fidgety while queuing for a train ticket, then your impatience can be the ideal means to put your focus on the present moment and calm your emotions. By "stepping back" and experiencing this agitation more consciously, you may discover that there is a sense of fearful anticipation of future issues, which stops you from enjoying your life right at this moment. By consciously embracing or experiencing the impatience rather than giving in to it, you will get in touch with its roots and be able to release it. Soon you will no longer create or attract situations that could make you be impatient.

The above procedure will help you learn from your emotions. Everything we need to know right now in our life in order to continue developing physically, materially, mentally and spiritually is contained in our emotions. Instead of searching for answers to your problems or questions outside yourself, you will gain much better results if you work with them inside yourself. Ask yourself why you are *really* impatient, irritable or unhappy, for it rarely is the current situation that is responsible for your emotional response. The very situations that make you impatient or unhappy are the ones you can use to regain your patience and happiness. This principle applies to every emotion. Simply stay with the feeling of irritation until it passes, observe your reactions and even verbalize them. Tell yourself exactly how you feel at each moment. This will bring the emotion to the surface and allow it to be released easily, permanently and without causing pain.

Don't Try to Change Anyone

One of man's greatest sources of emotional stress is his attempt to change other people. Our desire to change others is rooted in the need to change ourselves. We have expectations of others only because we have unfulfilled expectations of ourselves. What we don't like in other people is exactly what we need to correct in our own lives. Instead of wasting time and energy in trying to change others, we can use our personal power to improve ourselves. When we give up the need to change others, a great burden is lifted off our chest, which restores freedom in life.

We often use the argument that a certain habit or behavior of a friend, partner or boss causes us problems and if he only changed, then our life would be wonderful and successful; this is an illusion. By focusing our energies on other people's faults and discrepancies we will not get along with ourselves either. Imprisoned by the continual perception of other people's shortcomings, we only make our life dependent on them.

Yet as we learn to recognize these "faults" in other people as being mere reflections of our own inability to be who we really want to be, we begin to take the first step towards improving ourselves: We will notice that other people's attitudes towards us will start changing when we begin to improve our attitudes towards them. This requires self-appreciation, though. Once we feel better about ourselves, other people will begin to appreciate us as well. Because most people like to be around those who are happy, kind, compassionate, giving and strong, improving oneself is the *only* way to change somebody's reactions or behavior towards you. So the next time you catch yourself judging or criticizing someone, pause for a moment and reflect on the changes you may need to make in your own life.

Recently my mother told me about her new postman who never greeted her or even looked at her when he delivered the mail. His grumpy, hardened face expressed nothing but discontent. My mother felt compassionate towards him and stayed open to the possibility that one day he could become more pleasant and friendly. So she gave him an extra-friendly treatment. Several weeks later, this man was completely transformed. Today he is very talkative and has a happy smile on his face every time he comes around. He even wanted to make sure he was the first one to give a Christmas card to my mother. This incident shows that we *can* make a difference where relationships are concerned.

Conflicts are Opportunities for Growth

Most people try to avoid conflicts by all means. If there is a reason for conflict and you keep it all buried inside of you, the conflict is merely transferred to a deeper part of yourself and will continue to bother you in a number of ways. Avoiding conflict in a relationship never gives you the chance of expressing your frustration and making up again – a very important process in a healthy relationship. The so called "yes people" who never argue with anyone, bottle up a lot of "no" or resistance within themselves and thereby lower their sense of self. This may even prevent them from fulfilling their desires. Too weak to stand up for themselves, they often develop cancer or other debilitating diseases, which may be just another way of dealing with unexpressed conflicts. Since they try to please everyone around them in order to gain their love and attention, they transfer all their unresolved conflicts into the arena of the body.

If there are never any differences between partners or friends, one of them may be *giving in* all the time and trying to please the other, but not himself. Unless you are immersed in bliss 24 hours a day, difference is the dominating feature in life. Living with differences shapes our opportunities for greater change, growth and progress in our personal relationships.

If you always want to please everyone else because you crave their love and attention, you are creating a division within yourself. This is the time to make drastic changes in your life, even if it means that for the time being you can no longer fulfill the demands of those around you. Your loved ones may have taken you for granted for too long and may now need to learn to be more self-reliant as well. Since *you* have put yourself in the role of being "indispensable", only *you* can dissolve this illusion. Once you give yourself the time and attention you need, the urge to please others in order to earn their love begins to subside. This enhances your ability for true and unconditional love.

Depression – Anger Turned Inward

Depression afflicts millions of people in the industrialized world today. It impairs the digestive, nervous and circulatory functions in the body and depletes any remnant of joy and happiness. By itself, depression is not an independent emotion but is directly linked to repressed anger.

Traditional rules of social conduct promote the idea that it is better to conform to "proper" behavior than to reveal one's emotions, particularly anger. Many people have been brought up with the idea that anger is essentially bad and indicates an unbalanced personality. If you feel angry, then you should at least not show it. This unwritten law seems to apply even more to women than to men. It appears to be socially acceptable for a man to rant and rave, hurl objects about, shout at other people, and possibly become violent, but women are considered not "feminine" if they do the same. Many women have the tendency to become silent and withdrawn when they are angry. Their "quiet" nature, though, is deceiving. Unknowingly playing the victim and allowing men to dominate their lives, they may do whatever their partner or husband wants them to do without asserting themselves. Instead, they feel tremendous rage inside and subsequently suffer from depression, which can lead to a nervous breakdown. There is enough clinical evidence now to show that *depression is anger turned inwards*. Unless anger is expressed in a positive, active way, it accumulates in a passive way and becomes the "emotion" of depression. The effects can be devastating.

Dr. Philip Gold of the American National Institute of Mental Health was able to prove that stress and depression trigger the release of emergency hormones, causing brittle bones, infections and even cancer. Brittle bones are a major cause of death among women today. In many people these stress hormones are no longer merely triggered occasionally but they are kept at constant "hyper-readiness." When they are turned on and stay on for a long time, they destroy appetite, impair the immune system, block sleep, break down bone and shut down the processes that repair cell tissue. Research shows that chronically depressed women have high levels of stress hormones and enormous loss of bone density.

One particular study conducted at Ohio State University, USA, revealed that routine marital disagreements could trigger such hormonal reactions, especially among women. The stress hormone levels showed that women are more sensitive to negative behavior than are men, hence they are at much greater risk of becoming depressed and falling ill. According to the research, if the hormone levels stay up longer than they should, there is a real risk of infectious disease.

The latest findings in the field of Neuroscience have shown that levels of *serotonin*, an important neurotransmitter that is linked to the experience of pleasure (see chapter 4), are 20-25 percent lower in patients who are at high risk of suicide. *Serotonin* is particularly active in a part of the brain that controls inhibition, and a lack of the neurotransmitter, or its related chemicals, lowers the amount of control a person has over his actions. This predisposes a person to act on suicidal thoughts. Suicide is the eighth leading cause of death in the United States. According to the research, the tendency towards suicide may be aggravated by childhood experiences that can affect *serotonin* levels in the brain for a lifetime. In fact, people who commit suicide have a high rate of child abuse histories. Laboratory studies confirm that parental deprivation at critical points in childhood can diminish *serotonin* in an enduring way.

Social conditioning has taught many of us to repress anger right from the beginning of life. When small children don't get what they want, they have tantrums and are often told off by an angry parent. All the small instances of withheld anger or frustration build up to a highly explosive inner conflict, creating a strong chemical distortion in the body. Every new instance that triggers an emotional explosion reveals the entire past of unresolved conflicts. Anger, if it is dealt with before it turns into depression, can be a means of learning about the very weaknesses that we tend to project on others. Whenever you feel angry, you are never really angry with somebody else, but you are frustrated over your own inability to fulfill your desires, both past and present.

What Makes You Angry

Sometimes anger may well up when we see others become successful because they remind us of our own failures. Some people who lead unhappy lives may become annoyed when a close friend suddenly has a reason to be happy. Seeing someone else happy can reflect the emptiness or lack of happiness one feels inside. Consequently, a discontented person may become envious of those who have something desirable which he cannot have himself.

If you become annoyed about the way someone else is dressed or expresses himself, you may merely be projecting your own frustration because you don't dare do something similar or feel that you may be judged if you did. A parent can get on our nerves because he makes the same mistakes we make or have similar characteristic tendencies that we have.

We may become very angry when we see someone committing a crime, hurting a child or causing any other form of injustice. Anger, however, is not so much the result of an external event as it is triggered by the hidden memory of a past mistake of ours or the *unforgivable* hurt that a close friend has caused us. Anger can only come forth when there is still an old resentment buried in the heart. A person who is filled with love has no reason to be angry with anyone. Anger cannot teach him anything else about himself and therefore no longer arises.

"I Could" versus "I Should"

Another source of anger is the "should" in our life. Out of fear of being judged or criticized by a parent, friend or boss we may use the phrase "I should…" to justify our actions and behavior. Every time we use the word "should," we unconsciously admit that we don't have the choice or feel free enough to make our own decisions. This makes us resentful and lowers our self-esteem.

Instead of using the word "should" you can replace it with "could" which instantly increases the number of choices. The word "could" gives you the freedom to choose one way or another whereas the word "should" removes that possibility altogether. "I could visit my old aunt who I haven't seen for years" sounds very different than "I should visit my aunt who…" The two expressions have completely contrary effects on body and mind. Students, who feel that they *should* perform well during exams rather than just wanting to do their best, are found to have high levels of stress hormones and low levels of immunity. The same applies to all the jobs you do because someone expects you to do them.

By observing the various ways of expressing yourself through language you can become aware of all your self-imposed restrictions, some of which may even have manifested as physical problems.

Nobody but you allows the expectations of others to rule your life. Since these restrictions exist only in the mind you can change this illusion by reprogramming yourself in the following way: "Each time I say the word "should" I will pause for a moment and consider replacing it with "could." [**Note:** say it out loud; you only have to do this once]. This puts your awareness into the present moment - your only true source of power - and permits you to make changes and decisions that will be most beneficial for you and everyone involved. The result is a greater sense of personal freedom.

It's Okay to Say "No"

Anger or resentment can also be caused by our inability to say "no" when we really don't want to do something but agree to do it nevertheless. Many of us feel obliged to say "yes" because we feel that it is expected of us. And if we say "no", we may fear that this will cause problems in a relationship or we will no longer be liked or loved. The "yes-attitude" may be a result of deep-seated beliefs and codes of behavior that are connected with education, religion, gender and class. If you perceive someone as being more powerful or influential than you, such as your boss, you are more likely to say "yes" to a request of his than if it came from someone who is an employee of yours.

People who only know to say "yes" often have low self-esteem. Society may see them as the most selfless people who would do anything to help others. Their being selfless is, however, rather a sign of being low in self-worth. They sacrifice their lives for others so that they are loved and appreciated. However, these "saints" often become martyrs. The typical character traits of their personality are self-sacrifice, being a "good" person, always friendly and happy-looking, never having time for themselves. *Over-caring* is as harmful as is *under-caring*. Yet love is not about giving oneself away like a slave, this only causes resentment. It is more about honoring and appreciating one's life so much that love simply spills over to others. For such a person giving and sharing comes naturally without the need for acknowledgement.

Both, "yes" and "no" are parts of life. Say "yes" when it makes you feel good, but "no" when you do not want to do something. Going against your own gut feelings leads to conflicts and complications, whereas following them opens you to solutions and new opportunities. Even if you risk losing your job or breaking off a relationship, honoring your inner feelings will benefit you in the long run.

Self-honesty is the highest form of honesty and the only one that can bring you lasting happiness. Hiding your true feelings from yourself or others is an attempt of your ego to live up to an idealized image of yourself. Being honest with others means that you are not afraid to show them who you really are and what you really feel. As a golden rule, you can only be as honest with others as you are with yourself.

Since our cultural upbringing has associated saying "yes" to being liked and saying "no" to being rejected or disliked, most people tend to prefer the "yes-version" of communication, especially when they relate to a boss or a person close to them. Unlike small children who do not hesitate to say "no" when they feel like it – they know instinctively that they are still loved by their parents – we have learnt to buy our love with the little word "yes," yet this may make us increasingly resentful.

Saying "yes" when we mean "no" creates an internal conflict between what we really would like to do and what we are expected to do. Subtle blackmail, bribery and self-fulfilling rules and regulations formulated by parents, teachers and other authority figures have taught us to conform to manipulation. Saying "yes" seemed to be the only way to get what we wanted but we had to pay a price for it. Because we were afraid of facing the undesirable consequences a "no" would have triggered, feelings of frustration, anger, insecurity, anxiety and guilt gradually began to replace our innate spontaneous ability to be carefree and honest. As we continued growing up, we increasingly adopted the same or similar methods of manipulating others.

The irony of all this is that other people prefer you to be straight and honest about how you really feel rather than to be given last minute excuses or resentful acceptances for, let's say, an invitation. To say "yes" when you feel like saying "no" is called *lying,* but in reality, it is "self denial." So the next time when you say "yes" but really feel like saying "no", utter to yourself: "*I have said 'yes' again when I didn't truly mean it.*" This will take your old unconscious *say-yes-pattern* into your conscious awareness and allow you either to undo it and tell the truth or to transform it into a lesson of learning for yourself. *Becoming aware* is the fastest way of learning from your emotions and a safe way to overcome emotional problems in life.

Also, vigorous exercise can help you deal with repressed anger. It supports the body in its attempt to flush out the excess amount of *noradrenalin* – the chemical equivalent of anger. Exercise restores the chemical balance of the body and elevates your self-esteem. Talking to friends about how you feel, expressing your anger through writing, or counseling and minimizing it through meditation can all help in dealing with this unpleasant and destructive emotion. These methods act like letting the steam out of a pressure cooker, allowing you to gain deeper insights from your emotions.

Anyone who suffers from constant anger or frustration in life has accumulated large numbers of gallstones, both in the liver and the gallbladder. One of the fastest ways of clearing old resentments and repressed anger is to eliminate all gallstones through a series of liver flushes. As long as bile ducts are blocked and bile flow is obstructed, energy, joyful feelings will be subdued, and anger and frustration will be exacerbated. Gallstones are a constant source of recurring irritation; by removing them, the above methods of dealing with emotions become much easier and more successful.

Get a Pet –
It Can Make you Happy and Save your Life

Pet love can profoundly balance emotions and even prevent disease. A study on 5,000 people aged 20 - 60 years carried out in 1992 by the Baker Medical Research Institute in Melbourne, Australia, showed that male pet owners had significantly reduced cholesterol and blood triglyceride (high levels of which are associated with heart disease). In addition, the blood pressure of both sexes was significantly lower than in non-pet owners. This finding was independent of type of pet, the owner's diet or weight, or whether the owner smoked.

The positive emotions gained from simply stroking a pet can lead to dramatic reduction of major cardiac risk factors and calm both body and mind. When you watch your pet or play with him, you create a communication link that can trigger feelings of love and joy in you. At the same time your physiology undergoes profound changes. So pets can be good for us not only emotionally but physically as well.

Pets can benefit from us, too, provided we show them our affection. A classic study conducted 20 years ago on the effects of diet on rabbits demonstrated the therapeutic power of emotions on the health of animals. A large number of rabbits were fed with a toxic diet containing high amounts of fat. Consequently, all the rabbits developed arteriosclerosis – a condition when arteries become hardened and dysfunctional – leading to heart disease. However, there was one group of rabbits, in which only 30% developed the disease. This came as a total surprise to the researchers because there were no physical factors involved that distinguished the two groups. Soon they discovered that the student who was in charge of feeding this particular group of rabbits did not just throw the food at them but took them out of their cages, whispered sweet nothings to them, sang to them, stroked and cuddled them. The rabbits felt loved and cared for and although the food was toxic, they were able to metabolize it through different pathways than the other rabbits. Their immune systems thrived and were strong enough to handle even poisonous food. Although the food was the same for all the rabbits, this particular group had one very good reason to survive and live happily. It was the student's love for them.

What applies to animals in this respect also applies to human beings. A dog that licks your hand with affection or waits patiently for you to come home can flood your body with pleasure hormones and anticancer drugs. Animals can make you happy because they exhibit an innocent and natural behavior and they may also remind you that perfect health is a distinct possibility. Being near them and watching them helps us to reconnect to the natural world and generates balance in our emotional life.

Good Food – Good Mood

What Causes Mood Swings

Eating and choosing food is largely influenced by our emotional states. Our unconscious or conscious choice of various food items while shopping at the local grocery store, for example, is mainly based on how we feel at that particular time. If you feel there is not enough "sweetness" or satisfaction in your life, you are more likely to be drawn to the sweets and cake section than to the fruit and vegetable section. Your sugar reserves and blood sugar may be low, causing moodiness. To quell your spells of agitation you tend to look for quick fix solutions. A bar of chocolate, a piece of cake or candy will rapidly end the craving and raise your blood sugar levels to a high. Energy seems to return and moods improve.

Unfortunately, this situation is only short-lived. The quicker and higher your sugar level rises after you had a sweet treat, the faster and lower it will drop afterwards. Once again, your body will sound an alarm and you become nervous and agitated. The renewed cravings will tempt you to eat more sweets. You may even feel like you are cracking up. What's happening is that your central nervous system is running out of brain food.

Good food is brain food. Although the brain constitutes only about one-fiftieth of the body weight, it requires more of the following basic nutrients than any other part of the body:

- Energy, supplied as oxygen for combustion and as glucose for fuel.
- Enzymes and proteins which consist of amino acids.
- Vitamins that are required for the amino acids to function properly.

Other nutrients include metals, minerals, trace elements, and fats that help in the building of cell membranes. If our blood sugar level is normal and stable, our brain is able to function efficiently. This results in a good mood. When it fluctuates in either direction, we become emotionally unbalanced. If sugar levels are too high, we feel high and if they are too low, we feel low.

Because too much sugar in the blood can be damaging to the cells of the body, the body metabolizes and stores excess sugar with the help of insulin, which is secreted by pancreas cells. Since overstimulation, which is an abuse of the body's energy resources, is counterbalanced by "understimulation," more sugar is removed from the blood stream than is healthy and normal. The brain and all the other cells of the body are subsequently deprived of adequate amounts of nutrients, hence the cravings and agitated moods.

The Mood Chemicals

The chemical equivalents of thoughts are neuropeptides, neurotransmitters, and related chemicals. For each of your thoughts, your brain produces a neurotransmitter. These protein compounds consist of various chains of amino acids and can transmit the content of your thoughts from one nerve cell to another. This is necessary for the eventual translation of your thoughts into action like lifting up your arm or reading the words in this book.

Concentrations of these amino acids in your brain are directly affected by what you eat. Findings at the Massachusetts Institute of Technology, USA, have shown that the brain's chemistry is so changeable that it can be modified by a single meal. Both an unbalanced diet and poor digestion cause a shortage of nutrient supplies to the brain and thus weaken the inter-neuronal transmission of messages. Emotional trauma, accidents or other unpleasant experiences, all of which slow or shut down digestive functions, can trigger a similar effect. This greatly affects our moods and behavior.

One of the brain chemicals connected with feelings of well-being is the previously mentioned neurotransmitter *serotonin*. It has a calming effect and its concentration rises and falls in direct response to the kind of food being digested and assimilated in our digestive tract. Other neurotransmitters considered to be "positive" drugs are *dopamine* and *noradrenalin*; they are known to make us more alert and clear-headed.

We simply could not do anything without these drugs. However, high amounts of *dopamine* secretions are linked to schizophrenia and too much *noradrenalin* can trigger violent bursts of anger. Eating too many sugary and fatty foods depletes your body of vital nutrients and stimulates the brain chemical *acetylcholine*, which makes you sad and depressed. But by missing out on naturally *sweet tasting* foods (complex carbohydrates as contained in whole wheat, rice, fruits, vegetables, vegetable fats etc.), you can cause the very same problems. On the other hand, if you are in a very happy mood and you eat food that is considered harmful; your brain may nevertheless make "happy" chemicals. To add to the confusion, if you feel depressed and eat a healthy meal consisting of all the vital nutrients, your brain will still run short of the raw materials (amino acids) that make "happy" brain chemicals.

The relationship between mind and body is far too complex to be explained in simple words. Is it mind over matter or matter over mind that rules our life? The answer is that both hold true. The main question is: "What can I do to feel better?"

The brain's constant messages of comfort or discomfort determine how we live our lives. Signals of happiness and satisfaction show us that we are on the right track. Negative emotions can motivate us to return to balance again. This motivation is based on our natural tendency to be happy, which automatically results from living in harmony with the laws of nature. It is in our hands, therefore, to rediscover our inherent constitutional instincts and develop a healthy mind in a healthy body.

Our Constitutional Disposition Towards Certain Moods

Depending on your constitutional body type, you will experience different kinds of emotions when under stress. If you are a *Vata* type then your response will be fear, nervousness and a tendency towards worry. When *Pitta* is the dominating energy force in your body, you are more likely to become aggressive and angry. A *Kapha* type will tend to be withdrawn, lethargic, lazy, depressed or heavy going.

When the *doshas* are aggravated, the body searches for ways to pacify them. However, we may not always choose the right ways to accomplish this. Many people are not connected with their natural instincts. Because of inadequate health education, social indoctrination and insufficient nutrients in our diet we may no longer be able to rely on the body to guide us in our search for balance. Instead, we may solely use our mind to decide what kinds of foods we should eat. The mind usually tells us to get a quick fix to overcome emotional stress.

Accordingly, the *Vata* type may go and buy a bag of salted chips and/or eat a bar of chocolate. The hotheaded *Pitta* may decide to eat a plate of ice cream or have an iced coke, or else he may choose coffee, alcohol or cigarettes to escape the zone of discomfort. The unbalanced *Kapha* type may look for sweet and heavy foods like a cream cake or a sugary pudding to push down unpleasant feelings. Once one or all of the three *doshas* have been out of balance for a long time, your mind has lost conscious memory of what is supposed to be your normal condition. Consequently, you will begin to crave exactly those foods and drinks and do all the things that maintain the imbalance as if the unbalanced state was your natural one.

There are two ways to correct this situation and I would like to suggest that you use both of them:

1. Gradually replace unwholesome foods and drinks with delicious-tasting wholesome foods and drinks.
2. Change your desires and your way of thinking.

Two Important Things that Control Your Life

1. A Wholesome Diet

Most people who go on a diet do it because they want to lose weight or get rid of an annoying skin problem or a disease. But a special diet adopted for these reasons may neither be very beneficial nor procure lasting benefits. Unconsciously you may have linked this diet, however good it may be, with something you are afraid of. Every time you eat, your brain and digestive system produce "chemicals of fear" that act as suppressants of digestion, assimilation and elimination. You are actually afraid of the diet and your body will treat the food you eat as if it were an antigen (a foreign agent that needs to be destroyed). This may lead to food intolerance and even to allergic reactions.

Nevertheless, you can change the reasons why you want to lose weight or help a physical problem. One of the most important steps in this regard is to make improved well-being your number one motivation for introducing a healthy diet and regimen (to make this easier for you, use the guidelines described in the next section "the power that shapes your destiny"). What your body is really after is happiness. Happiness can be created by any activity, including eating food. Learn to make the eating process a means to increase happiness in

99

your life and begin to introduce those foods in your diet that are particularly pure and able to enhance your impulse to evolve; Ayurveda calls them *sattvic* foods.

Sattva, Rajas and Tamas –
Three Principal Forces of Life

Sattva is one of the three principal forces or *gunas* behind every phenomenon and activity in life. With regard to human life *Sattva* motivates us to grow, expand, progress and evolve spiritually, mentally and physically, and to find our higher purpose. Like everything in the universe, *Sattva* has its exact opposite, *Tamas*, which forces us to stay where we are. *Tamas* is the force that retards progress, causes stagnation and tempts us to hold on to past events and outdated beliefs. The third force, called *Rajas*, serves as a neutral link between *Sattva* and *Tamas*. *Rajas* urges us to act, take initiative, move and change, regardless of the direction, outcome or purpose.

All these three qualities are present in everyone and, depending on one's diet, lifestyle, thoughts, emotions and behavior, expressed in various degrees and intensities. The following are some characteristic descriptions of each *guna*.

A *sattvic* **person** favors progress above everything else. He derives great pleasure from being creative and innovative. He has a deep respect for life and nature and he always seeks a healthy and life-supportive environment. *Sattvic* people naturally have healthy habits and prefer pure and energizing foods.

A *rajasic* **person** favors action for action's sake, regardless of whether it is good for him or not. He has an inner urge to move, overwork his mind and body, be impulsive and impatient and look for an outlet for his nervous creativity. *Rajasic* people seem to have endless energy and are very extrovert. They prefer stimulating foods and drinks.

A *tamasic* **person** does not want to change and prefers everything to stay as it is. His inactive mind finds comfort in set routines and accustomed environments. *Tamasic* people tend to dwell on the past and try to avoid the present and future. They rarely develop new ideas or habits in life.

The three *gunas*, *Rajas*, *Sattva*, and *Tamas*, are mental qualities that correspond to the three physical *doshas, Vata, Pitta* and *Kapha*. Ayurveda had a clear understanding about mind/body medicine when it linked basic mental impulses to specific physical conditions, tendencies and disorders. It also categorised foods according to their effects on the mind.

Sattvic food is wholesome whereas *rajasic* and *tamasic* foods are unwholesome. *Charaka*, one of the founders of Ayurvedic Medicine, said thousands of years ago: "The body is constituted of food. Wholesome food is one of the causes for the growth of living beings and unwholesome food is one of the causes for the growth of diseases." In other words, if we want to progress in life, become vital and healthy and live in harmony with the laws of nature, we need to adopt a *sattvic* diet. Particularly those who would like to enhance their spiritual growth can benefit greatly from a *sattvic* diet. The following lists give you an idea about the different effects that food can have on body and mind. The quotations, which explain the three types of diet, are taken from the Bhagavad-Gita, a 5,000-year-old scripture that narrates in detail the interplay of the three *gunas* in a person who treads the spiritual path and reaches spiritual enlightenment.

The *Sattvic* Diet

"Sattvic diet is that which is unctuous, pleasing to the heart and mind, which stabilizes the body and gives long life, strength and health to the mind and body. A sattvic diet promotes happiness and love for all creatures." (Bhagavat Gita)

Sattvic diet is sweet in taste, light, unctuous (liquid-containing), and cooling (versus heating like in chilli, alcohol etc.). *Sattvic* foods include:

- Breast milk (for babies)
- Ghee (clarified butter)
- Butter
- Wheat
- Basmati rice
- Yellow mung beans

- Freshly cooked vegetables
- Ripened fruits
- Sesame seeds
- Rock salt or real sea salt
- Sesame oil
- Ginger
- Dates
- Almonds
- Honey
- Fresh spring water

Any food that has a soothing effect and is digested easily is *sattvic* by nature, provided we eat it in moderation. Please note: If any of the above foods do not pass the *Kinesiology muscle test*[5], they are not fresh, harvested too early, too old, contain harmful chemicals from fertilisation, are gassed to preserve them for longer periods, or have been combined with unwholesome foods or ingredients. You may also check with the list of foods for specific body types,[6] which will help you find out what kinds of fruits, vegetables etc. are *sattvic* for you. Ayurveda considers the *sattvic* diet to be the most suitable for promoting strength, vitality, a strong mind and lasting good moods, youthfulness and longevity. By beginning to include *sattvic* foods in your diet, unwholesome habits, addictions and ill-health will gradually disappear.

The *Rajasic* Diet

Rajasic diet is that which brings unhappiness, sorrow and disease. It contains mostly the pungent, sour and salty tastes, and it is too hot, sharp and dry, and causes burning sensation" (Bhagavat Gita).

Rajasic diet is too spicy, strong tasting (like cheese) and includes foods that have a *heating* effect such as chilli, garlic, onions, pepper, tomatoes, cheese (aged, salted), ripe eggplants, some pulses, meat, fish, sea food, eggs, alcohol, tea, coffee, cigarettes, sugary foods, soft drinks,

---

[5] See "Timeless Secrets of Health And Rejuvenation"
[6] See "Timeless Secrets of Health And Rejuvenation"

crisps and similar junk foods. If you are continuously attracted to these or similar foods, it indicates that there may already be a physical or emotional imbalance.

The *Tamasic* Diet

Tamasic diet is that which is stored and spoiled, which is without taste and has a bad smell; also leftovers and food, which does not look appealing" (Bhagavat Gita).

Tamasic food is heavy, cold, dry, tasteless, decayed, spoiled frozen or cooked in the microwave oven. People who do not mind eating tamasic foods are already controlled by the dulling influence of tamas, thus they are insensitive to purity and refined values. Poisoned by tamas and unable to appreciate pure foods and drinks such as water, *tamasic* people seem to be able to eat almost anything without a problem. Such people are likely to develop life-threatening diseases at some point in their lives.

2. The Power of Thought

A Change of Thoughts

Since every thought manifests as a powerful messenger molecule in your brain, by changing your way of thinking you not only improve your body but also your relationships and your destiny. If the pilot of an airplane decides to change its direction by even half a degree the plane may arrive at a completely different destination.

A change of thoughts can have a similar effect. Remember how good you felt when someone close to you told you how much he or she loved you or cared about you. By contrast, try to imagine how you would feel if your best friend turned around and told you how much he despised you. A little piece of information can be enough to change your entire life. If you don't like the way you live your life at this moment you can change its course by making a new decision right now. Take a few minutes to become clear about what you want out of life and then decide to achieve it.

If you face a major problem in life for which there doesn't seem to be a solution, you may feel that your whole world is collapsing. But if you could see yourself 10 years from now and looked back in time you would realize that life didn't stop after all. Simply move your attention away from what is not possible to what is possible and you are back on track. It is as easy as that. Whenever you are facing a serious problem in your life, go through the following simple exercise which is designed to take you into a more positive and constructive space than you are right now:

1. **Think of any one thing or person that makes you feel good. Begin to realize how important this one thing or person is for you and how fortunate you are to have it or him/her in your life.**
2. **Think of all the people who are not as fortunate as you are, like the homeless, sick and starving.**
3. **Now imagine how you would feel if you fulfilled your heart's desire(s).**
4. **What would you do as a first step towards achieving your goal?**

One of the main reasons we attract problems into our lives is because we don't do what makes us happy. We send out negative messages by saying "I wish I didn't have to work so hard", "How in the world did I deserve this?!" or "Life is a struggle!." Your life, and that includes the current condition of your body and mind, is the product of your thoughts and feelings. Thoughts influence everything far or near, material or non-material. If you want to examine what kind of thoughts you had yesterday, then look at your body today. If you want to know what your body is going to be like tomorrow, look at the thoughts you are having today. Every movement and activity in your body and mind is controlled or matched by the corresponding neurotransmitters. Not a single idea, desire, feeling, like, dislike understanding or misunderstanding can go through your mind without creating corresponding physical counterparts.

Happiness – Your Key to Nature's Drug Store

Your brain is capable of manufacturing any drug that could possibly be made anywhere in the world, provided it receives the "go ahead" signal from you, its master. The brain requires neither a sophisticated chemical laboratory nor much time to develop the most exquisite drugs for any type of physical or mental problem. With the few types of natural food ingredients mentioned above, it makes neuropeptides and related chemicals for every condition you could possibly develop.

For example, if you suffer from pain, your brain makes *endorphines* and *enkephalines*, morphine type compounds that are at least 40,000 times more powerful than the strongest heroin. If you injured yourself and your brain didn't instantly produce these drugs, you would not be able to endure the pain and would faint or go insane quickly. Since *endorphins* are also related to the experience of pleasure, you will make more of these drugs when you find joy in what you are doing. People, who suffer from emotional pain, soon begin to have physical pain, too; their brains are inhibited from making adequate amounts of painkillers.

If your body signals "cancer," your brain synthesises anti-cancer drugs or immune-stimulants that boost your immune system to take care of the problem before you even know it. Each day, millions of our body cells mutate and become cancerous but our immune system deals with them instantly and without the help of chemotherapy, radiation, or surgery. We do not have to concern ourselves with having millions of new cancer cells each day unless, of course, our body fails to destroy them. Cancer is the physical counterpart of an unbalanced emotion that contains a clear message: "There is an antagonistic element in your life, which is wasting away your body." This foreign element can be low self-worthiness, repressed emotions, a negative outlook on one's life, an unexpressed or unfulfilled desire, defensive responses to a hostile partner or environment, or an unbalanced diet. Usually, there is a combination of factors. Instead of trying to cut out this foreign element, you can learn from it and transform it for your own good.[7]

We generally tend to blame heart attacks, cancer, osteoporosis, AIDS etc. for causing most deaths in the world as if these diseases were

---

[7] To deal with cancer and its causes, see *Cancer Is Not A Disease – It's A Survival Mechanism* by the author.

powerful monsters that are out to destroy life indiscriminately. Only a few of the people afflicted with a serious illness question why they manifested it in the first place. Instead of deciding to put all your energy and effort into a particular problem, which tends to escalate it, you can direct your attention towards what you feel could contribute to your happiness. Make happiness your motivation and goal. Always seek happiness as the reward for your actions and the rest follows automatically. Wherever there is happiness, there are solutions and wherever there is unhappiness there are problems.

Energy Follows Thought

Energy follows thought is an excellent phrase to remember. Do not waste your energy on a disease, on a difficult partnership, on your financial troubles or on an annoying neighbour. You are practically feeding these problems with your energy and thus will maintain or even worsen them. This may give you the illusion that they are real. When you analyse the solution of any problem that has ever existed anywhere in the world, it was never found by dwelling on the problem. Conflicts, wars, economic struggles, disasters etc., ended when the involved groups, or people began to focus their attention on what was possible rather than what was impossible. We always have the choice and freedom either to argue over who or what is responsible for our problems or to look for real solutions. There is no need to know what causes the darkness of the night when we know that there will be a dawn of a new day.

You may remember how downcast you were when your life was in a state of crisis and how remote and insignificant that problem became a while later. A problem begins to dissipate when we take our attention away from it. For example, if you suffer from a sleeping problem, instead of worrying over the fact that you cannot sleep, you could bring your attention to your breathing or think of things or people who bring you happiness. Suddenly you will find that not sleeping isn't so bad after all, and then you will drift off naturally. Should the problem persist, use it as an opportunity to take a closer look at your life. If you are not happy at nighttimes, it indicates that you have not been happy during the day either. Use the sleeping problem to find out what doesn't make you happy in life and then think about how you can change it.

You may decide that you want a better job that inspires and fulfills you more. Be daring when it comes to fulfilling your desire but do not admit defeat before even trying. The argument that you would not be competent or clever enough for a better job is illusory. You will always be good enough for a job you feel attracted to as long as you put your undivided attention on it. If you keep telling yourself that you are not good enough, you have created the exact limitations that will keep you there until you come up with the courage to say that you deserve much better.

We let ourselves be so easily persuaded to believe that it is another person, society, the government or even destiny that holds us back from achieving our dreams. But it is only our limited thinking that keeps us confined to failure or lack of success. The old saying, "where there is a will there is a way" is a law that holds true for everyone under any circumstance. The three *P's*, *P*atience, *P*ersistence and *P*erseverance, have been the dominating qualities that helped transform common people into the most successful and pioneering personalities the world has ever seen. It was Mahatma Gandhi's vision of a better society that propelled him to endure the difficulties of his life. Stephen Hawking became one the most brilliant physicists in the world despite his total speech deficiency and paralysis. Instead of dwelling on his incapacitating disease or feeling sorry for himself, he made an enormous contribution towards understanding and utilising the most fundamental laws of nature.

The greatest athletes of the world had their fair share of major difficulties before they managed to rise to the top. Most famous artists and musicians had to go through periods of failure and rejection before they were acknowledged to be among the best. Many of the truly successful people share one common principle of living; they want to be more and more creative because they know that being creative is the only source of happiness. We all share the same infinite potential that creates and maintains the entire universe. What makes the biggest difference between people is that some have decided to use their potential and apply the three P's in their life, whereas others have not. You, too, can make that decision. You can make it right now! All it needs is a shift of attention.

CHAPTER 6
The Principles and Technique of Primordial Healing

This chapter explains the principles and technique of Primordial Healing which has a myriad range of effects on all levels of body, mind and spirit. The Technique of Primordial Healing is effortless, easy to practice, and almost as automatic and simple as breathing itself. It combines breathing with specific healing sounds and is practiced in two consecutive parts. Part one of the technique, which you can learn in this section, deals with conscious breathing; much of the second part deals with primordial healing sounds. To be able to practice both parts of the technique, it is necessary to have a good understanding of conscious breathing.

Part One
The Miracle of Conscious Breathing

Breath is All There is and Much More

Our physical existence depends entirely on the breathing process. Life begins anew with each new breath we take and ends with one final exhalation. We inhale external air 15 times or more per minute to supply each cell of the body with oxygen and vital energy or *Prana*. Each of the trillions of chemical reactions that occur in our body every second requires *Prana*-carrying oxygen. Therefore, breathing does not only take place in the lungs of our chest but also in the "lungs" of our cells. We breathe with every part of our body. Oxygen, which makes up about 21% of the atmospheric air, is involved in a series of chemical events that result in the release of energy from nutrient materials. This energy is essential for all cellular activities.

Every physical problem involves a restriction in the flow of oxygen to the affected area. Under normal conditions, breathing happens

108

automatically and is sufficiently effective to take care of all the body's needs, from its very first to its last breath. Yet we also have conscious control over the process of breathing – for a good reason. Under stress – due to the release of stress hormones – normal breathing is no longer efficient. To meet the increased demand of oxygen, we require a greater expansion of the chest during inhalation, which, however, can only be enforced through voluntary muscular activity. But during times of distress most people tend to do the exact opposite: they breathe in a shallow way, hold their breath, or breathe through their mouths, which triggers the release of *adrenaline*. Consequently, the body suffers lack of oxygen and *Prana* energy. This can be avoided. The negative effects of stressful events, emotional tension or physical exertion, which may develop into disease, can be reduced, brought under control and even eliminated through "conscious breathing."

Whenever you find yourself in a difficult situation simply put your attention on the area of your nostrils, and begin breathing deeply. Although exhalation occurs automatically and usually effortlessly, it is under your conscious control how much air you take into your lungs during each breath. You may mentally follow the movements of your chest as it expands and contracts. Within just a few moments, your mind will find pleasure in the peacefulness during the brief moments of pause after each exhalation or before each inhalation. There is nothing else you have to do but to merely put your attention on the breathing process. You might not yet be able to change the situation that made you tense in the first place, but you can certainly change your response to it by allowing your mind to become increasingly settled through conscious breathing.

Apart from physically relaxing and unwinding, you have tapped into something much greater than you possibly could have imagined. You have contacted the creator of the breath, who is the sustaining power of your body. He is the cosmic intelligence within the silent depth of your awareness. He is you.

How do I Start?

The technique of Primordial Healing is practiced in a comfortable sitting position and with the eyes closed. It is best to sit straight to make it easier for the body to breathe without strain. For maximum results, you do this exercise for about 15 minutes twice a day, in the morning and in the evening, preferably before or at least 2 - 3 hours after eating food.

As you close your eyes, simply bring your attention to the end of your nose or to your chest and experience the movements of inhalation and exhalation. Breathe easily and naturally. The longer you practice, the more readily will your mind follow the rhythm of breathing and become relaxed. To go into a peaceful state, your mind does not have to stop thinking. In fact, the only mistake you can make with this practice is trying to stop thinking or prevent thoughts from coming. If you are carried away by thoughts, feelings or emotions do not do anything to stop them. Simply bring your awareness back to the breathing, to your nose or chest, and if the thoughts continue to be there, fine. An increased thought activity during the practice indicates that stress is released from the nervous system; stress release naturally results in more physical activity which in turn increases mental activity, i.e. thoughts, feelings, ideas etc.

Continue this process until you feel 15 minutes have passed. There is no reason to be anxious about doing this correctly. Breathing is natural and having your attention on it is natural, too. There is nothing you can do to improve upon what nature is already doing perfectly. Also, don't try to breathe with greater emphasis or deeper than you would normally do in the sitting position.

By repeatedly allowing your mind to follow the inhalation of fresh air into the body and the exhalation of used air out through your nose, your mind will become increasingly quiet and peaceful. If for a brief moment your mind becomes still altogether, you will only be aware of yourself, without a thought or feeling. For this moment you are Self-realized or "Self-referral" because your Self is the only thing to which you can refer. It is for this instant that your mind has given up thinking; your body follows suit by becoming completely relaxed. This is the time when body and mind are perfectly coordinated and primordial healing takes place. There is nothing you can possibly do to produce or experience these moments. They occur when you expect them the least, i.e. when you are totally relaxed about the process, with no expectations or effort.

With regular practice of conscious breathing, you will find that this peaceful and relaxed state of your mind will extend in time and accompany you during mental and physical activity throughout the day. There will be a strong sense of calmness and of being centered and self-confident even in stressful situations or amidst noise and chaos. The depth of this experience will increase to the point where your own unbounded awareness will coexist with the most dynamic activity of your body and mind.

The Key to Success is "Letting go"

The above breathing technique is the simplest technique of self-development that exists, yet it is also one of the most powerful ones. However experienced or inexperienced you may be in the field of meditation or other techniques of self-development, *conscious breathing* is equally beneficial for everyone, since progress never stops but is increased and accelerated with regular practice. In the field of meditation, the level of achievement it controlled by the rule "do less and accomplish more;" and not by how much effort or concentration you put into it.

All that is required is the ability to let go. Letting go is a constant feature of creation. Something old has to go for something new to emerge. A thought appears on our mind's screen and then disappears again. Similarly, we take a breath and then we let it go. To be able to release a breath is a great relief for the body and the mind. We can only take another breath after having released the previously inhaled air from our lungs. With *conscious breathing* we "sink" deeper and deeper into a restful mode of "letting go" which gradually creates the experience of feeling free, relaxed and centered even during the most active and challenging moments of life. The result is a stress-free mind and a healthy body. We cannot train ourselves to let go through increasing willpower or intellectual efforts, but we can spontaneously master this, perhaps most important, ability in life when we release each breath with full awareness.

For many people breathing is no longer a conscious experience. Due to stress and tension, exhalation becomes shorter and inhalation shallow and insufficient. With insufficient inhalation and exhalation,

111

the body begins to suffer from oxygen deficiency and retention of waste products, including carbon dioxide in the lower lobes of the lungs. This turns on the body's stress responses, which makes our nervous system even more "nervous" and agitated.

Healthy babies still have the natural experience of effortless breathing. Their abdomen rises and falls as if their lungs were located in their stomach. This is an indication of their carefree, innocent and blissful nature. However, when fear creeps into their lives because of pressures from the educational establishment, parents, nutritional deficiencies, emotional trauma etc., breathing becomes unnatural and strained; their carefree spirit and joyous nature diminishes, too.

Just as negative or frustrating experiences in life cause breathing to be deficient, *conscious breathing* can gradually release bottled-up emotional stress and unresolved problems. Through the mind/body connection, emotional toxins create their physical counterparts; this may eventually manifest as psychosomatic disease. *Conscious breathing* improves circulation, which helps to remove impurities and their corresponding emotional stress. The secret of success of this technique lies in its regular practice of at least 15 minutes twice a day. Breathing is natural and putting the attention on it is natural, too. This is all there is to know to make *conscious breathing* an effective technique for spiritual growth and self-development.

The Power of Attention

Attention is the single most powerful tool we have at our disposal to accomplish anything in life. Since energy follows thought, whatever we put our attention on will receive energy and grow stronger. We would not be able to perceive the world had we not our attention on it. You may have read a book but if your attention was elsewhere, you have neither truly read it nor understood its contents. Similarly, you may be eating a meal but if your attention is focused on the TV news or on reading a magazine, you may not even notice what you eat and your food won't get properly digested and assimilated either. Attention makes all the difference. It is required when you visit the bathroom, when you drive a car, when you cook a meal, or when you play a musical instrument. Your relationships require attention, too;

otherwise, they may "wither" from lack of love and care. Whatever lacks your attention becomes useless for *you*. Such it is with your body.

Muscles become depleted if we do not use or exercise them regularly. In truth, your whole body requires attention to be healthy. If you neglect it, it begins to malfunction. Although you may not be aware of the cells of your body or of the complex processes occurring within them, on a very subtle level your attention is present in even the tiniest part of your biological organism. This is due to your desire to live and the awareness that you are alive. All the cells, molecules, and atoms in your body are held together by this subtle form of attention.

Unless we feel an ache or a pain somewhere in the body, we may not realize how important the body is for us. Our subtle awareness of the body suddenly becomes more pronounced when it cries out for help and we begin to put our attention on searching for a remedy. Carelessness about food, digestion, elimination and hygiene and being unmindful of the body's messages of discomfort lead to a disruption of this delicate connection between the body and mind.

Since the vital breath is needed in every part of the body and sustains all its functions, conscious breathing is a direct way to bring the attention back to the disconnected and malfunctioning areas, tissues and cells. The *energy* that *follows thought* or *attention* helps to reawaken them to their original vigor and vitality like dry fields begin to bloom when irrigated by a stream. By putting your attention on the breathing process, you bring vigor and vitality to your body, mind and soul.

Part Two
Primordial Healing Sounds

You are What you Perceive

All the primordial vibrations responsible for every aspect of the physical and non-physical creation are located in the silence of one's awareness just like a tiny seed that contains all the information it needs to bring fourth a giant tree. This field of silence is not empty or chaotic but organized, purposeful and active. It is made of invisible designs that

113

are perfect and flawless, translating themselves into the building blocks of our physiology. It is here where the frequencies of primordial impulses – primordial sounds – become form, where "the word becomes the flesh." Because the transformation of sound or vibration into form or matter begins on the level of our awareness, we can learn to correct any malfunction in the body merely through *intent* or desire.

We all ingest, metabolize, and become everything that we perceive within and outside ourselves. We literally become the thoughts we think, the emotions we trigger, the knowledge we understand, the sounds we hear, the shapes and colors we see, the air we breathe, just as we become the food we eat. Wherever your attention goes to, the mere mental contact with it absorbs its very essence and makes it an integral part of your life.

Through mere observation of natural scenery, you create the same healing effect within you that it (the scenery) generates for all the surrounding creatures. Looking at a sunset or a snow-covered mountain may have slightly different effects on each one of us yet its overall influence is soothing and calming. By contrast, you may figuratively become as cold and hard as a jungle of concrete and steel if you live in one or see it often enough. Studies conducted in American hospitals have revealed that patients staying in rooms that face natural scenery such as a lake, trees or mountains, recover much faster and require less medication than those who are faced with the lifeless scenery of concrete buildings or cannot look out of the window at all.

The vibrations emanating from sounds, words, colors, shapes or forms are waves of various lengths and frequencies. They are basic to all organic and inorganic life forms and have a profound influence on our lives, too. We merge with whatever we perceive through our mind, intellect or senses of perception. Waves are not only playing an important part in the world of physics, they are the basic energy patterns that make up our thought forms and feelings as well. They become part of us and form a new set of information in our awareness, which in turn can reshape our destiny on every level of life, physical, material, and spiritual. Sound waves have perhaps the most powerful effect on our well-being.

The World of Sounds

Every sound produces sound waves or disturbances in the air, which travel at about 332 meters per second. Through complex internal processes, we can pick up these sound waves through our ears and eventually perceive them in the cerebral cortex of our brain. Our brain is capable of receiving an enormous number of various kinds of sounds that are generated in our environment and, what is most intriguing; it can make sense of them. It knows how to differentiate all the numerous sounds and link them to our auditory memories. Some sounds are words, which we call language, others we call music, and again others we consider just noise.

Every sound that our brain cells perceive stimulates them to make neurotransmitters that subsequently translate these sounds into specific physiological responses in the body. For this reason, you may feel elevated and cheerful when you listen to your favorite music or you may become nervous and agitated when you hear the jarring noise of a machine or the scratching of a nail.

Some sounds affect different parts of the body more than others. Instrumental music for instance stimulates the right hemisphere of the brain and its related left side of the body more than it stimulates the left hemisphere and its related right side of the body. If vocals are part of the music, then the whole body is stimulated. All the cells in the body can "hear" these sounds because they have receptor sites for the same neuropeptides that the brain makes when it perceives sound. This also means that the cells in our body are capable of producing the same chemical messengers as the brain and they use them to communicate with each other through sound.

Our skin, for example, is a very apt receptor for music. If sound waves reach and touch the skin, which they do when you listen to music, the skin cells respond by secreting "pleasure hormones" and other chemicals that enhance immunity and vitality throughout the body, provided the music suits your psycho-physiological body-type. This fantastic ability of skin cells may be rooted in the fact that they are identical to brain cells, except that they die after one month whereas brain cells can live for as long as a hundred or more years. Some people report a pleasant tingling sensation running through their skin while listening to music. Jarring noise on the other hand can make your skin shiver and your hair stand on end. In that case your skin cells make stress hormones.

There is ample evidence now that all the 60-100 trillion cells in the body listen to and respond to all the sounds we perceive (that includes the cells of a fetus carried in a mother's womb). Harmonious and coherent sounds make you feel healthy and alive. For this reason, music has played a major role in all the cultures of the world, throughout time. Every culture has developed its own particular type of music to suit the specific requirements that are formed out of the various geographic and climatic conditions in each area.

Music is not just a fundamental need of every culture but a physiological one as well. In the field of health, music has been found to reduce the time of recovery after surgery and to strengthen a patient's ability to fight infection. Patients are found to need less medication for pain, fewer tranquillizers and sleeping pills when they listen to their favorite music. A large number of American hospitals are already using music for therapeutic reasons. There is music that can reduce appetite, lower blood pressure or put you to sleep.

Of course, not all music triggers a healing response. There is a musical frequency for everything that exists, even to cause disease. If you regularly listen to hard rock music, your lymphocytes begin to drop in number, leaving you more prone to infection. Low-pitch sounds can make you feel sad and depressed. For this reason, funeral music uses low pitch sounds. On the other hand, high-pitch sounds can make you feel happy and enthusiastic.

Yet again, as is the case with every other external influence, the responses vary according to body type. If you are a *Vata* out of balance (impatience, anxiety) then slow, low-pitch music may benefit you more than fast, high-pitch music because it reduces hyperactivity and nervousness. A lethargic *Kapha* type, on the other hand, can do with lively high-pitch sounds to get his circulation and metabolic rate going. A fast tempo is likely to increase your heart beat and an irregular tempo can cause an irregular heart rhythm and even lead to *cardiac arrhythmia* as seen in the cases of some pop singers.

The Body – A Symphony Orchestra

Medical research has revealed that each organ in the body creates a specific sound that can be amplified by highly sophisticated measuring devices. The liver, for example, produces a certain sound when it is healthy. If the liver gets diseased, it produces a distorted sound. If you play the recorded healthy sound back to the liver, it can be restored to health. The liver sounds are different from the sounds generated by the heart, the spleen, the lungs, or any other part of the body.

All the various types of cells make their own characteristic sounds. Their specific electrical broadcasts differ from each other with the frequencies they produce. In the case of an infant the measurable frequencies range from 1,520,000 to 9,460,000 Hz (cycles per second). The lower end of this fairly high human frequency overlaps the radio frequency range of AM radio broadcasts, which are from 540,000 to 1,600,000 Hz; FM is 88,000,000 to 108,000,000 Hz, out of the human range, which means that we cannot hear these sounds, at least not consciously.

As a whole, a healthy body "sounds" like an enormous symphony orchestra with millions of different musical instruments. All disease processes begin with a distortion of these sounds and can lead to a near-total loss of synchrony as in the case of cancer or AIDS. Can you imagine a symphony orchestra with millions of instruments all playing out of tune? What is needed are a few master musicians and a conductor who can lead and coordinate all the other musicians.

Name and Form Relationship

There are several "master sounds" which command the major functions of the organs and systems in the body, others control the tissues, and again others are in charge of the body's energy centers. These sounds are identical to the basic vibrational frequencies that the various parts of the body produce when they are in perfect balance. Ayurveda, the ancient science of life, is the one of the ancient sciences that knows of the therapeutic value of such primordial sounds.

Brain research has shown that the thought of an object such as an apple or an elephant and actually seeing it creates the same chemical

117

changes and brain wave patterns. In other words, whether you think of an elephant or actually see one makes no difference with respect to the corresponding biochemical changes in your body. All material objects have their basis in non-material vibrations, i.e. sounds; in truth, both kinds are inseparably one. In the not so distant future we will be able to make use of this intimate relationship of name (or sound) and form and spontaneously materialize an object such as an apple, an elephant, or even a diamond, if need be (see section on Primordial Siddhi Sounds). Today's miracle will be tomorrow's reality.

The situation is similar with Primordial Sounds. By using these sounds, you can restore the original forms and functions of the tissues, organs and systems. The regular use of the sounds can promote profound healing in body, mind, and spirit because they are projected from our own pure awareness or Higher Self. The sounds become the channels or beams of energy from our Higher Self and are used to perform their assigned duties and responsibilities. Their regular use does not only induce specific healing responses but also stabilize pure awareness and make it increasingly available in daily life.

Summary of the Technique of Primordial Healing

The technique of Primordial Healing which takes advantage of the intimate relationship that sound has with matter can be summarized as follows: Every bit of matter, whether it is a piece of stone, a bacterium, or a complex human nerve cell produces specific and unique vibrational frequencies or sounds.

The various cellular tissues, organs and systems in the body differ from each other in as much as they produce different sounds or frequencies. The low-frequency sounds produced by toxins, viruses, harmful bacteria, pollutants, repressed negative emotions and stress responses, interfere with and lower the body's own frequencies leading to weakness and instability.

Disease occurs when a particular part of the body has been disconnected from its original primordial vibrations, which carry vital impulses of information. Loss of contact with this inherent vibrational information leads to chaos and confusion, as is the case with isolated and malignant tumor cells. By contrast, the high frequencies pertaining to primordial sounds can correct imbalances at their most primary stage of development and thereby induce profound healing. Primordial Healing Sounds restore the frequencies of their corresponding parts of the body and through repeated use re-establish their healthy functioning. Combined with "Conscious Breathing" and/or "Ener-Chi Art," they are invaluable assets in the balanced development of our body, mind and spirit. The healing sounds that I have personally created for my healing system, *Art of Self-Healing*" will be made available during the course of 2006.[8]

There are, however, a number of Primordial Sounds that a person can generate himself for balancing the energy centers of the body and other parts as well. Contrary to the chants used, for example, in *Art of Self-Healing* or during a *Sacred Santémony* session (see information in the next section), you can chant these sounds aloud in your home or while walking in nature. The following primordial sounds can be learned quickly and practiced daily. They are as follows:

The Primordial Healing Sounds of the Seven Chakras

1. **Lam** *Laaaammm......*: located at the root or base of the spine, *Lam* controls the legs, feet, genitals, anus, base of spine, kidneys; the body's life force.

2. **Vam** *Vaaammm......*: located between the navel and the groin, *Vam* controls the pelvis, belly, sex organs, nervous system, low spine; adrenal glands, and sex glands (ovaries or testes).

3. **Ram** *Raaammm......*: located at the Solar Plexus, *Ram* controls the stomach, liver, diaphragm, gallbladder; spleen and pancreas.

4. **Yam** *Yaaammm......*: located in the heart area, *Yam* controls the heart and chest, circulation, lungs, arms hands; thymus gland.

---

[8] *Art of Self-Healing* is a unique approach that gives a person instant access to his/her own healing powers. The approach consists of a series of 32 light-ray-imbued pictures (Ener-Chi Art) created by the author, and specific healing sounds (Sacred Santémony) that he has recorded on CD for the purpose of removing any obstacles to healing one's body and mind and emotions. The supplied CD is synchronized with viewing the pictures for about half a minute each.

5. **Hum** *Hummm.......:* located in the throat area, *Hum* controls the neck, voice, lungs and chest, mouth; thyroid and parathyroid glands.

6. **Om** *Oooommm......:* located between the eyebrows, above the bridge of the nose, *Om* controls the ears, nose, left eye, the nervous system, skull base; pituitary gland.

7. **So-hum** Sooo-hummm…: located at the crown of the head or on top of the skull, *So-hum* controls the upper skull, cerebral brain, right eye; pineal gland.

The Five Hr... Sounds

1. **Hrim** *Hreeemmm:* Throat
2. **Hrum** *Hrooommm:* Liver, Spleen
3. **Hraim** *Hraheemmm:* Kidneys (diuretic)
4. **Hraum** *Hrowmmm:* Organs of elimination incl. bladder, colon, skin
5. **Hrah** *Hrah:* Heart, chest

Directions of use: When chanted, the above sounds resonate with their corresponding areas of the body and thus enliven and maintain their proper functioning. They can be practiced anywhere and at any time but preferably on an empty stomach. Begin by taking a deep breath and while exhaling chant all the seven sounds related to the seven energy centers in the sequence given above. Repeat as often as you like. This will help align your chakras, endocrine glands, and their functions and improve your breathing patterns as well. The sounds cleanse your *etheric body* from impure influences and make you feel more comfortable within yourself.

Should you require extra healing for any specific areas of the body you can use the 5 *Hr... sounds* in the same way. Take a deep breath, chant while exhaling. Then repeat five or more times. If circumstances do not allow you to chant these sounds aloud you can use them mentally instead.

Primordial *Siddhi* Sounds

There are nearly two dozen Primordial sounds, which in ancient times were used to develop physical and mental abilities that were out of the *ordinary* experience. These are known as *Siddhis,* or supernatural powers. *Siddhis* develop key areas of the brain that are responsible for extraordinary perception and abilities and previously inaccessible knowledge.

The purpose of practicing the *Siddhis* is to unfold one's infinite potential and to stabilize unbounded, pure consciousness in daily life. The skill of spontaneously fulfilling one's desires by mere thought develops as a natural result of regular practice of conscious breathing and these sound formulas. The sounds correspond to and fully develop the 192 bundles of nerve fibers known as *Arcuate* or association fibers located in the largest part of the brain (*cerebrum*). The *cerebrum* includes control of sensory perception and voluntary motor activity.

One set of *Siddhis* is designed to develop *divine perception* by refining the five senses to a degree that they can fathom the deepest and million times richer areas of colors, shapes, sounds, smells and tastes. They can open us to the fifth and sixth dimensions of reality, where every thought becomes realized instantly. Other *Siddhis* are directed towards unfolding the qualities of the heart e.g., compassion, love, and happiness. Some *Siddhis* deal with gaining knowledge and direct perception of the inside of the body and its condition and of objects hidden from view or being at far distance. There are also *Siddhis* to develop concrete insights of the universe by seeing its structure and purpose in a flash.

Several other *Siddhis* are linked with unfolding the power of intuition, physical strength, knowledge of the mind and one's Higher Self, and mastery of the five elements earth, water, fire, air and ether. One very powerful *Siddhi* bestows the ability to physically levitate.

It is not advisable to learn *Siddhis* from books. To learn them properly and practice them effortlessly one needs to find a teacher who knows this ancient art, which is based on the *Yoga Sutras of Patanajali* (book of the Vedic literature relating to the practice of Yoga). The organization that spreads Transcendental Meditation offers Siddhi courses, albeit they are very expensive. There may be others groups that teach them..

121

After 25 years of practising *Siddhis*, I developed a unique channelling gift, called Sacred Santémony – Divine Chanting for Every Occasion. The sounds that pass through my vocal cords consist of primordial sounds of ancient languages. The sounds have distinct healing abilities. For more details on Sacred Santémony and how to how to arrange for a phone session, see *Other Books, Products and Services by the Author*.

CHAPTER 7
The Five Senses – Fountains of Youth

Healthy Senses for a Healthy Life

We keep contact with the outside world through the senses of sight, hearing, touch, taste and smell. The senses "feed" our mind, which in turn drives our body into action. To live a healthy life we need to have healthy senses. Any deficiency in sensory perception such as weak eyesight causes disturbances in both mind and body. Whatever enters the nervous system through the senses, i.e. food, air, water, sights, sounds, smells, tastes, warmth or cold, dryness, softness or roughness, is translated into the appropriate neurotransmitters or related chemicals in the brain and instantly alters the functioning of our mind and body.

For example, a beautiful landscape or sunset can lower an elevated blood pressure and an irritating noise can raise it. A violent movie or bad news shown on the TV screen may release stress hormones, suppress the immune system and even trigger a panic attack. The reduced resistance to disease can make a person more susceptible to infection, heart disease or cancer. Delicious tasting food can raise the production of digestive enzymes; on the other hand, spoiled food or bad odors cut down their production, reduce appetite and raise heart rates etc. Ayurveda claims that mind and body can only stay healthy if you are able to derive a certain amount of pleasure and happiness from *all* the five senses. Both *over-indulgence* and *under-indulgence* of the senses generate imbalances in body, mind and spirit.

For the body and mind to be healthy and efficient, the senses must be healthy and efficient, too. Through natural and simple techniques and exercises, we can develop the senses to an even higher degree than what is considered normal, and in this way increase our inner happiness and enjoyment – prerequisites for long continued health, youthfulness, and material and spiritual success.

1. Inner and Outer Vision

Limited eyesight (both shortsighted and farsighted) reduces the pleasure and enjoyment of life and causes detrimental chemical changes throughout the body. Eyesight, however, is only one part of what we refer to as vision. The other part of vision has to do with how we see others and ourselves in a non-physical sense. Inner vision and outer vision intimately connect to everything that takes place in our life, whether it is outside or inside of us. A faulty vision is linked to an imbalance on a deeper level of our personality, as well as to poor functioning of such as organs as the liver, kidneys and intestines. This imbalance generates or attracts corresponding circumstances and situations in life. We then may find ourselves addicted to certain substances or foods or unable to give up a harmful lifestyle. The lack of "in-sight" into our true nature, which is unlimited potentiality, can impair also our ability to properly see with the physical eyes.

There may be people in our lives we try to avoid. On the other hand, we may consistently ignore the impulsive reaction we have each time something happens that doesn't suit us or that we don't want to see. Limited eyesight may not only be related to resisting to deal with certain pressing issues or problems but also with wanting to see too much or being impatient in life. In all cases, the result is strain in our eye muscles, which inhibits both nourishment of new eye cells and the removal of dead cells and metabolic waste products from the eyes. The accumulation of metabolic waste and cell debris in and around the eyes are among the leading physical causes of eye problems. This congestion results in rigidity, stiffness and aches in the eye muscles. The eyes may also become hypersensitive to sunlight, causing excessive straining, even headaches; or they become too dry, leading to infections; in some cases, the eyes become watery, causing blurred vision.

The Importance Liver Cleansing and Balanced Diet

Dietary mistakes also play a major role in causing eye problems. The eyes require large amounts of oxygen, glucose, and micronutrients such as vitamin A. When AGNI, the digestive fire, is weak, then digestion and absorption of these nutrients become impaired which leads to deficient elimination of waste material through feces, urine and perspiration. The resulting accumulation of acidic and toxic compounds is increased beyond the level of tolerance and the blood is no longer able to dissolve and remove the waste products efficiently. They combine to form a sticky, glue-like colloid substance (AMA) which congests or occludes the tiny blood vessels (capillaries) that supply the eye cells. This results in defective circulation to the eyes and impairs their normal functioning (in many cases the eyes look red or "bloodshot").

Most eye problems are caused by a weak digestive system. Vitamin A is the major vitamin necessary to maintain the cornea of the eye in a healthy state; it is amply available if digestive and assimilative functions are balanced. If the liver bile ducts and gall bladder are congested with gallstones, digestion, assimilation and metabolism of food remain inefficient and eyesight deteriorates. To make vitamin A and other nutrients sufficiently available to the eyes and restore proper vision, I recommend cleansing the liver and gallbladder from all stones first. When cleansing of the liver is combined with following a balanced diet and eye exercises, eye problems usually disappear very quickly.

Good vegetarian sources of vitamin A are carrots, butter, pumpkin, green leafy vegetables, pineapple, peas. Since 70 - 80 percent of the body is alkaline, fruits, vegetables and salads – the key components of alkaline forming foods – should ideally make up the major part of our diet. Eating too many *acid-forming foods* such as animal proteins, dairy products, wheat and its products, other grains, sugars, fats, oils, nuts etc., thickens the blood and has a damaging effect on the entire body, including the eyes. Those with eye problems do better following a *Pitta* pacifying diet and particularly avoid tomatoes, vinegar, pickles, onions, garlic, yoghurt, cheese, meat, pork, fish, eggs and hot spices.

Eye exercises can help restore proper and complete eyesight when the causal factors are eliminated first or at the same time. The following simple eye exercises (A1-7) stimulate the cells of the retina making them more receptive to white light, improve color perception, increase the flexibility of the lens and eye muscles, and thereby improve any visual problems. Those suffering from cataracts (opacity of the lens) can greatly benefit from an exercise that uses human saliva.

Another set of eye exercises (B1-8) comprises fixed eye positions which, apart from strengthening the eye muscles, help access and improve visual memories as well as memories of conversations, music, smells, fragrances, tastes etc. Holding the eyes in these various fixed positions for 20 - 30 seconds has been shown to significantly increase EEG brain wave coherence, thus creating a harmonious influence in the entire body as well as increasing creativity, concentration and learning ability. Simply follow the instructions below.

Note: for all exercises it is best to take off any corrective lenses.

Eye Exercises
A 1-7

To enhance your sensory perception, to improve your eyesight, sense of color perception, memory, creativity, attention span and learning ability.

1.   Look at the sun or full spectrum light with your eyes closed for about 20 seconds. This stimulates the cells of the retina and makes them more sensitive to light.

2.   Then gently massage the eyeballs with your fingertips for about 20 seconds and slowly move your head away from the sun or the source of light and again towards the sun or source of light. By doing this you will experience in your awareness one or several colors. Now hold your attention and observe the color or colors in your awareness until they fade away. These subtle colors will stimulate the *cones*, which are responsible for color perception. Consequently, the colors in your environment will become more rich and alive, causing a profound healing effect. In a way, this exercise can be seen as a personalized form of color therapy.

3.   To increase the flexibility of the lens, look at an object which is close to you and then look at an object that is distant. (For example, look at the hand in front of you and then look at the horizon). Perform this exercise 15 – 20 times.

4.   Pin up a sheet of printed material on the wall. Then stand away from it as far as possible for comfortable reading. Each day, move back just a little bit but still close enough to read the text comfortably. If you

126

do this gradually, you will be able to improve your ability to clearly see objects at far distances.

5. Take the same printed material and read it from as close a distance as comfortable for your eyes. Then gradually bring it nearer to your eyes or move closer towards it every day until you are eventually able to read it even when it almost touches your nose.

6. Stare at the moonlight without blinking for 30 seconds or as long as is comfortable. The moonlight has a soothing, calming and strengthening effect on both the eyes and the nervous system.

7. Brush your teeth and wash your hands. Then imagine biting into a lemon, producing saliva. Bring the saliva to your fingers, close your eyes, and generously rub it into your eyelids. You can do this in the morning or before bedtime or both. *Note: this exercise is especially good for cataracts. The saliva contains enzymes that can digest the dead protein accumulated in the eyes (a major cause of cataracts).*

B 1-7
To strengthen *the entire* eye muscles
hold each eye position for 20-30 seconds.

1. Look with your eyes left and up and keep this position for 15 – 20 seconds. This is a movement you spontaneously make when you try to recall a visual memory, (if you are right handed). The position strengthens your ability for visual recall.

2. Looking down and left accesses auditory memory and auditory recall. This position will improve your memory of conversations and music.

3. Looking down and right accesses the experience or memory of touch and strengthens this ability.

4. Looking up and to the right strengthens your ability to create new visual forms, which is especially useful for artists.

5. Looking horizontally and right will strengthen your ability to create new sound forms and symphonies that a musician would create.

6. Staring towards your nose will strengthen the olfactory memories –the memories of smell and fragrance – thereby enhancing enjoyment of food.

7. Moving your eyes towards your lips and having the idea that your eyes are pointing towards the tongue will enliven and strengthen your memories of taste, thus improving digestive power.

8. Turn your eyes upwards and inwards and look at the space between the eyebrows. This will help to open your "third eye" or sixth sense, which is the power of intuition.

Holding the attention on these fixed positions for 20-30 seconds each has proven to increase EEG brain wave coherence dramatically and thereby enhance multi-sensory experience.

Sunlight Eye-treatments

The sun which allows natural vision and color perception to take place, offers the greatest help in overcoming all sorts of eye problems. Apart from removing gallstones, there cannot be any superior method for improving eyesight than natural sunlight. Eyes cannot function properly without adequate and regular exposure to the sun and most eye problems result from sunlight deficiency. Living beings, which live under the ground, like earthworms, have no organs of vision. Where there is no light, there is also no need for a sense of sight. Fish living in dark caves require no eyesight and therefore become blind.

Most miners develop defective eyesight and inflammatory diseases of the eyes. In fact, all people who live in dark places, indoors or under artificial lighting most of the time, develop weak and insufficient eyesight. After living in these or similar conditions for a certain length of time, the light receptor cells of their eyes begin to deteriorate. All cells in the body, including those constituting the eyes, require sunlight, especially ultraviolet rays, to stimulate proper cell growth and cell division. According to the saying "use it or lose it", eyes that lack regular exposure to sunlight gradually "wither" away like flowers which are kept in the dark.

Similar to the eyes of fish living in a dark sea cave, human eyes, which are no longer exposed to sunlight, literally develop an aversion to it. They hurt, burn and become torn from exposure to normal sunlight. Some people's eyes can become so sensitive to sunlight that they "insist" on protection while being outdoors or else they shut altogether. Although sunglasses provide such a protection and provide temporary relief, they also make matters worse. After a while, the eyes will require even darker glasses, thereby weakening eye cells and further interfering with their functions. To escape this vicious circle I recommend the *Liver and Gallbladder Flush* and the following eye treatments. The exercises can be done by anyone who has developed sensitivity to sunlight and wishes to improve their eyes:

C 1-4

1. Sit outdoors in a comfortable position and face the sun with eyelids closed. Let your body sway gently and make sure that your eyeballs move according to the movements of the head and body, and not in the opposite direction (swinging prevents your eyes from staring). Do this for a few minutes and then turn away from the sun or move into the shade while keeping your eyes closed. Now cover your eyes with your palms for about 5 minutes. When you open your eyes you will feel an immediate relief. The more regularly and more often you do this treatment, the faster your eyes will recover.

2. Once your eyes have become used to natural sunlight, you can repeat treatment 1 but this time with your eyes open. Again sway the body from side to side, but make sure at first that your eyes are looking down. Then gradually raise your head while blinking frequently, bringing your eyes towards the sun but don't not look directly into the sun. While swinging, imagine that the sun and other objects are moving in the opposite direction. Do this for a few minutes and once again "palm" your eyes for about five minutes afterwards. If you feel that the rays of the sun are still too strong for you, you can place your feet in cold water, which quickly absorbs the heat rays and keeps your head cool. Note: try to avoid doing this exercise between 10 a.m. and 3 p.m., unless it is during winter or springtime.

3. Gazing at the morning sun for a few minutes and then "palming" the eyes for half a minute exercises the iris through alternate contraction and dilation of the pupil. The light stimulates the retina and darkness relaxes it again.

4. This treatment combines water with sunlight: Fill a bowl or a basin with water that does not contain chlorine. Dip your face, keep

your eyes open and blink frequently. Remove your face from the water to take a new breath. Then gaze at the sun for a few seconds with eyes open. Repeat this procedure ten times or more. The sun cannot harm the eyes because the layer of cold water in front of the eyes absorbs the heat rays. In addition to this treatment, you may want to gently splash your (open) eyes every morning up to twenty times right after waking up with cold water. This treatment helps blood circulation to and from the eyes and aids removal of toxins; it can be done anytime whenever the eyes feel tired.

Note: Begin any of the sunlight treatments with the mild rays of the sun and gradually expose the eyes also to the stronger rays, but avoid sitting in the sun when it is hot. If the sun does not shine on certain days, substitute a full spectrum light and if that is not available, a strong electric light. Keep the eyes about six inches away from the light, or as close as is comfortable. After every sun-treatment wash your eyes with cold water which greatly enhances circulation. Facing the sun for 5 minutes a day is sufficient to keep your eyes healthy and shining.

To develop your inner vision, strengthen the eyes, and improve outer vision you may also use the following ancient Vedic techniques:
- Place a candle about one foot away from your eyes while the rest of the room is dark. Keep looking at the flame and gently move your body forwards and backwards following the rhythmic patterns of respiration. You can count from 25 to 100 breaths according to what feels comfortable.
- Put two candles nine inches apart and about one foot away from your eyes. Look at the candle to your left while inhaling and as you exhale move to the candle on your right, then inhale while looking at the candle to your right and move to the left candle while you exhale again. Repeat 25 – 100 times.

2. The World of Hearing

Hearing on all Levels

The sense of hearing is located in the ears. The human ear is a complex organ of remarkable sensitivity. It enables us to be aware of the position and movement of our head, and by giving us a sense of gravitational direction, it facilitates our capacity for balance and motion and allows us to make co-coordinated, smooth movements.

Our outer ear can collect vast numbers of sound waves and through extremely complex processes, some of them become audible to us. We acquired this ability when we were a four-and-a-half month old fetus in our mother's womb. From this early age we were able to hear quite well and respond to sounds, especially to music.

Sound waves cover a vast range of frequencies, from fractions of a Hz (cycle per second) to millions of Hz. Many animals such as dolphins, bats, cats and dogs have a wide range of hearing, extending to 200,000 Hz and above. Humans can consciously respond to a frequency range from about 20 Hz to a maximum of 20,000 Hz. Sounds lower than 17 – 20 Hz can be merely felt as vibrations, but sounds higher than 20,000 Hz are too high for us to hear or sense, hence they are known as ultrasonic.

The rest of our body can detect *all* the frequencies of sound and in fact is able to resonate with the sound energies around it. We are constantly exposed to and influenced by a vast amount of unheard sounds to which we respond in an unconscious way. The sound exercises described below help us to make this process more conscious and enhance our hearing abilities to far beyond what is considered normal, thereby linking up with a much wider field of the ultimate and complete world of sounds and their precious meanings. The word that can best describe such a heightened sense of hearing may be "divine hearing" since it comprises the most beautiful symphonies of nature at the subtlest levels of creation.

The science of cymatics is a discipline that studies wave energy, Through photographic images it can reveal the patterns and forms inherent in sound. In fact, all matter or form is created through sound (see primordial healing sounds, chapter 6). Our body is but a product of numerous natural laws that express themselves through the vibrations of sound, shaping the vast complexity of our physical existence. When the cells of our body no longer function efficiently, it is because their ability to perceive and follow the specific codes and instructions contained in the sounds of nature is impaired.

The build-up of toxic residues in the body leads to the thickening of cell membranes, thereby restricting the ability of the cells' receptor sites to receive sound information from the surrounding cells, organs, systems and environment. Being increasingly cut off from the world of sounds, the cells begin to degenerate, which can lead to aging and diseases of the tissues and organs. By removing the layers of toxins that thicken the cell membranes through cleansing methods[9] and using certain sounds we can improve our sense of hearing and enhance our perception of sound through every cell of our body. This can be achieved through the "bio-resonance effect."

Some of the most powerful sounds that the cells of our body receive are generated when we speak. The sounds include the five vowels, which are common to all alphabets in the world. This is no coincidence but a necessity for survival and constant regeneration. We all use these vowels to resonate with all the cells in the body and thus keep them energized and alive. The following exercises are very beneficial for waking up the "sleeping" cells in the body and restoring them to balance.

Sound Exercises

Vowel power

A as in *art* - **E** as in *may* - **I** as in *he* - **O** as in *no* - U as in *you*.

Begin by taking a deep breath and "chant" all five sounds out loud as you exhale, **ah, aye...ee...oh...oo,** or you may choose to take one vowel at a time. Repeat 3-5 times. This will help to restore balance of all the 60-100 trillion cells of your body. For maximum results, this should be done every day. The following sounds are used in the same way but have more specific effects on various parts of the body.

---

[9] As described in "Timeless Secrets of Health And Rejuvenation"

Humming

One of the best sounds we make is simple "humming." We naturally hum when we feel contented, happy, and in harmony with others and ourselves. There are three natural ways of humming.

1. "mmm" , when your lips are closed and your tongue lies on the floor of your mouth. While making this sound you will feel the vibrations in the palate at the roof of your mouth. This sound resonates with the lungs, nasal passages and sinuses and the skull. It is beneficial for all problems in these areas, including asthma, sinusitis and sinus headaches. It also enlivens and harmonizes both hemispheres of the brain, and improves memory, concentration and learning ability.

2. "nnn", when your tongue touches the hard front part of your palate. The vibrations produced by this sound spread up into the ears and help with any ear problems, including earache and deafness.

3. "ngngng", when you hold the back of your tongue against the softer rear part of your palate. This produces nasal humming: these vibrations travel into your throat and neck, helping all throat problems and pain or stiffness in the neck.

Jaw sounds

Yaa as in spa   -   Yoo as in who   -   Yay as in play

These sounds resonate with the tissues of the jaws and help to relieve tension and rigidity. They are useful to help with migraine and tension headache.

Throat sounds

Kaa as in spa   -   Gaa as in spa   -   Huh as in hut

These sounds resonate with the tissues in the throat and speech center. They are beneficial for any throat problems and /or speech deficiencies.

Stomach sound

Huh Huh Huh ..... as in the sound of laughter.

The sound of laughter resonates with the stomach cells and helps with any stomach problems including nausea, hyperacidity, ulcers and cancer. This sound generates emotions of happiness and is known to trigger powerful immune responses helpful for any type of illness.

Note: in addition to creating powerful physiological and psychological effects through these sounds, the almost complete elimination of carbon dioxide from the lungs at the end of exhalation while uttering a sound, helps to strengthen lung functions and improve oxidation of all the cells in the body.

Sound Therapy

Sound therapists and biologists have extensively researched the effects of sound vibrations on living cells. Research has shown that by using tuning forks as a sound source, the different frequencies of the musical scale caused red blood cells to change their color and shape. The musical note C, for example, which is also part of our natural spoken voice, causes blood cells to become longer; the note E makes them spherical; the note A changes their color from red to pink. It seems that the frequencies contained in the musical notes are similar to if not the same as the cells' own natural frequencies. By producing the notes, the cells set up sympathetic vibrations, reinforce resonance and break up disruptive interference patterns.

This effect can be used in a number of ways. It was demonstrated several years ago that cancer cells in test tubes burst when exposed to the sound of "hum." The latest research in this field has shown that cancer cells, which in comparison with normal cells are weak, floppy and overweight, gradually become disrupted and disintegrate when subjected to a sequence of rising frequencies at 400-480 Hz (A-B above middle C). The resonance seems to strengthen healthy cells and tissues yet discourage unhealthy cells from growing. The research has identified specific sound frequencies that correspond to and affect certain parts of the body; whether the sounds are produced vocally or by an instrument, both can have very profound healing effects.

Note C : For colon problems such as constipation, diarrhea; cystitis; prostate problems; all circulatory problems including cold feet; swollen ankles, feet, and legs; knee problems; stiffness in joints; low back pain; sciatica; iron deficiency; anemia; and melancholia; weak sense of smell.

Note D : For lung and bronchial problems, including asthma and bronchitis; obesity; gout; gallstones; blockage of lymph ducts and lymph nodes; difficulties in removing toxins and poison from the body; kidney and bladder problems; lethargy and passiveness; weak sense of taste.

Note E : For intestinal disorders; all problems of the stomach, liver, pancreas, spleen and skin; constipation; headaches; cough; boredom; sluggishness; weak sense of sight.

Note F : For heart conditions; high blood pressure; immune problems; hay fever and allergies; ulcers; head colds; trauma and shock; tension; back pains; colic; exhaustion; dry skin; weak sense of touch.

Note G : For eye problems; headaches; laryngitis; tonsillitis and throat infections; skin problems and itching; vomiting; muscular spasms; menstrual cramps; fevers; weak sense of hearing.

Note A : For all problems of the nervous system; balance disorders; dizziness; breathing difficulties; convulsions; obsessions; excessive bleeding and other blood disorders; swelling. Lack of trust in one's intuition.

Note B : For all glandular disorders; goiter; low immunity; cancers; deficient vitamin absorption and processing; nervous disorders; cramps and inflammatory pains. Low self-worth and self-respect.

Music Therapy

Natural sounds are extremely important for maintaining balance on all levels of existence, that is, mind, body, behavior and environment. Unless deaf, we cannot even remotely imagine what this world would be like without sounds. An environment without the gushing sounds of a waterfall, the singing of birds, the humming sounds of bees, the rustling of leaves, the swishing of grass, the murmur of a river, or the chirping of crickets is unattractive, to say the least. Natural sounds are essential for sustaining the decisive frequencies that guarantee continual evolution and existence of our natural world. We, too, are the evolutionary products of nature. Nature's sounds contain the information and instructions to create and organize all of matter, including our bodies. The sounds emanating from dolphins or whales have upheld growth and evolution on our planet for eons and so have the "minutest" sounds generated by insects, amoebae and microbes. Natural sounds form the basis of all life in the universe.

We can use nature's sounds to restore life wherever it has been distorted or damaged by sounds that have adverse effects. Life disintegrates wherever nature's sounds are subdued. Plants, animals and humans require nature's "music" to follow a pattern of healthy growth. This inner need for nature's "symphonies" has instilled in every culture the desire to create a unique traditional type of music under the direct influence of the particular geographical conditions and specific climates prevailing in different regions of the planet. Like other beings, humans are also able to create music and they can be very good at it. Music harmonizes differences and has a happiness and love-generating effect on our environment and us. The frequencies of happiness and love are the most powerful antidotes to disease, disharmony, crime and environmental destruction.

For example, greenhouse and field plants grow faster when soft music is piped to them. Carefully controlled studies with plants showed that germination, growth, flowering, fruiting, and seed yield are affected by sound waves, particularly by musical sounds ranging in the low frequencies from 100 Hz to 600 Hz. Cows also respond to music by giving more milk. Listening to music helps people to relax, normalize blood pressure and balance moods. By listening to music at least once a day you can find and keep your inner balance.

You can do this in two ways. Find a quiet space somewhere out in nature and focus your mind on the natural sounds around you. You may even want to write down what sounds you hear and your reactions to them. This makes the sounds more concrete and meaningful for you and helps you become more aware of the sounds around. Some sounds are more obvious than others. Do you prefer to hear the loud, dominating ones or the ones in the background? Do you find low-pitched sounds more comforting than high-pitched sounds?

Becoming aware of the sounds around us can reflect how we feel about ourselves. They help us to correct imbalances within us. If the sounds bore you, it only reflects that you are bored within yourself. So simply listen to these sounds until the discomfort passes. This gives you an opportunity to move closer to your true essence, which can never be boring. Natural sounds can serve as a wonderful therapist, always available when we need one. Thus, the sound of a river can instill patience and peacefulness in the listener. The singing of a bird can cheer you up, and the gentle sound of a breeze can create clarity in your mind.

The second method of regaining balance is to listen to music of your liking. For best results it is best to do this with full attention, which means sitting or lying with eyes closed. Music can be a very powerful therapeutic tool. Listen with your heart and mind. When you listen to great music with your full attention and allow it to touch you in many different ways, you can enter a profound state of bliss. This can remove mental stress, emotional upset and ill health.

Let your feelings guide you when you select a particular piece of music; don't go by what others think is the best music (fashionable). Let the tunes "soak in" and "filter" through your skin into your blood, bones and nerves. The music will realign your cells and make them stronger and healthier.

Tuned to Heal

A healthy body is composed of numerous rhythmic patterns, all of which are harmoniously linked to a happy mind. When we become angry, these patterns of internal music become distorted and lead to physical problems. Feeling angry is not merely a thought, but it is an all-body sensation where every single cell of the body is forced to deviate from its normal style of functioning. When we are angry, we are literally "out of tune." The result is that our eye and facial muscles tense up, the skin begins to redden or become pale, heart beat rises, and the body posture changes, reflecting how we feel inside. This micro-muscular response to emotional states is what was described as body language in chapter 5. In a way, our body tries to remain tuned to its natural sounds and rhythms which produce happiness but once it is thrown off balance, harsh words, a raised voice and ill feelings signal that we are no longer tuned to the music of perfect balance or health. This also cuts our links with nature, hence the feeling of poverty, loneliness and loss of spiritual awareness.

Dr. David Aldrich, head of a clinical team researching music therapy, has shown that heart disease patients have difficulties in co-

coordinating and empathizing with the rhythms of music makers. That music has therapeutic value has been known for a long time, but it is becoming increasingly clear that music is a necessity for creating and maintaining health rather than just a means for gaining pleasure.

Dr. Ralph Spintge, head of a pain clinic in Germany, has produced a database that reveals the powerful effects of music on over 90,000 patients. All patients showed measurable improvements in both quality and speed of recovery. Other effects of music included a 50% reduction in recommended doses of sedatives and anesthetic drugs needed to perform otherwise very painful operations. Now there are even some procedures that, with the aid of music, require no anesthetic at all. Although a certain part of the value of music helps the patient to distract his mind from his sickness or pain, most of its healing effects emanate from restoring the important biological and neuro-physiological rhythms that underlie the vital functions of the body. Music soothes and relaxes anxieties, helps to trigger natural painkillers in the brain, and improves the performance and clarity of the mind.

Research has shown that music activates the right-brain temporal lobe, which is associated with emotion, movement, and meaning. This is particularly important in our left-brain society where logic, rational behavior, and analytical thinking are considered the preferred keys to success. Music can stimulate our right brain which comprises the intuitive and artistic faculties, and this may turn stress and tension into opportunities for positive change in life. After all, we were not born with only half a brain. Our right-brain temporal lobe has many astonishing abilities in store; however, our predominantly left-brain oriented educational system has not sufficiently encouraged their full development. Music has the capacity to fill this gap. There is a desperate need to develop right-brain activities in our society, which is a major reason why so many young people spend all day listening to music.

Tony de Blois is a typical example of a right-brain musical genius. Born brain damaged, blind and autistic, Tony at the age of twenty-one is not even able to tie his own shoelaces, but he has a remarkable musical memory for over 7,000 songs. His ability for playing and singing incredibly complex jazz improvisations has made up for the lack of intellect. His memory for music is extraordinary. He can play any one of his 7,000 songs in any possible style without making a mistake and leap without transition from classical music to the most modern compositions of pop. When his mother gave him his first electronic keyboard she hoped that this would stimulate him in some way. At first, she was disappointed when Tony only produced random notes and their possible combinations. After about six weeks, he began to play the first three notes of "Twinkle Twinkle" and his gift for music was born.

Playing musical instruments has a profound influence on the performer himself. If you possibly can, try to learn an instrument. One does not need to be autistic, artistic or intelligent to play music. Tony, too, had no previous skills. The random and seemingly meaningless musical notes he produced prior to developing his musical skills had served as a stimulant to trigger his right-brain functions. Everyone who has a right-brain temporal lobe is artistic and musical by nature. By playing a musical instrument, you can develop this important side of our brain. You don't have to be a good performer of music to reap the benefit from the frequencies of sound, but by merely producing sounds you bring about profound changes in your brain. Playing music creates happiness and contentment, both essential for a healthy mind and a healthy body. That producing music or singing can have an anti-aging effect is clearly demonstrated by such artists as Tina Turner, Barbara Streisand, Andrea Bocelli, David Bowie, Cliff Richard and Diana Ross, among numerous other performers. They seem to have stopped aging years ago.

Ear Coning

Perhaps one of the fastest and most profound methods to improve and refine hearing is known as *ear coning, ear candling* or *ear cleansing* – a technique that was used by the cultures of India, China, Tibet, Egypt, Aztec, Mayan and Americas and Southern Europe for both physical and spiritual reasons. Ear coning, which has aroused great interest in recent years and is now recommended to German medical students as a remedy, promptly and without any discomfort removes large quantities of fungus, yeast, and ear wax from the ears. This not only removes hearing problems, sinus infection, and lymph congestion, headaches, migraines, and numerous other disorders but also cleanses the seven layers of the aura and strengthens the link to our higher self. Directly after a coning session most people experience a new sense of clarity, openness, and balance in body and mind. Ear coning can release old traumas and create a wonderful sense of well-being. Many alternative health practitioners are offering this treatment and it is easy to learn and to apply.

3. Touch for Health

Touch has a many times stronger effect than verbal or emotional contact. Since the skin is one of our richest reservoirs of both hormones and immune cells, the sense of touch can be the most influential of all the senses. Experiments on prematurely born children known as "preemies" have shown that regular stroking three times a day, called "kinesthetic tactile stimulation", caused a daily increase of their body weight by 49 percent.

Growth factors such as growth hormones are abundantly present in the skin. Ayurveda teaches us daily-performed do-it-yourself massages that help to release a "shower" of healing chemicals into the blood stream, a powerful effect useful for both prevention and cure of illness. The massage techniques also remove harmful fatty acids and other toxic waste products from the tissues and the skin, improve general circulation, enhance flexibility of the joints and have now shown to be effective in helping with reversal of arteriosclerosis (hardening of arteries). The techniques I refer to here are "dry brushing," and "Abyanga" or daily oil massage[10].

Begin by brushing your whole body with a dry body brush made of natural bristle or a good natural loofah. This will improve circulation, strengthen and rejuvenate the skin, and help with lymphatic drainage. The brushing of the skin also opens the pores and increases effectiveness of the oil massage. Then massage yourself for 5 – 10 minutes (from head to toes) with sesame oil or with coconut or olive oil (all cold pressed and unrefined, available from health food stores) to draw out toxins and improve circulation, followed by a warm bath or shower.

---

[10] See "Timeless Secrets of Health And Rejuvenation"

A third major Ayurvedic body technique is known as *Marma therapy*, which is described below.

Marma Therapy

Marmas are junction points between consciousness and the body. Ayurveda describes 108 points where the Prana energy or vital force is most concentrated, often referred to as acupuncture points. There are three major junction areas on the body, also known as Maha-marmas. They control all other functions in the body. Gently massage them with cold pressed, unrefined sesame oil for *Vata* and *Kapha* types or with jojoba, coconut, or almond oil for *Pitta* types, using clockwise circular motions for a few minutes each (do not apply any pressure). This can establish a healthy mind/body relationship and thus ensure good health. So gently massage a little oil for 2 – 3 minutes into

- *the place between the eyebrows.* This induces a state of calm, restful alertness and triggers other profound biochemical changes throughout the body.
- *the central area overlying the heart.* This has a balancing influence on emotions such as anger, impatience and sadness.
- *the area over the stomach.* This improves digestion and appetite and eliminates false cravings.

Other very important marmas are the *soles of the feet.* When gently massaged, they balance the entire nervous system and stimulate all other functions in the body. If applied in the morning the foot marma massage helps to improve motor sensory activities and when done in the evening it stimulates the sleeping center in the brain, which induces sound and uninterrupted sleep (this is especially good for children and adults who have difficulties with falling asleep). Other major marmas are located at the back of the neck, the top of the head, the palms of the hands, the insides of the elbows, the back of the knees, and the coccyx area.

Apply oil on each of the marma points for 2 – 3 minutes or as long as it feels comfortable. Use circular motions without pressure, as marmas are very sensitive areas. *Vata* and *Kapha* types benefit most from using sesame oil, *Pitta* types *with* skin problems do better using jojoba, coconut or almond oils. These base oils can be made more effective by using specific Aromatherapy oils for each *dosha*:

Vata oils: Basil, rose geranium, orange, lavender, neroli, patchouli and frankincense.
Pitta oils: Sandalwood, lavender, peppermint, jasmine and ylang-ylang.
Kapha oils: Eucalyptus, mustard oil, clove, camphor, marjoram, juniper and bergamot.

If you are not sure which ones are best for you, use the Kinesiology muscle test to find out or dowse if you are into dowsing.

Body Techniques

There are many different body techniques available today that attempt to restore balance of energy to both mind and body. They include Shiatsu, Aromatherapy, Reflexology, Metamorphic, Bowen, Osteopathy, Sacro-cranial therapy, Rolfing, Trager, Thai Massage, Biodynamic Therapy, Applied Kinesiology, Tuina, Tibetan Massage, Chi Nei Tsang, *Neural Organization Technique* etc.

I have found that different people respond to different techniques in different ways. What benefits one person may not be helpful for someone else. If you are not sure which body technique is suitable for you, let your intuition guide you. Simply ask yourself if the particular method you are thinking about is beneficial for you. If your first impulse makes you feel good, start looking for a qualified and experienced practitioner. As your body begins to improve, you may find that after a while you need another method to help correct others types of imbalances.

With any of these techniques, the benefits will increase tremendously after you have done liver, kidney and colon cleanses, since gallstones in the liver and gallbladder, stones in the kidneys, and accumulation of toxic waste in the intestines are the main source of discomfort, pain and illness in the body[11]. Once these obstructions are gone, the energy will flow more freely in the body. This makes it much easier for a therapist to make the necessary physical adjustments.

One very profound and comprehensive self-healing techniques I have learnt is Chi Lel, an ancient healing art from China. Chi Lel is composed of a number of 5,000-years-old Chi Kung practices that were kept as secrets within families and religious temples. In 1980, these methods of healing were revealed to the general public and have since helped over 8 million people worldwide curing their illnesses, many of which are considered incurable.

The Huaxia Zhineng Qigong Center near Beijing, China, which is the world's largest medicine-free hospital, has so far treated over 100,000 patients with 180 different diseases, and achieved a success rate of 95 percent. Monitored by modern ultrasound technology, Chi Lel has been able to make large tumors disintegrate and disappear within less than a minute, as can be seen on ultrasounds. People who were paralyzed for many years, regained full mobility, blind people regained their vision and deaf people their hearing. What is most remarkable, however, is that Chi-Lel seems to heal the soul of a person.

Chi Lel can be practiced by anyone. There is a book, videotape and a number of audiotapes that can instruct you to learn and practice the techniques[12]. In the Unites States, there are also short courses one can follow. Persons who suffer a terminal illness and are able to travel to the Chi Lel Center in China can expect the same recovery rates as those suffering from the flu. Many other types of Chi Kung have similar effects.

4. Taste – An Intimate Source of Pleasure

The sense of taste provides us with one of the most enjoyable experiences in life, "eating", something we all have to do to sustain life. Deriving pleasure from eating has been shown to be crucial for

---

[11] See "Timeless Secrets of Health And Rejuvenation"
[12] Contact the Benefactor Press, 9676 Cincinnati-Columbus Road, Cincinnati, OH 4524, USA;   Tel. 513 777-0588, Fax. 513 755-5722.

maintaining good health. The pleasure that arises from tasting and eating food triggers the release of "pleasure hormones", including *endorphins* -- the body's own natural morphine and painkillers – as well as *interleukin* and *interferon* – the body's natural anticancer drugs. Loss of enjoyment from food results in insufficient secretion of these important hormones and can be seen as one of the root causes of illness ranging from a simple cold to a malignant growth; it can impair digestive and metabolic activity, cause weight problems and decrease energy and vitality.

Located on the tongue, the sense of taste regulates the body's secretion of digestive enzymes by informing the brain of the exact types and quantities of foods that we ingest and feeds back to us our requirement for food nutrients. The tongue accommodates six different kinds of taste buds to detect six different kinds of tastes, namely *sweet, sour, salty, pungent, bitter and astringent*. The reason why we have taste buds is to experience and process all the six tastes at least once a day. Regular consumption of meals with all the six tastes supplies the body with all the nutritional values it needs. Food that has only little natural taste, e.g. food that is grown with chemical fertilizers, refined, processed, preserved, artificially flavored etc., also has only little or no nutritional value for the body.

The body has no system that is able to count calories or determine the exact amounts of daily-required amino acids, vitamins, minerals or trace elements. Despite this "weakness" or maybe because of it human life has continues to exist for millions of years. The body knows perfectly well what it needs to maintain its equilibrium. If we had not been fooled by "masked" foods, we would rarely suffer from nutritional deficiencies and know instinctively what type and amount of food we need to sustain healthy growth.

If your body requires, for example, more bitter taste which has important blood cleansing properties, you would naturally be drawn towards eating bitter greens such as endive, romaine lettuce or other green leafy vegetables; or your body may crave tonic water, lemon rind or spices such as turmeric or fenugreek. Coffee and chocolate are also dominated by the bitter taste but are unpalatable when taken in an unaltered form. Processing as well as adding sugar and milk makes the bitter taste of these substances sweet and desirable. This, however, can lead to an overdose of bitter foods and in fact poison the body, which consequently triggers a strong immune response (mistaken for an increase of energy). Such a situation only arises because the taste buds have been misled into believing that the food is sweet (whereas in reality it is bitter) and is therefore "acceptable" in larger quantities than is acceptable for the body.

The lack of one or more of the six tastes gives rise to nutritional imbalances and causes discomfort and finally disease. For example, if a *Pitta* type is only getting sweet, sour, and salty tasting foods and misses out on bitter, astringent and pungent foods, the body responds by generating food cravings to satisfy its needs. However, since the tongue's taste buds only had contact with the first three tastes they will urge the body to eat even more foods that contain sweet, sour and salty tastes, such as a hamburger with French fries and tomato ketchup. The continued lack of the other three tastes leads to a further decrease in the supply of basic nutrients, which causes addictions to certain foods and substances.

Ayurveda has a clear understanding about the six tastes and knows how much of each taste an individual needs (every person's body type is different, giving rise to different dietary needs). Regular supply of all the six natural tastes allows the body to extract the right amount of basic nutrients, such as vitamins and minerals, in order to maintain all its functions and avoid deficiencies of any kind. Once balanced, the body will instinctively look for the right kind of food to maintain its balanced state. This will make dietary rules unnecessary. To get there, however, we may need to practice a few simple rules of eating.

Simple Rules for Healthy Eating

The sense of taste is responsible for our enjoyment of food. Weight problems and other physical imbalances are due to loss of enjoyment from food. If we could truly enjoy food, we would never have a weight problem. The following awareness techniques maximize the enjoyment of food, improve digestion and metabolism, and increase energy and vitality:

- **Whenever you eat or drink anything, however little it may be, make it a rule to sit down.** Food can only be digested properly

145

when we eat in the sitting position. To eat while in the lying position impairs blood and lymph flow throughout the gastrointestinal tract, and eating while walking or standing causes indigestion.

- **When you eat, don't do anything else such as listening to the radio, watching television, reading or driving a car**. A major reason for having taste buds on the tongue is that the brain can receive signals as to what type and quantity of food is entering the digestive system. This enables the body to produce and release sufficient amounts of various enzymes required for the digestion of the food. If we didn't have such a facility, our digestive system would secrete enzymes indiscriminately which would be a wasteful action the body cannot afford. When we turn our attention to anything else but the food we are eating, our taste buds cannot make sufficient "conscious" contact with the various foods and their tastes. This restricts the release of the appropriate digestive enzymes for each particular taste and reduces AGNI, the digestive fire. It also confuses the body for it will no longer know when the saturation point for a particular type of taste, such as salty or sweet, has been reached. Hence, foods cravings begin to emerge which are linked with insufficiently digested and absorbed foods, as well as with the lack of pleasure hormones, normally secreted when food is eaten with full attention. Since eating is an act of enjoyment, we might as well do it with an undivided mind. As a golden rule, everything we do with joy and attention is beneficial, and everything we do with displeasure and lack of attention generates problems.

- **Eat only when the stomach is empty**, otherwise you interfere with the enjoyment of food. When the stomach is still full or is in the process of digesting food, the taste buds are desensitised to prevent a person from eating. Natural hunger only occurs when the stomach is empty. On the other hand, false hunger or food cravings emerge when the basic natural rules of eating have been violated for a long time and emotional imbalances exist; both these causes override or suppress the normal signals of satiation coming from the stomach and taste buds. The urge to eat food while the stomach is still digesting, is often connected to occurrence of gallstones in the liver and gallbladder and disappears once they have been removed through a series of liver cleanses.

- **Do not put food into your mouth till the previous bite has gone into the stomach.** The process of eating is a unique opportunity to practice mindfulness and patience. By chewing the food until it has been masticated enough to produce a sweet tasting liquid, greatly enhances the enjoyment of food and keeps your attention on the present moment, which is the key to all happiness. Mahatma Gandhi advised people to "drink" their food and "eat" their drinks. Eating and drinking in this way is one of the most powerful methods of overcoming emotional problems in life.

- **Don't speak while there is still food in the mouth.** When you speak while there is food in your mouth, you tend to swallow before it is properly masticated, and you miss out on enjoying your food. It is better to speak only when there is no food left in the mouth.

- **For your first helping, take about two cupped hands full of food.** This will fill two thirds of your stomach; the rest is empty space that is needed to propel the food and mix it with digestive juices. If you are still hungry, wait for 5 minutes. If the feeling of hunger has not subsided by this time, you may take some more food. Leaving the table slightly hungry is a good method to increase one's will power, determination and self-confidence. Completely filling the stomach leads to indigestion, dullness, lethargy and food cravings.

- **Make certain to have all the six tastes of food at least once a day.** This can effectively help to reduce food cravings and prevent nutrient deficiencies. Be careful not to eat more than 3-4 main ingredients in one meal at a time or have more than one type of starch or protein in a meal.

Better Taste

There are two methods to improve the performance of our taste buds and to lubricate and sensitize them for greater enjoyment of food:

1. When your tongue is coated white or yellow, clean it with a tongue scraper or a tablespoon every morning after awakening

147

and every evening before going to bed. This removes sticky AMA (with billions of bacteria) from your taste buds.

2. Swish 1 – 2 tablespoons of cold pressed and unrefined sunflower or sesame oil in your mouth cavity for 3 – 4 minutes every morning, and perhaps also in the evening before bedtime. The oil draws and absorbs toxins and microbes from the throat, tonsils, ears, eyes, blood, chest etc. Then spit it out and rinse your mouth with water. When the tongue is clear and the taste buds are unobstructed, we tend not to overeat because the natural satiety level or satisfaction from food is reached more easily. Those who tend to overeat or smoke cigarettes have dull taste buds. They have a "high-flavored" threshold, which means that they need much stronger and more stimulating foods to be satisfied; this may lead to food cravings and substance addictions.

5. Sensing through Smell

The sense of smell is closely linked to the sense of taste. Eighty percent of the flavor of food is because of the sense of smell. Therefore, the enjoyment of food also depends on this sense. The sense of smell directly influences the hypothalamus, the brain's brain, where most of the body's functions are regulated. Thus, a heightened sense of smell can positively influence the entire physiology. Ayurveda uses this faculty to increase the sensitivity of smell for greater enjoyment and to strengthen the body's natural resistance to disease by using certain aromas appropriate for specific body types. These aromas help to release the body's own natural healing chemicals and increase overall well-being.

Techniques for Improving your Sense of Smell

Gently massage the inner nasal cavity with a little bit of sesame oil once or twice a day. You may use cotton wool buds or your little finger. This lubricates the receptors in the nose and increases the awareness and sensitivity of smell and at the same time lowers the susceptibility to colds. When you travel in airplanes this technique can be applied more often and reduces jet lag and prevents sickness.

The use of aroma oils sends specific signals to the hypothalamus to balance *Vata, Pitta,* and *Kapha* as follows:

Vata is balanced with a mixture of warm, sweet, sour aromas such as basil, orange, rose geranium, clove, and other spices.

Pitta is balanced by a mixture of sweet, cool aromas such as sandalwood, rose, peppermint and jasmine.

Kapha is balanced by a mixture of warm aromas, but with spicier overtones, such as juniper, eucalyptus, camphor, clove, and marjoram.

In general:
Floral aromas balance *Vata* and *Pitta*
Minty aromas balance *Pitta*
Musky aromas balance *Kapha*
Note: You may use these aromas by adding a drop or two to your massage oil, diffuse them with an aroma dispenser, or if mixed with a base oil such as jojoba, as perfumes.

CHAPTER 8
Spiritual Wisdom –
Man's Ultimate Lesson from Nature

Discovering the Love Frequency

Our main purpose here on Earth is to discover, live and express love in the purest sense of the word. Love is the key to access a treasure of information that has the potential to create Heaven on Earth – a paradise of unimaginable splendor and beauty. Man was put here on Earth for a much greater purpose than merely passing his time, acquiring wealth and possessions or having a little bit of fun. Whatever happens here on Earth, automatically and simultaneously influences the rest of the physical universe and every other dimensional reality. All the living beings residing within the various levels of universal life are eagerly awaiting the day of our collective spiritual awakening.

Nature is helping us in this process. She serves as a perfect mirror reflecting back to us who we are, what we are doing to others and ourselves and what changes we need to make at each moment. If we dislike ourselves, we will find nature to be boring, unsupportive or even life threatening. If we love ourselves, nature will take care of all our needs like a loving parent who attends to the needs of his child.

Most of us have heard of such excessively unhappy and angry personalities as Adolf Hitler or Stalin whose immensely destructive power made their own lives and that of many others a living hell. On the other hand, some of us may have met personalities who displayed another form of power, the power that lies in the frequency of love. Mother Meera, for example, is an expression of pure, unconditional love. Being a living Avatar (Divine Incarnation), she radiates the warmest and most penetrating, powerful form of love. Her service to humanity is beyond human description and the value of her deep work (all done in silence) cannot be fully comprehended by the human intellect.

There have been, or are, many other examples of individuals who have mastered the love frequency like Jesus Christ, Sri Aurobindo, Mahatma Gandhi, Albert Schweitzer, Mother Theresa, Bruno Groening, etc. Princess Diana instilled the love frequency into many a heart while alive and still does. Millions of people have been inspired to follow their example. The world would be much different today had they not contributed their "loving touch" to the awakening process of humankind. Perhaps, we would have already destroyed ourselves.

Lesser known and understood are the contributions made by the great civilizations of the past, including the Mayas, Incas, Native Americans, Egyptians, some of whom visited our planet only for relatively short periods of time but long enough to maintain the love frequency in different parts of the world. Their emergence was necessary to prepare for the day when humankind as a whole would be ready to discover the essence of love and rise to the same height of development if not higher. The great teachers of the past have brought us to this point, but now mankind is as if thrown into a deep pool and forced to learn to swim without the help of (external) teachers or systems of learning.

We all have learnt much about our material world through teachers or systems of learning and their various disciplines. Yet to find out who *we* are we cannot depend on anyone else but ourselves. Because we were relatively helpless and dependant, we needed external guides in life, but the era of the teacher-student relationship is now ending. The real teachings in life take place from within us.

As a human race, we have distanced ourselves from nature by believing that we are superior and nature is inferior. We were taught that we had to subdue or fight nature in order to survive. By taking the animals as our slaves and slaughtering them without respect and appreciation, we have disconnected ourselves from the rest of nature. By burning down forests and by polluting our water and the air, we have denied ourselves access to the wisdom contained in the trees, plants, flowers, insects, even mountains and streams. Very few people know that the Native Americans or other ancient civilizations were able to communicate with all that there was on the living planet in the same way as we communicate with friends or loved ones. They had no concept of being superior or inferior to nature, they experienced themselves as equal to or one with the animals, flowers, birds and trees.

Their deep respect for all the life forms came as a reflection of the respect they had for themselves and each other.

Consciousness permeates every fiber of creation. Whatever *is* has consciousness at its basis. Since most people don't know who or what they are, they project the same veil of ignorance that stops them from discovering their true identity on external objects or beings, thinking that cats, dogs, cows, ants, flowers, trees, body cells, atoms etc. are not aware of their existence either. This self-induced lack of communication with nature has reinforced our belief system that man is incapable of communicating with other beings, animals or plants. However, it is the nature of consciousness to be conscious. This applies to everything that exists.

Consciousness is the Key

Universal Consciousness, often referred to as God, is the essential "ingredient" of everything and can therefore not be more important or valuable in one of its expressions than in another regardless of whether it uses a highly developed human brain or the relatively simple nervous system of a an ant. All of existence is held together by the intelligence of consciousness. Its presence in our body allows us to live a physical existence. In the same way, the presence of consciousness in the body of an ant allows the ant to live its life, too.

The intelligence of an ant's DNA or that of an amoeba is not so much different from ours. The reason for that is that the intelligence of consciousness operating in an ant cell has to know nearly as much as the one in a human cell in order to survive in this world. Both the types of DNA have recorded vast amounts of information not only about the complex functions of their own bodies but also about the intricate connections that exist between the microcosm and the macrocosm, plus millions of years of planetary evolution. All this is necessary for both an ant and a human being to live and to survive.

We generally believe that animals, plants or insects are not aware of any of that. But then most of us are not aware of it either. We use intellectual, scientific concepts to understand reality, yet this has prevented us from actually experiencing it. In fact, plants, minerals, insects, birds, springs, oceans and mountains are much more aware of and in tune with their existence and interconnectedness because they do not use a mind or intellect to understand their world.

Reality, as it is, cannot be understood intellectually. Any intellectual framework or theory will always be too small to describe the vastness and complexity present within every grain of creation. Recently, Australian scientists have revealed the first *biosensor* capable of determining whether a patient was suffering from indigestion or a heart attack. All they need from the body to diagnose a specific condition is a drop of blood or saliva. One particle of blood contains all the information of the entire body. Even the smallest subatomic particle contains the blueprint of the whole cosmos. It has to know the whole story in order to know where it belongs or what it should do. Without this intrinsic wisdom, the universe and we would collapse like a house of cards. This set-up or wisdom can be called "nature."

When we say, "nature knows best how to organize" we refer to her as a conscious being, a form of intelligence. All the species of animals, plants, flowers, insects, minerals and even atoms have their own form of intelligence or soul. Fairy tales have been descriptive of various types of beings we no longer recognize to be real. Fairies, nature spirits and angels have been as if banished to the "unreal" world by our inability to see them and communicate with them. Trying to sound realistic and scientific, we may emphatically state: "I only believe what I can see!" Yet quite the opposite is true: "I can only see what I believe." My brain permits me only to perceive what I already know and believe is true and real, the rest of the information is automatically filtered out. What gets through to my conscious mind will merely confirm what I already know to be true.

It is time to let go of *all* the belief systems that have such a limiting influence, for they are castles in the air. To rely on what we think is true and real means living in the past but may or may not be relevant in the "now" which is the *only* reality. The present is new at every coming moment and cannot be fathomed, relived or understood by memories from the past. Belief systems are just memories about what we have learnt or experienced some time before. The experience always comes first and is followed by an intellectual concept or understanding that can explain what we have experienced. But because intellectual understanding cannot relive the experience it is always outside the reality.

Animals Know Something We Don't

Animals, on the other hand, seem to be much smarter than we are. They don't behave as if death was the end of their existence. Not fussing over where they will die, they also don't organize big funerals for other animals that die, however strong and powerful they might have been in the past. Furthermore, animals don't set aside money as a pension for the times when they can no longer provide for themselves. Animals, plants, trees etc., do not share the same fear of death, which drives man into fighting for a piece of land or acquiring power and wealth. They are in contact with their source and therefore have no need to follow a certain religion to tell them that their souls come from God.

Animals, plants, insects, forests, clouds, streams, oceans, the sun, the moon, the stars are all interconnected through the element of consciousness. Unless we are aware of our own consciousness, we can only perceive their three dimensional physical appearance but miss out on perceiving their underlying consciousness which is not any different from ours. We may not be aware of the tremendous work each aspect of creation is involved in on the inner planes of existence, but without its contribution, the wheel of evolution would stop turning. We may even believe that we are superior to animals, plants or minerals, and even to other human beings. This distorted understanding of reality is at the root of humankind's socio-economic problems today.

We are equal and one with everything, not superior to it. Animals live this oneness. They operate in the love frequency even if this includes killing other animals. They know instinctively that by increasing or decreasing the numbers of their own or other species, they contribute to ecological balance, harmony and evolution of the whole. A key purpose of theirs is to teach us how we can do the same even if it means that they have to sacrifice their lives to help us. A dog that has found a master and has learned to love him may continue to love him unconditionally after having been mistreated. Cows, chicken and other animals know in what way and how long their kind has been abused, and still most of them give themselves to man. Yet more and more animals can no longer tolerate the abuse and prefer to leave the planet by contracting diseases that make them unfit for human consumption. It may still take a while before scientists will acknowledge that cattle

154

diseases, for example, are manifestations of severe distress in these animals in the same way as psychological problems generate psychosomatic diseases in us.

The collective departure of entire animal species helps us to learn to love what we took for granted. We didn't appreciate them when they were here but we will appreciate them once they are gone. A planet without animals would be a very lonely planet. They are departing in large numbers because they have nothing to gain any more from being here, except teaching us a final lesson. Many people are now becoming aware of this tragedy and are feeling the plight of those animals on the planet that for the time being have great difficulties in sharing the planet with us humans. Over 50 percent of the various species that have used Earth as a habitat for thousands of years are already extinct and more and more of the ones left behind are also endangered or are on the verge of departing. This drastic change of planetary vibration has an unsettling influence on humanity as a whole. Yet there is also great learning in this.

Message from the Whales and Dolphins

Among the most highly developed species of animals that have made the collective choice to leave the planet now, are whales, dolphins and cows. Whales and dolphins are the most advanced living beings on earth. Unlike us human beings who still need to create most of what we need externally; whales and dolphins create everything internally. The whales have inhabited the planet for 500 million years and are responsible for holding its memory. Without the whales, all planetary life forms would simply cease to exist. Dolphins are not less developed than the whales but have been on Earth only for about 35 million years.

Whales and dolphins are mammals, not fish, and they have an amazing relationship with their human counterparts. They differ from us in the sense that both their brain halves are fully functional, whereas we still only use 5-10 percent of our brain capacity and only one hemisphere at a time. Their enormous brain capacity and 24-hour unity consciousness allows them to keep in close contact with all life on earth at all times. Since they have direct access to the higher dimensions (spiritual realms) they can materialize their thoughts instantly.

Whales and dolphins produce the highest form of love frequency that exists on Earth. Most humans take a liking to them as if they were our brothers and sisters (which they are) and swimming with the dolphins and whales has become an attraction for this reason. Many dolphins are extraordinary soul healers and by touching humans, they help them overcome emotional or psychological problems on the deepest level.

Unattached to their physical bodies, many dolphins and whales are now throwing themselves into fishing nets or onto the shores of the sea. By killing themselves in this way they remind us that we are doing the same when we destroy animals on land and in water as well as the forests and our natural environment. The dolphins and whales are killed or kill themselves because they want to hand over to us the responsibility as the guardians of this planet.

The love frequency must now become the dominating force behind all our thoughts and actions. Through their collective departure, the dolphins, whales, cows, tigers and other animals feed this message directly into our subconscious which helps us to gradually kindle this powerful force in our own hearts. The message says that it is within our power now to heal, restructure and refurbish the Earth. We have been given access to unlimited resources but it is up to each one of us to reclaim this birthright of ours. The more we trust that this is so, the more readily and abundantly we will receive the knowledge and organizing power that can transform life on earth. The external changes we are witnessing today but reflect the internal changes we are going through at the moment. The "cow's drama" can shed some light on this transformational process.

Perhaps the Cows *Are* Holy After All

Cows are amongst the most intelligent and good-natured animals around. They have developed and radiate a high degree of the love frequency and are very sensitive to how they are treated. Their innocent looking faces and gestures are inoffensive. Only in countries like India where religion considers cows to be holy, are they treated with the same respect as human beings. In the more practical so-called civilized world, cows are largely seen as food-producing machines or a good source of leather ware, which, however, is not their purpose at all. Slaughtering them and selling them as meat is the most degrading thing that could possibly happen to them. Yet they don't mind working for humans if they are treated with respect and love.

Cows have a strong positive effect on their surroundings. When we look at a cow as an important and valuable piece of God's creation we translate the goodness and gentleness it radiates into neurotransmitters which can trigger profound healing responses in the body. Just by observing them you can effectively normalize an elevated blood pressure, balance hormone secretions and calm and relax body and mind. However, cows do much more than please the environment. Their unconditional love for mankind has helped to avert some of the most serious catastrophes in the world.

Cows are here to feed us with the love frequency, which is expressed symbolically and practically by their ability to produce milk. However, the milk that comes from cows that are kept in large halls without sunlight and natural environment, are fed with growth-enhancing hormones and antibiotics and are milked by electronic devices instead of human hands is no longer suitable for human consumption. The *polluted* milk is responsible for causing many of today's diseases including those of the kidneys, the heart and the joints. An alarming number of people are no longer able to break down milk protein or milk sugar (lactose) or develop allergies to milk and dairy products for this reason.

Unhappy and imprisoned cows are no longer able to produce healthy milk. Normally, a mother cow will produce milk that is nourishing and wholesome because of the deep affection it has for her newborn calf or the families it has "chosen" to sustain. However, when cow's milk is no longer a product of love but is spoiled by the experience of abuse, fear and captivity, it becomes harmful for us.

What applies to milk also applies to the meat derived from cows, except that some of the diseases accruing from meat consumption are as terrifying as AIDS. One of them is the fatal brain disease *Creutzfeldt-Jakob* (CJD), the equivalent of mad cow disease or *bovine spongiform encephalopathy* (BSE). Modern medical treatment is helpless against the disease since its real cause is unknown and there are no known methods to diagnose it. It spreads through infected but healthy-looking meat, and maybe even through milk.

But as in the case of so many other diseases, including AIDS, we tend to immediately blame a virus for a dreaded infectious disease. Yet it is much more likely that cows that have been slowly poisoned by chemical fertilizers, drugs, flesh feeds and hormones succumb to BSE than those raised naturally. Any animal that is consistently fed with non-physiological substances and feeds, abnormal to its species, develops genetic mutations and eventually suffers a deadly disease.

Learning the Hard Way

The 'involuntary' mass departure of cows is both a message and a gift to us. Cows mirror to us how we are treating ourselves by eating polluted flesh and ingesting poisonous drugs. Those who are able to decipher the message will change their attitude towards cows and other animals and will refuse to participate in the collective and individual *Karma* that arises from killing them unnecessarily. Others will continue to blame governments, scientists or farmers for destroying our cows whose value for us is only measured by how much milk, meat and money they can bring us.

Many people justify their actions by the outdated myth that we need meat to live. Yet most of the world's population lives perfectly well without it. In my youth, I believed that meat makes us strong and vital. However, before long I became a victim of this doctrine and developed several debilitating diseases. Even though I have not eaten any meat, chicken, fish or eggs for over 30 years, I feel as youthful, healthy and strong as ever.

Cows, which are a symbol of love, have no intention of causing the death of humans or make them ill. They feel "misunderstood" since their purpose here on Earth is quite a different one. They are meant to maintain ecological balance and promote harmony and happiness among all living beings. The mass slaughter of millions of cows every day is a very ugly way of ending their lives, undeserved for such highly advanced animal beings.

Animals need love and respect in the same way as we do. Because they are equals, they want to be treated as equals. Once the love frequency is established as the principal force behind our thoughts and actions, animals will share with us their great spiritual wisdom and inter-dimensional connections.

Respect for all Life

On m first visit to Morocco, I saw a group of camels riding through the desert. One camel rider spoke to me about the sensitivity of camels and why they need to be treated with care and respect. He said that a camel would never forget the person who rode it. Camels can remember anyone who has treated them badly, even forty years later. Because of the fear of being abused again, it will kick the offender when he comes near. In the same way, the camel will always recognize a friendly rider and may follow him with obedience and loyalty for the rest of its life.

Animals still love us but most of them are terrified of the human race. Their fear of humans may make them defensive, hostile or aggressive. Before man began abusing animals (about 25,000 years ago), they used to be very friendly and even the lion and the buffalo were tame. Every unnecessary killing of an animal anywhere in the world increases fear and hostility in the rest of them. Unlike us, they are able to sense and pick up all that is happening to the other animals on the planet.

Plants are no less developed. They can "broadcast" global events just like radio stations do. Even the rocks, which serve as the bone structure of the Earth, contain vast amounts of information that can be accessed and utilized by those who have developed the love frequency. The stones contained in the Great Pyramids in Egypt, the Acropolis in Athens, Stonehenge, and in the sacred sites of the ancient civilizations in South America, such as Machu Picchu in Peru, know more about the universe than we could possibly imagine. They were chosen to serve as ancient "computer chips" because of their high density, stable and orderly structure and long life span.

Crystals in particular are highly developed memory depots. Their fantastic ability to store vast amounts of information will eventually replace microchips altogether. So far, we have only been using quartz crystals in watches and communication devices, but soon crystals will be valued for their ability to absorb and process information much faster than the currently available computers. We will be able to store information in crystals and recall it without the need of any other technologies than mental ones.

As we begin to recognize and experience our oneness with Earth, we will realize our true status and utilize the secret knowledge that made the ancient civilizations so great. Their "mind-technologies" were far more advanced than our modern technologies. They knew how to construct and materialize anything through mere thought. The irony is that *we* were these ancients but have no or only little conscious memory of that. Yet gradually we are beginning to get glimpses of the true nature of things.

As any observant person would see it, not only man is an intelligent being but also everything else in the universe is an expression of intelligence. "Being" implies that it is intelligent; otherwise, it would and could not exist. "Being" is everywhere, although this may not be obvious to our senses. There is "Being" in a grain of sand as there is "Being" in an amoeba and in a lion. The micro-constituents of a piece of stone zoom about its inner space no less forcefully than the ones found within our body cells. Coordinated and held together by the same all-pervading consciousness or Being, they play a very important role in creation. We are in no way superior to the water contained in the earth or the oxygen molecules in the air; without them, we would be nothing but a heap of decaying, dried-out cells.

Every part of creation has an important role to play in sustaining the whole planet, no less or more important than our role. The key to enlightenment or spiritual awakening lies in the intuitive and cognitive realization that everything that exists is necessary. "Know thyself" also means to know your purpose or role. When we see ourselves as being essentially equal with everything else, a blissful oneness begins to develop in us, which treats all forms and expressions of life with deep and loving respect. This is the onset of humbleness and inner peace, the master key to unlock the secrets of life.

Earth knows Everything

The Earth is aware of everything that is taking place in the world. She can read the people who walk over her just like we read books; and she computes and records all our moves like a computer does. Everything is stored in the rocks, the soil, the water, the fire and even in the air; nothing goes unnoticed. Strictly adhering to the laws of nature, Mother Earth returns to us what we have given to her. If we ignore and neglect her, she will ignore and neglect us. If we love and honor her, she will reward us with health, abundance and wisdom. Because we share the same source, i.e. universal consciousness, there exists no real separation between the Earth and us.

The state of the Earth simply reflects the state of our collective consciousness. A sick person creates sickness in the Earth and a healthy person strengthens the Earth's natural immunity. Everything that is taking place outside of us also occurs within us because consciousness is the same within and without. The threats that we receive from nature result from the threats we have created against others and ourselves. Similarly, the abundance of the Earth's natural resources reflects the level of our inner abundance. The more generous and giving we become, the more freely Earth will give us what we need and what we desire.

At present, the collective consciousness of humankind is still composed of a mixture of all kinds of values from destructiveness to unconditional love, giving rise to a large variety of natural phenomena on the planet. The lack of unity and closeness with nature is at the root of all conflicts and disasters. Now is the time to give up any sense of superiority over nature or other beings and recognize that we, as beings of consciousness, are equal to and united with all of existence.

The Healing Power of Mother Earth

Mother Earth is suffering from global fever caused by pollutants accumulating in her lungs, her veins and her flesh. We have all directly or indirectly contributed to the destruction of her rain forests to give way for cattle breeding or to make paper and build houses etc. We are contributing to the contamination of ground water, the rivers and the

161

oceans by purchasing products containing chemical toxins. Every day we pollute our air, causing acid rain and other forms of environmental destruction. We are also exploiting Earth's natural resources such as oil, gold, minerals, precious and semiprecious stones which she needs to sustain her electromagnetic balance. Crystalline deposits in the Earth balance the electromagnetic forces that are connected through lay lines. By removing them from the Earth's interior, we confuse the energy grid of the planet, which leads to a build-up of stress points within the Earth and causes "accidents,' such as car or airplane crashes. We have lost our respect for Mother Earth and have treated her like a slave. However, Mother Earth is far from being sick or helpless, as little as a person who is struck by fever. Our planet is passing through a major toxicity or healing crisis.

At first sight, Earth does not seem to resemble a living organism. But since every bit of the body is derived from the planet and life can only be sustained by living things, the Earth must be alive. The same laws of nature that control the organism of the planet also control our organism. Our bones carry the body mass with all its connective tissues and blood vessels in a similar way as the rocks and stones of the Earth carry the earth masses, the oceans and the rivers. The atoms that constitute a handful of sand have no less life in them than those that make your heart or your brain. If God is everywhere, He, She or It is as much in the subatomic particles that form a piece of rock as he is in a microbe, in the air we breathe or in the cells of an elephant. Whether a carbon, oxygen, or hydrogen atom sits in a piece of fruit, my eyes or a piece of wood does not make it any more or less alive.

The incredibly complex activities that take place within the structure of a single atom resemble the collective activities of our body and even of the entire universe. Trillions of subatomic particles such as the *tau*, a heavier cousin of the electron, decay into other particles in less than a trillionth of a second. They all react with other trillions of particles within the same atom to give rise to an infinite number of possible combinations, permutations and applications as is demonstrated by the continuous creation and destruction of the visible world. There is infinite power within an atom because it is never in isolation, always connected with the rest of the universe. There is also infinite intelligence to control and supervise all these complex activities in close relation to everything else that goes on in creation.

To make life meaningful, a supreme form of intelligence, which many people have given the name God, must be present in the tiniest of particles within every single atom. Even the slightest mistake occurring on this level of existence could potentially destroy the entire cosmos. Our planet is far from being inert or lifeless. The same supreme intelligence that sustains a tiny particle also sustains the whole universe and moves everything towards higher states of evolution. It acts out its power not only to restore balance on our globe but in fact to create a much higher life form than has even been possible before.

The Planet is Alive

Because of our outdated belief system that matter as such is devoid of life or consciousness, we have ignored the basic truth that our planet is as much alive as we are. Those who see themselves only as a physical body without a soul or spirit will also see the planet only as a mass of matter without a Being in it. But many people are beginning to recognize that every physical object also has a non-physical aspect – a body of consciousness or Being – and they feel an increasing sense of respect, admiration and love for the grand Being that we call Earth.

Each one of the astronomical number of atoms that are miraculously held together in this vast space occupied by our planet is in the right place at the right time in order to serve life as a whole. Nature has made no mistake when some of them were concentrated in certain areas to make streaks of gold, silver or emerald. Others are used to serve as food for the plants or to make up the correct balance of air so that our fellow beings and we can breathe the vital oxygen. An organization that has to co-ordinate an almost infinite number of atoms with each other and not make mistakes is certainly more than super intelligent. We cannot even begin to imagine what must be going on in a mind that has to keep track of the exact number of photons contained in the various color rays of the sun in order to supply each plant or flower with the correct dose necessary for its growth and color intensity.

For Earth to continue being a habitable place every tiny aspect of the planet has to be balanced, and it is for this reason that the supremely intelligent Earth Being, called Mother Earth, attends to the minutest details with utmost precision. All the various species of microbes, insects, plants, animals and human beings (the different races) are part of the whole, each one equally necessary and important. Together they give rise to higher life forms and evolution. Earth tolerates any interference in this universal organization only to a certain degree, which is the level of saturation when a toxicity crisis occurs.

Like our body, the planet was designed to go through times of upheaval and toxicity crises; these help correct the imbalance superimposed on her. The crises trigger powerful responses by her immune system. The increasingly unpredictable fluctuations of temperature and climate are mere cleansing procedures initiated by the planet in co-ordination with sun activities.

A fever in the body may be accompanied by shivering or intense heat. Such self-help programs are based on natural laws that begin to take over when the originally employed laws of nature are no longer effective enough to maintain balance. It is incorrect to assume that the current dramatic changes in global weather and consequent disasters are signs of global dissolution and destruction, although some individuals or population groups may experience them as such; they are rather attempts by the holistically acting Earth to rid herself of all the stress, tension and pollutants caused by humankind over a long period of time.

All Earth Changes Favor Life

If we could understand the current changes occurring on our planet for what they really are, we would not panic or try to resist Earth's efforts to cleanse herself. Our stress and fears carry frequencies of destructive energy that have a disturbing influence on the magnetic field that sustains the balance of the planet. This makes the effects of cleansing more destructive than would otherwise be necessary. By suppressing a fever, which our body requires to employ and activate large numbers of immune cells and antibodies in order to remove toxins or infection-causing microbes, we push the toxins deeper and literally suffocate certain parts or organs in the body. This situation and the continued weakening influences caused by an unbalanced lifestyle, over-stimulation and fear, lead to more serious crises of toxicity. They may manifest as cancer, AIDS or MS and require a more drastic approach of purification. Likewise, the Earth, being bombarded with "missiles" of anger and fear and her laws being violated day by day by millions of people, is forced to respond with stronger measures to overcome the effects of man's disharmony.

It is not the Earth, the sun or life as such we should be afraid of, it rather is the constant violation of the laws of nature that causes all the problems we are facing in the world today. Many scientists and experts tell us that global warming and other phenomena endanger life on our planet. This sounds as if our planet was in bad shape. However, this is not true; the planet and we are simply going through a healing crisis.

The more people believe in or support the theories of those who promote the frightening idea that our planet is deteriorating fast, the worse the side effects of global healing will be. Each emotion of fear caused by the people feeds the global energy grid of fear and negativity even more and makes the forthcoming times of regeneration a greater challenge for large proportions of the population. When Darwin observed the behavior of plants and animals, he formulated a law to clarify nature's scheme of survival; he called it "Survival of the fittest." The same law applies to the current time of global transformation. Only in this case, "fit" means *without fear, honest, spiritually oriented, abiding with the laws of nature and healthy in mind and body*. In this sense, it would be beneficial for us all if we adopted a more positive viewpoint of our global situation than is generally presented by the theories of modern science and prognoses of psychics and fortune-tellers.

The Shifting of Earth Poles

An increasing number of people, including scientists, speak of the sun becoming dangerous to man, but such statements only undermine her true value. All growth on our planet is oriented towards the sun. If we collectively create an aversion to the sun, the fear frequency will begin to interfere with the sun's electromagnetic frequencies and disturb basic growth processes on our Earth.

The sun can read and absorb every vibration that occurs on the planet. The tremendous shifts that are recorded as taking place within the sun now are a mystery to most scientists. In December 1994, *NASA* launched the spacecraft *Ulysses* to measure the magnetic activity of the sun. The scientists discovered much to their astonishment that the magnetic readings taken at the sun's north and south poles were totally identical and that the sun has completely lost its polarity. In addition, the increase of solar flares is about to reach unprecedented levels. The energy of the sun will burst and burn, sending us massive amounts of gamma rays. The change in the rays coming from the sun is in direct response to the (positive) shifts taking place in our collective consciousness.

The bursts of energy within the sun directly affect the Polar Regions on our planet. They resemble extremely powerful nuclear explosions sending jolts of electricity deep into space. Earth poles are powerful magnets, which are able to catch this energy. Due to the magnetic force, they arc the energy either around the equator or inward to the core of Earth. At the moment, the locations of the poles are not in their proper positions and therefore unable to catch all the energy. The current pole alignment cannot serve as the correct "lighting rod" and would lead to a short circuit and cause a burnout of the planet. In order to avoid annihilation, the poles are shifting. In fact, they have already shifted.

On June 4, 1996, scientists detected major deviations in the Earth's magnetic field. Since then the magnetic poles have shifted between five and 13 degrees, which in terms of physical distance means between 600 and 1,000 miles off their normal position. In the past few weeks (January 2006), the media reported that the magnetic north pole is now in Siberia. Although this phenomenon has been described in network news and science journals as very unusual, pole shifts are not so unusual on the planet at all. They occur every 12,500 to 13,000 years which when compared with the Earth's age, is a rather frequent event. At times, they have reversed themselves altogether and pole caps were even at the equator. This explains why you can find seashells almost everywhere on the planet whether you look on the top of the Rocky Mountains or in 12,000 feet high Lake Titicaca. Scientists gather much of their information about pole shifts by taking six-inch, eleven foot-long core samples out of the ocean floor and reading the sediment just like tree rings.

This time the pole shift is going to be substantial. Once the shift occurs, which has already begun, the people on Earth need to adjust to the new energies, otherwise they will "burn out." Some are in fact burning out already. They are those who cannot yet harmonize with themselves and with nature. They are being "poisoned" by their own thoughts and create havoc in their bodies because the new energies magnify the effects from every kind of experience, mental, physical and emotional. The pole shifts make our thought and speech extremely powerful. Anger, jealously, hate, aggression and fear turn into missiles of self-destruction and through the mind/body connection generate multiple forms of disease symptoms. If we respond to the sun and the elements around us with fear and disagreeable energy, we invite powerful waves of destruction into our lives. On the surface, it may appear that the sun causes skin cancer but in truth, it is fear that generates the genetic chaos underlying the disease.

Another way of stating this is that love, honesty and trust will soon be recognized as being the only effective means of success in life, including the creation of perfect health, abundance and spiritual wisdom. The sun is helping humanity to adjust to a new life form that will be free from pollution and in harmony with the laws of nature. She is certainly not our enemy, although it may appear that way to many people. The shifting of the Earth poles will unleash great powers that will sweep the globe. The violent storms raging in several parts of the world may still intensify. We know that the element of fire is composed of both water and fire qualities. The intensifying sun energies empower the water element, which will acquire tremendous cleansing properties. Although we may see this power as being mainly destructive, its real effect is to raise planetary vibrations to such high levels that everyone on the planet will be motivated by love only.

Scientists attribute the current dramatic melting of ice caps in the Antarctic to global warming, but also these and many other climatic changes and natural disasters are part of Earth's deeper restructuring process. Our environment is so toxic that we cannot survive without combining our own efforts of cleaning up the planet with those instigated by the sun and the Earth.

The situation of the current global phase transition requires a completely different composition in the rays of the sun than there has ever been before. The regions with thinner levels of ozone allow this new and different quality of the spectrum of light and radiation to penetrate the Earth's atmosphere. We are all influenced by this. When

167

we experience a different spectrum of light, our bodies translate the new rays into chemical responses on the deepest level of our physiology, which is subatomic. This has a profound effect on our genes. As our DNA is gradually being upgraded from two strands to twelve or more strands, our bodies will respond with great change and adjustment.

Entry into the New World

Those who will make the quantum leap into the new age of all possibilities – which will predominantly be ruled by the love frequency – are at present undergoing a massive transformation, physically, emotionally and spiritually. This transformational period may be accompanied by chaos, a general sense of insecurity, breaking down of long-term relationships and confusion over the real meaning of life. Most people now, and especially those who have been working in the field of spirituality, will find their physiologies going through unusual periods of "adjustment." Digestive troubles and symptoms of disease that suddenly appear and quickly disappear again are signs that our bodies are in "transition" – a period of transformation and restructuring that is characterized by instability.

Old values of living are in the process of becoming redundant, whereas new ones have not yet fully established themselves. We currently live in a kind of "no-man's land." Our ego identity is being separated from our soul identity and we haven't quite made up our minds, so to speak, which one is the real Self. Nature seems to reflect our fears, confusion and instability through a monumental imbalance of climate and seasons. The currently experienced unstable weather conditions, the coming back to life of hitherto extinguished volcanoes and the moving of earth masses tells us that Mother Nature is active and alive. Her earthquakes, flood waves and storms show us how vulnerable and superficial our security really is if it is only based on money, concrete structures and emergency exits.

In order to relinquish our sole reliance on physical security and teach us how to rely on natural law instead, we may have to go through some more drastic global transformations. Earth is changing because we are changing (collectively). She reflects the chaos and turmoil we are currently going through but also the tremendous spiritual progress we have made up until now, although not everyone may be aware of this. It is certainly not fear that Earth wants to instill in us. Like the sun, the dolphins or the cows, her purpose is to serve and sustain life, by all means. She wants to completely heal herself so that humans are able to rise to higher states of consciousness. The planet is meant to become a vast communications center for all the life forms in the universe. To achieve this immensely complex task she has to remove every obstacle that hinders the prospering of healthy and unpolluted crops of love, progress and happiness.

Our planet is going through an extraordinary transition and will enter a source of energy previously untapped on Earth. All pollutants that have contaminated our air, water and soil will be removed within a short time. The "upliftment" of human consciousness into higher dimensions, namely the fourth and fifth will reveal our true spiritual nature and resourcefulness. It will also make us self-sufficient regarding energy and other resources. We will find that whatever we think, as soon as we think it, will materialize instantly.

People like Sai Baba who at some stage in their lives were able to create any desired object from the ether are here to demonstrate to us that accessing the higher dimensions of our existence is both practical and real. Whenever he materialized a large diamond, a watch or ashes through mere thought, he shook up the foundation of our materialistic experience and view of the world. Such demonstrations can teach us that we all are truly one with the spirit or essence of everything and that we can create anything through spirit once we lift the veil of ignorance and remove the illusion of being separate from nature. Humans will recognize themselves as true guardians of Earth rather than her masters.

When the main transformation takes place, it will happen very fast. It is similar to switching from one TV channel to another. When you tune your TV set to a different wavelength you will see a different picture. The world is different in different states of consciousness. Our current state of consciousness allows us only to perceive the world as two and three-dimensional. This, however, does not mean that this is its *only* reality. The world simultaneously exists in all the different dimensions and time lines – an infinite number of them. Once we perceive a wavelength other than the one most people are currently able to perceive (7.21 cm), we will live in another reality aspect of the same world.

The reason why everything is so difficult in the three-dimensional part of our world is that our thoughts and desires take time to become realized. When we are not able to fulfill our desires quickly and effortlessly, we become frustrated, anxious and even hostile towards others who we believe prevent us from achieving our goals. The exploitation and destruction of our natural resources and the subsequent pollution of the environment, as well as conflicts of any kind, are rooted in our inability to fulfill our desires immediately. The feature of instant fulfillment of our thoughts belongs to the higher dimensions, which we are about to enter collectively. Our main technology will be "mind technology" and the need to fight for material things or control in life will simply vanish. Exactly when this will happen is completely up us and can, therefore, not be foretold.

It's Time to Make a Choice

The time of making a choice for promoting life rather than destruction and death on Earth is now. Those who begin to love themselves and take care of their most precious possession, the human body, will be protected, loved and honored by the Earth. They will be "initiated" into the world of spiritual wisdom. Some people like to call this process, the "Second Coming of Christ", others name it "The Dawn of the Age of Enlightenment", "Heaven Descending on Earth", the "Onset of the Aquarian Age," or "The End of the World (of Ignorance)." It is not important by what name we call new time. What is important is that the Earth will become a true home for those who are ready to live and express love.

This is perhaps the most important time humankind has ever experienced because the choices we are making now will affect our future more dramatically than ever before. This is the time of learning; learn to serve your body, your heart, your friends, the animals, the plants, all life forms, and the planet, in whatever ways you best can. By doing this, you intensify the love frequency within and around you, which can be considered to be the most important work anyone can do at this moment in time. There are already millions of people who have recognized both the need and the power of service. Even on the mass communications network "Internet" you can find numerous people who, without any financial return of their expenses, pass extremely helpful (spiritual) information to numerous subscribers. They have no other intent than to raise the love frequency in those who receive it. These *light* or *love workers* will be rewarded amply and in ways which will become more apparent *after* the *Great Transition.*

Many people have the impression that self-work is difficult and that it requires discipline and a lot of patience. The truth, however, is far from that. Everything we do in life is self-work, although most people may not recognize it as such. Your thoughts, feelings, attitudes, desires etc., occur on many levels simultaneously. In the body, for example, they occur as neurotransmitters, which trigger profound physiological responses. In the ether, they become powerful energy fields that affect our body, other people and the environment. Therefore, when you move things out of your wardrobe or room for which you have no need any more, or when you tidy up your garden, basement etc., you do the same on all levels of existence. If one corner of your house is always untidy, dirty, or full of things you no longer need but cannot let go off, there is one part in your mind and body that needs attending to as well. The state of your environment reflects the state of your body and mind. If your present environment does no longer "suit" you it is because you have moved on, physically, emotionally and spiritually, and you may need to create or move to a new environment that reflects the "new" you.

There is a great deal of restlessness among people on the planet at the moment, which is expressed by the desire to change home, job and/or partner. If you feel like them, it is best to go with the flow and not stick to the old beliefs or principles of how you *should* live your life. Make the increase of happiness your main focus in life. Happiness comes naturally when your focus is on serving others, your body and nature in whatever way you can. For example, if you see rubbish lying on the ground, you have the choice of both ignoring it and saying that it is other people's responsibility or picking it up and throwing it into the nearest dustbin. If we decide to pick up rubbish that others have carelessly left behind we develop humility, strip our ego of false pride, and create a powerful energy field in the ether which will quietly inspire other people to do the same (similar to the hundredth monkey effect).

By attending to your body, cleansing it, feeding it properly, by listening to its subtle messages and learning from them, and finally seeing it as a divine instrument, you will automatically grow in the desire to help others to do the same. This is what is meant by true service. As a reward, you will see Earth in a different light, too. Those who choose to develop this love frequency regardless of whether they express it through cleaning up a beach or healing another person will receive the very best that nature can offer. Heaven is a perceptual reality, which we can create by tuning into the most blissful frequency of living, the frequency of love. The current period of global transformation allows us to develop the love frequency more easily and more quickly than was ever possible before.

Owning the Wisdom of Nature

Your body is the key to your soul. Learn to use your body wisely and with appreciation and it will turn out to be your very best teacher and your very best friend. Give it nourishing foods, good air, healing sunrays, lovely sunsets, inspiring music, clothes made of natural fabrics, uplifting fragrances, oil massages, internal cleansing, and supportive environments. Don't let fear be the motive for your actions. You are worthy of receiving the very best that life can offer.

Spend time in nature, touch the trees, the plants, feel the ground of the Earth under your feet, breathe in the breath of nature. Mother Earth thrives on your loving contact and she greatly values your presence. She needs us to be channels of divine energy and suffers if even one channel is blocked. Every one of us is equally important to her. Those who are blocked and cannot feel her presence but continue to harm the environment are given the opportunity now to open up physically, emotionally and spiritually. For them, the experience of sickness and suffering becomes a way to reconnect to natural law. Thus, developing a cancerous tumor can neutralize all negative vibrations (*Karma*) a person may have accumulated during his current life or previous lifetimes. At the same time, this quite drastic method of burning off old *Karma* significantly raises planetary vibrations.

One thing is for sure, nature is never out to punish but to heal. Everyone is loved and needed, regardless of whether he plays the role of a saint, a beggar or a criminal. Everyone who works through *Karma* in whatever way deserves the highest form of respect and admiration. Judgment has no place in this for it does not recognize the larger picture which often is opposite to what its seems.[13] Those doing the "lowest" kind of jobs like cleaning toilets or removing garbage, are souls that help humanity more than you can imagine.

Likewise, the young people who roam the streets, use drugs and even become aggressive and harmful are often very advanced and wonderful beings. Since they are unable to sustain their sensitive mental and emotional natures in a world of harshness, senseless materialism and cruel competitiveness, they attempt to drown their pain in such physical sensations as drug abuse, forced sex and violence. They are actually amplifying and dramatically playing out the outdated but still powerful concepts, attitudes and belief systems that control modern society. It is important now that the older generation starts to give them the respect, love and appreciation they deserve because they are the ones who do the "dirty work" which is destabilizing the stuck, rigid patterns of social conditioning. Judgment is quite irrelevant in all this; whatever wrong anyone has done in the past, now is the time and opportunity to let go of it and start afresh.

Conversing with Nature

Imagine that you could have a conversation with the plants. In actual fact, they respond to your thoughts, your feelings and your touch by releasing their specific pheromones (hormone-like compounds) which fill the airwaves and inform the immediate environment of your presence. Depending on the quality of your thoughts or feelings, these chemicals can trigger either hostile or friendly responses in the other plants, trees, insects and animals. Once you have gently touched a flower and spoken to it with kind words, the entire environment is informed that there is a friend of the Earth.

---

[13] See "Lifting the Veil of Duality – Your Guide to Living Without Judgment" by the author

A healthy human aura has a radius extending to about fifty meters. Our aura changes its colors, shape and width according to the quality of our thoughts and feelings, the foods we eat, the air we breathe, the clothes we wear and numerous other factors. When we walk through a field or a forest, the plants, flowers and trees around us are literally touched by our aura. The experience of fear and anger changes the color and shape patterns of the aura and can induce fear and defensiveness in the animals or plants that are nearby. Feeling happy and content, on the other hand, generates a greater sense of peace in the environment. Walking through a forest, swimming in the sea, eating fresh foods, or mediating can cleanse any distortions in the aura and restore balance of mind and body. Especially cold showers have the effect of stripping the aura of negative emotions and unpleasant thought forms.

Plant beings are highly evolved and have a great purpose here on Earth. Their way of communication is through silence and it requires a quiet, peaceful mind to hear their silent "words." When we realize that we are on equal par with them, we will begin to receive and channel their wisdom. They love to share with us what they know and they can help us on our journey to higher consciousness. They reciprocate our appreciation of them by energizing and realigning our connection to Earth. This can lead to profound healing of our body, mind and spirit.

In our center for health and healing, which will start to operate in Cyprus at the beginning of the new millennium, we will create a garden in which the flowers and plants are arranged in such a way that their collective effect will be powerful enough to cure diseases. There will be instructions on how to be with the plants to receive their healing energies and audibly perceive their symphonies just as we can listen to a concert of classical music.

Vegetables and fruits willingly give themselves to human beings and to animals who respect them for what they are. Their purpose is to spread and by eating them we disperse their indigestible seeds to other places, at least this was the original plan of nature. Yet even today, traditional and organic forms of farming use manure from animals to fertilize new crops. The wind and rain takes the seeds and carry them to other areas and help the spreading of new plants, flowers and trees.

Vegetables and fruits become resistant to our digestive enzymes when they are grown for purely commercial reasons. This also applies to greenhouses where plants have only limited contact to the natural elements. When they are fertilized with pesticides, their auras shrink and their life energies diminish. Whenever a field is sprayed with these chemicals, all the plant beings leave the field in horror. This leaves the plants very dependent on chemical fertilizers. If chemicals are not applied, they are eaten up by insects and snails or destroyed through diseases.

Conversing with nature and its beings, on the other hand, can be much more effective in preserving the life of vegetation and animals. As experiments with plants (see chapter 2) have shown, our attitude towards them changes their growth pattern quite dramatically. The love frequency can turn everything into gold. This applies also to animals. Even if you have to slaughter and eat an animal for lack of food, by blessing the animal with your gratitude for saving your life, it is likely to surrender to you willingly and help you regain your strength to whatever extent is possible. This was a common practice of the Red Indian, for example, when other sources of food were unavailable.

Imagination Shapes Personal Reality

Whenever you direct your loving attention to someone or something, you are recharged and rejuvenated. By looking beyond the façade of physical appearance, you can see the vast intelligence that works in everyone and everything. Imagine a Great Spirit within a flower that makes the flower look fresh and perfect. Begin to trust that whatever you can imagine is also real. *Lack of imagination is the cause of all limitation in life.* If you cannot imagine that there is a Great Spirit within the flower, then for you there is none.

Imagination is the most wonderful tool we have at our disposal to create and achieve anything in life. A car engineer can only create a new and better car if he is able to imagine one. A computer scientist will develop a faster and more sophisticated software program if he can imagine it in his mind. A good songwriter keeps coming up with new songs because his imagination takes him to the infinitely creative world of music.

Everything you create comes from your imagination. You are free to imagine anything you like. To achieve what you imagine, simply trust your imagination and witness it come true. Express gratitude for what you have created in your imagination. Gratitude is the energetic payment for what you have received. Since everything has must be created first on the energetic level before it can manifest itself in the physical form, the fulfillment of your desires depends on how much you trust yourself.

If you doubt your ability to communicate with plants or animals, then this effectively cuts your ties with the natural world. The doubt only reinforces your belief system that man cannot have a conversation with anyone but human beings. Yet this is only a limitation we have learnt to believe in and accept as reality when we were young.

Doubt originates in fear and fear restricts our ability to imagine. Do you remember the days of your childhood when it was very easy for you to imagine things? Some of you even remember having seen angels, fairies, faces beaming at you from within trees and flowers, voices whispering to you through the wind, clouds smiling at you, raindrops singing their songs. Who says that all that was, or is, not true? A rationally thinking scientist would argue: "Well, if you can't prove it, it isn't real, because only what is scientific can be claimed to be real. Children are only imagining these things because they don't know yet what the real world is like. Who could possibly believe that angels are riding down a rainbow, or little elves are dancing around mushrooms?" The answer to that is that those who can imagine these and similar etheric beings are the ones who actually see or feel their presence, and learn from them.

There are scores of angelic presences on every level of creation. Without their specific energies and vibrations a carrot, a flower or the human body would collapse into heaps of useless matter. The difference between a vitamin C pill and an orange is that in the vitamin pill there are no angelic beings present, whereas in the orange there are many. The pill may contain the typical ingredients of vitamin C but it has no or only little life force in it. The life force of anything is relative to the presence of free and happy angelic entities. An organically grown orange is occupied by very happy nature spirits and angels, whereas one that has been sprayed with chemicals is loaded with etheric beings that are "imprisoned"; they are chained or live in (etheric) cages. Due to their sadness, they radiate very little light, hence the depressed aura surrounding this orange.

Your "password" to the *real* world is your imagination. As we change inside, the world changes outside, too. There are exactly as many worlds as there are people in this world. Each one of us lives in a different state of consciousness and therefore imagines the world in a different way. By having gone through more or less the same system of education, most of us have made a collective agreement about how the world is supposed to be or look like; yet each of us lives in his own personal reality.

If you imagine the world to be a chaotic, frightening place with no hope of survival, then that is exactly how it will present itself to you. It is much better and no less real to imagine the world to be one great challenge with the enormous potential of becoming a paradise. *Your approach* to life makes all the difference.

It is time for us all, now, to wake up and claim our birthright for achieving everything that fulfills our purpose here on Earth. Each one of us has a different and unique purpose in life; to find and live this purpose we require perfect health, abundance and spiritual wisdom. Use your imagination as a tool to create your personal heaven while here on earth. To help you do that I suggest that you deeply anchor *"The Twelve Gateways to Heaven on Earth"* as outlined in the following chapter in your awareness. Read them again and again, without strain and anticipation of results. Once these basic principles of a successful and fulfilling life are established in your awareness, they will spontaneously create a new reality for you and the world, which is going to be Heaven on Earth.

CHAPTER 9
The Twelve Gateways to Heaven on Earth

By opening and applying the following twelve gateways to Heaven on Earth, any individual, society, government or nation can rise to a problem-free life, continued affluence and freedom from limitations.

1. The Gateway of Oneness

Oneness is a state of awareness that knows no fear. It is the most natural and powerful reference point for knowing that all things and all people exist in the closest possible contact with each other. We all share the same consciousness or intelligence that controls all life forms in the universe. The natural world with its vast number of different species, particles and types of energy behaves as a coherent whole where love and purpose hold everything together and united. You and I have sprung from the same soul consciousness. We are like flowers of the same tree or individual waves of the same sea. All that separates us from each other is the fear that arises from not knowing that we are one and of the same origin.

The need for competitiveness exists only in a fearful mind. The trusting mind knows that there is a place and time for everyone and hence he cannot fail to always be in the right place at the right time. The knowledge and experience of being one with everything and everyone prevents us from having to compete or defend ourselves, materially, physically, verbally or emotionally. You only require protection when you send out vibrations of fear, which others around you may interpret as threatening. The generation of fear is the most common cause of conflict in life. However, a person who sees oneness in everyone remains untouched by it.

When you begin to value yourself and all life around you, you will receive the spontaneous support of all the laws of nature. All your needs will be taken care of automatically. We often label certain events in our life as being "bad", but in nearly all instances bad things turn out

178

to be good for us. Problems are merely opportunities in disguise. There is no need to determine what is good for you or what is bad for you. You always receive what is best for you and your personal growth, even if it seems unfavorable to you at present.

Now is the time to draw into your life only what pleases you and what makes you happy and content. A river cannot flow upwards. The stream of natural law can only support us if we see other people and nature as equals. Everything belongs to each one of us because we are the expression of universal consciousness. Oneness is that natural state of life that allows the river of life to flow through you. This will deliver to you all the power, nourishment and wisdom necessary for your soul's development at this point in time.

By keeping in your conscious awareness that all things are essentially one, you can free yourself from the pain of restriction. Before you came into matter (human body), you may have chosen to be black, yellow, or white for whatever reasons of learning. Your choice of profession reflects the lessons you need to learn for your soul's completion during this lifetime. Whether you are an artist or a scientist and I am a writer or a beggar, we are all part of the same "tree of life." The consciousness that keeps everything and everyone alive does not know the difference between color, creed or profession. It is not important what you are or to what religion, political party or nation you belong, but it is important that you are *yourself*. Restrictions, rules and regulations are not part of your soul essence or your Higher Self. The fact that you *are* is enough to be one with everything, and it is merely a matter of remembering to regain your lost awareness of unity. When you look at the objects and people around you, try to imagine the underlying oneness that permeates it all. This will remove the imaginary appearance of separateness and difficulties in your life.

Many of the atoms that compose the piece of jewels you may be wearing zoom into your body in the flicker of a moment. They replace those that currently make your eyes, your skin, your heart or the air you breathe. The air that is between your body and the book you read connects and unites you with the book. The river of life flows through everything, whether it is "alive" or not, and holds everything together. By recognizing the interconnectedness of everything, we gain the benefit of being consciously linked to all of existence and we can direct the river in any way we choose.

179

The fear of doing something wrong or hurting someone who is close to us does no longer arise when we open ourselves to the river of life that brings nourishment to everyone. Whenever we recognize the underlying oneness, fear begins to subside. To be fearless is to be free. When we feel free, the heart begins to open. An open heart spreads love and unites differences. Love heals old wounds, removes hatred and discord and brings waves of happiness to everyone, including the giver of love. Whatever does not spread happiness is not worth living for. So make oneness your priority in life. See it in every stone, every, insect, the clouds, the rain, the sun and see it in yourself. It is just a matter of regaining the memory of your connection to the river of life.

Opening the First Gateway

I will open The Gateway of Oneness by increasingly putting my attention on the underlying oneness that connects all people, objects and nature with myself. I recognize that there is a greater purpose in all that happens to me and that the river of life flows through me and all of creation. This deep connection makes all forms of life equally important, useful and valuable. Since there is oneness in all of diversity, I have no more reason to be afraid, to be intimidated or to defend myself. I will focus on increasing happiness in life. This will allow me to become a channel for unconditional love and thereby contribute to a more harmonious world. I am asking for oneness to become the dominating experience in my life.

2. The Gateway of Solving All Problems

If we are faced with a seemingly insurmountable problem in life, it means that we are not able to see the larger picture for the time being. Problems are not there to make us suffer; they are lessons in disguise that can reveal to us where we have gone wrong and what we can do to correct our mistakes.

Problems of any kind in life indicate that we are resisting the flow of vital energy. Our first response to a given difficulty may be to ignore, suppress or fight it. If the problem persists, we may blame others, circumstances or even ourselves for bringing it about. When a baby keeps crying, we may find ourselves shouting at it so that it stops being such a "nuisance" or we may shut it up by putting food in its mouth.

If we experience pain in the head or in other parts of the body, we tend to "solve" the problem by taking a painkiller. If the pain keeps reoccurring, we go to the doctor to get it "fixed" just as we go to a mechanic to fix our car. We may try "overcoming" a financial difficulty by taking a loan. If a partner is no longer the way he used to be, we may decide to separate from him or get a divorce. An unwanted pregnancy may be terminated through an abortion. If the nation faces an enemy, he is fought with weapons of mass destruction.

It seems logical at first to believe that the problems afflicting us individually or collectively have their causes in external factors that are beyond our control or power of influence. Yet all problems that we encounter in our lives have been caused by us individually or collectively. The "thread", which connects the symptom of a problem with its cause, however, is invisible to most people. This may give rise to the impression that difficulties always arise from outside. Although the skin and the blood are two completely different aspects of our body, the skin erupts, ages or dies off if the blood becomes toxic. The outer part of our body only mirrors what is going on inside the body. If a problem affects us in any way, we can be certain to have contributed towards it.

We all attract towards us our own problems. This is an important insight to learn during this period of global transformation. If we worry about something or project our present fears into future events, we will manifest these incomplete and unhealed aspects of ourselves as personal difficulties.

Since problems are opportunities in disguise, unless we have recognized them as such, we will carry them with us wherever we go, into every new relationship we begin and into every new job we take up. Running away from our problems or ignoring problems makes them only more persistent. On the other hand, their very persistence can turn out to be our greatest asset. Once we have dealt with them and

181

learnt from them, they disappear by themselves and new opportunities begin to unfold.

All the so-called "negative" experiences in life have a deeply hidden purpose, which is up to us to discover. The bigger the problem, the greater is the meaning of its purpose or message for us. Problems only exist in relation to us and they "pursue" us to remind us that there is a greater purpose in life than what we are currently aware of. Problems can shake up the core of our being in order to awaken us to the need for major change. Since the world is made up of polarities, problems always bring their solutions along with them. If we want to see light, we have to accept that there will be shadows, too, because it is the shadows that defines the light.

For centuries, man has been taught that problems are bad for us and should be avoided by all means. Consequently, we generally see them as unnecessary, useless and harmful. This is an unfortunate assumption because problems are like a map that can guide us towards our destination. The *first step* to solving problems in life is to give up the wrong notion or idea that someone or something out there is creating problems in my life. The *second step* is to become aware that all problems are associated with a sense of uncertainty. In the case of an illness, this uncertainty could either become a serious issue or a harmless situation. It is up to us to determine the outcome. *The third step* consists of simple *being or mindfulness*. Once you consciously feel the uncertainty that accompanies a problem and *be* with it, your fears begin to subside and with them the necessity for the problem.

Problems always teach us to be more patient or to stay in the present moment. Problems can also work as a braking system when we move too fast or wear ourselves out. By slowing down and staying with the problem rather than running away from it or pretending that it isn't there, we enter the "nothing is happening phase" of the problem. These times or moments of suspension and uncertainty serve as a means for transcending our own fears, limitations and weaknesses. They actually form the most important part of solving problems. There is always light at the end of the tunnel. By going through the fear or staying with the problem from its beginning to its end, you can emerge enriched, more self-confident and with newer and greater opportunities in life than ever before.

For example, if you are with a partner who controls your life, suppresses your freedom of choice or criticizes every move you make, hard as this may be to accept, his "harsh" attitude towards you is identical to the one you apply to yourself. By suppressing your own feelings, holding on to a pattern of low self-worth, or not feeling in control, you have unconsciously chosen someone as a partner who represents this subconscious aspect of your personality. By consciously going through this difficult period in your life and by seeing your relationship problem as your personal one, you automatically relinquish your need to change your partner. This results in a better image of yourself and attracts a supportive behavior towards you, not only from your partner but also from everyone around you. If your partner is not able to work out his own problems in a similar way, the relationship may break apart. What is most important in either case is that you have made a quantum leap in your personal growth.

Albert Einstein saw problems as a need to change one's thinking. He said: "One cannot solve a problem with the same kind of thinking that gave rise to it." By changing our way of thinking – something we all are free to do at any time – we deprive a problem of its cause. This opens up new opportunities for us to move forwards in life. To open the Gateway of Solving all Problems does not mean we will never have problems in our life, what it means is that by changing ourselves, our response to a problem will change. This will give us the space and energy to effectively deal with the problem and what is even more important, to learn from it.

Opening the Second Gateway

I will open the Gateway of Solving all Problems in Life by seeing and understanding that every problem of mine is a unique and personal opportunity to change a stuck notion or emotional pattern within me. I recognize that going through the experience of a problem from beginning to end can make me a stronger, more competent and self-reliant person. I say thanks to all the opportunities in life even if they come in the disguise of a problem.

Since problems can help me deal with my fears I understand that there is no advantage in finding hasty

183

solutions to them. Whenever I face a personal problem, by fully experiencing it, I will become aware of the fear that the problem brings up in me. This will allow me to let go of the fear altogether. If I am afraid of the dark and always need to keep a light on even during sleeping, by voluntarily switching off the light for a few seconds to begin with, I can become more aware of my fears and feel the emotional effects they have on my body. By applying this principle to every difficult situation in my life I can gradually and in my own time release all the fears that I may have accumulated in this or a previous lifetime.

By asserting that I will not take shortcuts when I need to solve a problem or overcome an illness, my fears will disappear and with them the current difficulties in my life. My attitude towards problems is a "friendly" one because they could turn out to be the best teachers I have ever had. I know that each problem in my life can contribute towards making me more self-sufficient, happy and free.

3. The Gateway of Gaining Mastery over Time

The message of this gateway is to stop being a slave to time. Time is only a gauge or measure of perceptual change. Some things change within a millionth of a second, other things take more than a lifetime, but you, the perceiver, *is* and always will be. *Being* is set in the *now* which is eternally there and since you *are now*, the Being in you is truly timeless.

The feeling of being driven or controlled by time is caused by the fallacy that there is not enough of it. If this is your experience, it indicates that you have lost the sense of the eternal moment of timelessness or that you are influenced by the fear of the unknown. The sense of timelessness creates oneness, whereas fear of the unknown creates the illusion of separateness. Your mind may be dwelling solely on future events rather than being anchored in the present moment.

This can give you the impression that, as these events come closer, time becomes shorter too. The constant fear of not being able to meet deadlines or the apprehension of missing an airplane can trigger enough stress hormones in your body to speed up your perception of time to the degree that time is literally running out, for you. When we use such expressions as "I never have enough time for myself" or "time is too short", this may foretell an imminent problem, which will force us to slow our pace or change our concept of time.

You metabolize *your* experience of time similar to the way you metabolize food or the air you breathe. Your perception of time becomes your personal reality. If you are among those who wish they had more time for themselves but don't seem to be able to "find" the extra time, it may be necessary for you to change your priorities because your happiness is at stake. Put yourself first even if it looks selfish to others. People who are "driven" by time become increasingly unhappy and begin to neglect their health, their spiritual needs their relationships and forget that they have free will and freedom of choice. There will always be time for everything in life if you give yourself enough time. The time you spend on yourself is an investment in you. This investment dissolves the illusion that time controls your life.

All things take their time. If you try to push things or speed up time, you will somehow lose whatever time you have gained. Someone may argue: "The faster I finish a project, the more time I will have left for the next one." This is the basic concept of modern time management. However, the illusion of time saving creates what can be called "time slavery." The principle of time saving speeds up the treadmill of our lives. To attain a better position with more responsibility at work we are required to produce or perform faster than we did before because workload increases with responsibility. Modern technology which is believed to "speed" up progress also reduces the amount of time we have available for *living* our lives.

The benefits of time saving methods are hardly worth mentioning. They are measured in terms of earning a little more money that we may spend on things that cannot replenish the vitality, health and happiness we have lost because of time pressure, i.e. stress.

Those people who set aside time for attending to their health, emotional well-being and spiritual needs, or who spend time in nature, meditate regularly, play a musical instrument or play with children are

185

often rewarded with the bliss of the moment when time stands still. Life is not about how fast you can live it or how quickly you can accomplish a given task, it is about how much happiness you can derive from doing it.

Truly creative people have no concept of time. Creativity is only available to us when we are centered in the timelessness of the moment. Since creative performance itself produces so much joy, there is no need for the performer to look towards the future or to remain enchanted by the memories of past events. That is when we gain mastery over time. To master time means to be free from all limitations. Limitations only exist when we "fall" out of the present moment of eternity and get caught up in the so-called "real" world where money, time and competitiveness rule. But the "real' world lacks what satisfies us – the joy of creating.

The gateway to mastering time helps us to focus our attention on only that one thing we are doing at the moment, whether it is small and unimportant or big and important work. When your mind wanders into the future, gently bring it back to the now. Whether you drive a car, hold a seminar, paint a picture, deliver mail, collect berries, or pull weeds from your garden, just keep you mind focused on what you are doing. *What* you do is much less important than *how* you do it.

Regular meditation helps to create the habit of staying in the present. Conscious breathing, both as a meditation or a method of mindfulness during activity, helps to maintain the focus on the present moment. Learn to *listen* to others instead of merely *talking* to them. Take a step back from a given situation and observe how it unfolds at every step. Painting a picture (you don't have to be good at it), helps center your mind, too. Let silence infuse your life instead of noise. This removes the rush of the past and the pressure of the future.

Opening the Third Gateway

The next time I feel pressured by time, I pause for a moment, close my eyes, and feel the effect this pressure has on me, my body, relationships, sense of well-being and happiness. I will open the Gateway of Mastering Time by setting new priorities in my life, regardless of what others may think of me. I am beginning to understand that my happiness and that of my family, friends and colleagues depends on how much time I spend on or with myself. My surrounding can only benefit from me if I am happy and content. I start to see and appreciate every activity – whether it seems important or unimportant – as a unique opportunity to experience the timeless moment of the present, the source of all happiness. I feel no need to rush, for haste only takes me away from this moment of timeless contentment. By holding my attention on every new moment as it slips into the presence of my experience, I become the master of time and I can live my life to the fullest without fear of future or past events. I see myself as the central point of a wheel, changeless, timeless and always in charge all movements, whether they are backwards or forwards in time. I realize that I have all the time in the world because at each moment I am truly timeless.

4. The Gateway of Abundance

Both abundance and poverty are projections of our mind. Outer poverty reflects inner poverty and outer abundance reflects inner abundance. The amount of material possessions, including money, however, cannot be seen as a reliable measure of abundance in life. There are many wealthy people who suffer from "poverty consciousness" which is expressed in their incessant drive for more and more material possessions. Their restless feeling of never having enough makes them truly poor, unable to enjoy their wealth. They possess less than a poor man who may take great pleasure in the little he owns. The fear of losing what they have earned makes them dependent on material things that could lose or gain in value at any time.

True abundance is something entirely different. Abundance is the kind of consciousness that has no fear of losing anything. Abundance is present in a person who does not feel the need to hoard money or possessions. His awareness is established in the deep trust that he always gets what he needs and what he desires. Moreover, if a desire does not get fulfilled he knows that there is a good reason for that, too. He never worries about the future and he gives freely for he knows it will be returned to him in many ways. The abundant person is connected to the river of life, which never stops flowing, wherever he may be, or whatever he may do. Poverty occurs when we cut ourselves off from this lifeline which is the connection to our inner self. Self-reliance, trusting oneself and appreciating oneself restores abundance in life.

Abundance becomes a living reality when we give up the *urge* to hoard possessions or money, although having access to a lot of money *can* be a sign of inner abundance. If fear is the motivating factor behind saving money, poverty consciousness results. Saving money for a good purpose, however, can be a sign of prudence and have an "enriching" effect. Someone who saves money may argue that he is poor because he feels it won't last very long, whereas another person may feel happy and more affluent when he puts aside some of his earnings. This is the difference between poverty consciousness and affluence consciousness.

A newborn baby sucking its mother's breast has no sense of poverty, although it has no possessions either. The secret in all this is that if we stop trying to possess something, it will come to us. Abundance can only exist in abundance consciousness. Holding on to money for the sake of just owning it indicates that we have already lost it. It is no longer a source of real pleasure or energy; in fact, it can have a draining effect on us. If we save money out of fear of not having enough in the future, we may jeopardize our feelings of abundance. We may even think of money as if it were the goal of life and hence are terrified of it slipping away.

Money is a form of energy. As long as it flows, it is healthy and productive. If we keep holding on to money this energy begins to stagnate, which gives us the impression that we are wealthy, whereas in reality we are quite poor. The longer we hold on to money the greater will be the fear of losing it again. That's when material wealth can no longer serve as a source of happiness for us.

To gain true abundance, apart from serving our own interests, it is a good idea to use a small percentage of our money to help and serve others in whatever little ways it is possible. This will allow the energy to flow and gather momentum. When we give money for a good purpose and without expecting something in return, it enriches our heart and increases material wealth. In this way, money can become a source of creating real abundance in life.

Our mental attitude towards money is the most important tool we have to attract this form of energy into our life. Abundance is naturally present when you give up your attachment to material possessions, which doesn't mean we should give up our possessions. Abundance will always be there when we need it. The river of life will flow through us when we stop resisting it. The resistance is nothing but fear of not having enough. If money or material wealth is scarce in your life, you are given this opportunity to face and overcome your fears of poverty. By allowing yourself to only have little for some time and really appreciate what you have, you will develop inner abundance and soon also outer abundance. As a result, you will have the experience of abundance on every level, e.g., abundant health, abundant wealth and abundant wisdom.

Opening the Fourth Gateway

I will open the gateway of abundance by becoming a channel for the abundance of the universe. I recognize that poverty is only my resistance to accept abundance into my life. As my self-worthiness and self-appreciation increases, the wealth and abundance present in every nook and cranny of the universe will be directed towards me. As I begin increasingly to trust in the law of giving and taking, I realize that the more I give from my heart, the more I receive an abundance of love, appreciation, opportunities, and material wealth. I further realize that money and possessions are not the cause but the effect of abundance in my life. It rather is the ability of letting go of my attachment to anything I own which bestows on me the freedom to give and receive what I need to achieve a higher purpose in life. True abundance is the complete trust that I am at the right place at the right time. I know that I am and always will be connected to the river of life, which knows all my needs and desires wherever I will be and whatever I will do. This is my status of abundance.

5. The Gateway of Success

Success is the spontaneous result of an activity that makes us happy and content. Each person has a unique purpose and plays one or several specific roles during each lifetime. My purpose is no more or less important than anyone else's is. Before we were born, our soul made the agreement to develop and fulfill that particular purpose. This purpose is called *Dharma.* Many people spend their entire life trying to find their *Dharma,* which can be a very unsettling and stressful experience. By contrast, once we are attuned to our *Dharma* we become balanced and peaceful. To live our *Dharma* or purpose, we need to align ourselves with the infinitely creative power of natural law. This alignment is the true source of success in life.

Success structures a personality that is able to manifest and communicate the wisdom of nature and set the physical and emotional preconditions for the development of higher states of consciousness. This kind of success is characterized by unique expressions of creativity that bring you happiness and continued inspiration. Acquiring wealth alone is not necessarily a sign of success. On the other hand, when it is accompanied by the spreading of harmony, happiness and abundance all around you it assumes real meaning in life.

The level of true success is proportional to the amount of joy you derive from completing a given job or task. Joy and happiness, however, rather result from the creative act itself than from the achievement of the goal. Most people live *goal-oriented* lives and therefore miss out on the pleasure that arises from the act of "creating." Needless to say, the satisfaction they derive from having achieved a certain task or goal is only short-lived. On the other hand, being *process-oriented* opens up whole new aspects of one's creative potential which brings lasting benefits, regardless of whether the goal is reached or not.

By putting your attention on each moment of your work, you will spontaneously tap your source of creativity, even though it may take some time for this to become apparent outwardly. Expressed in practical terms, if you are a student in a school or college, your performance will drastically improve if you don't focus on the marks or grades you could achieve but instead try to discover what benefits you can derive from the learning process. If you like your job but change it for another because it can bring you more money, you may sacrifice quality for quantity and create a lot of stress in your life. Job satisfaction is extremely important for our physical, mental and spiritual well-being. It is better for the whole of you if you choose a job that you love doing.

Money alone cannot not solve your problems. If you are working on a production line, you might greatly benefit if you took your attention away from the money you will be getting at the end of the month, and instead centered your mind on what you do in each moment. You will be surprised to discover so many precious insights about yourself, your job and your life.

Teachings come in many disguises. Since every person on Earth is always in lesson you can take it for granted that you are always in the right place at the right time. By keeping your mind on what you do at each moment rather than on the goal ahead of you, you begin to consciously connect with your higher self; this can turn into a fountain of creative thoughts. You may suddenly get an idea how to improve a particular product or service, which consequently could promote your present status. To be really creative requires one's full attention. Listening to music while working *does* enliven the right (artistic side of the brain) but also divides the mind and weakens the body. People who use such distractions may do so because they don't like their job, but this in fact only increases their dissatisfaction. Strikes and other forms of social protest mostly indicate the deep frustration that results from goal-oriented, unsatisfactory success. They also imply inefficient use of one's creative potential.

Everyone is equipped with the same source of infinite creative intelligence regardless of whether he is a garbage collector, a homemaker, a lawyer or a head of state. Seen from the perspective of the Creator, no person is a better person than another. The infinite creative power of the universe is available to us at each moment of the day. However, as long as our focus is on the goal, we have no or only little access to this pool of creativity. The saying "energy follows thought" applies also to creativity and success. If we *only* think of the pay check, our creative skills will not develop fully and our *Dharma* or purpose in life will remain unclear.

Of course, it is much easier to be creative when there is a lot of external stimulation. Yet sometimes we are given a stressful and boring routine job in order to develop the more unusual creative streaks within us. Since necessity is the mother of invention, our creative genius is expressed more likely in problem situations that demand an innovative solution or when we are no longer satisfied with the status quo. Out of the inner urge and need to be creative, new opportunities can open up for us which will align us even further with our *Dharma* – the source of unique creativity in life.

Those truly successful people who have made a difference in this world were rarely concerned with the goals of their creative activities. It was rather the creative performance and the joy they derived from sharing their skills or insights with other people that made them so successful. Constantly inspired by their own creativity, they achieved what others considered miraculous. A Beethoven, Einstein or Michelangelo were not after fame or glory, they loved what they were doing. They were in tune with their *Dharma*.

Like these great minds, you too, have a unique specialty that only wants to be expressed. By seeking to be of service in whatever little or big way is possible, you create the necessity for becoming more successful in your own life. The timeless law of supply and demand or give and take is the secret of all success and abundance. By giving freely and generously without expecting anything in return, you become truly successful and affluent. The more people your activity, product or service influences in a positive way, the more fulfilling success you will reap for yourself.

Opening the Fifth Gateway

I will open the gateway of success by finding and living my natural purpose or Dharma, for which I will take the following steps:

192

- *Whenever I do something, I will check whether my attention is on the product (goal) of my activity or on the process of achieving it. If I see money as the means of achieving my goals, I will ask myself whether I derive pleasure from earning it.*

- *I will begin to make the increase of happiness the prime motivation for everything I do in my life. If I am not happy at work I will think of and implement ways of improving the product, working environment, relationship with colleagues or whatever else I don't like about my work, regardless of whether this will lead to a pay rise or not. Should my work still remain a source of stress, fatigue or depression, I will set aside some time each day to think of ways towards a more fulfilling and satisfying work activity elsewhere.*

- *I let go of the idea that only struggle and hard work can provide comfort and happiness; instead, I trust that success comes easily when I am at ease with myself.*

- *I understand that using my skills to serve other people's interests apart from my own will sustain continued success in my life.*

- *I recognize that by keeping my focus in the present moment of activity, I will derive much joy and satisfaction, for there is no effort or stress involved in creative action.*

6. The Gateway of Non-Judgment

Any attempt to correct or improve somebody else stems from the belief that such a correction is necessary. The need to judge someone reveals a lack of love. Love cannot judge, it can only forgive, which is a form of "overlooking" another person's mistake. Love cannot judge because it perceives everything and everyone in the light of oneness. Love cannot be where there is judgment and there cannot be judgment where there is love.

When we judge someone for what he has done to us or other people, we unconsciously admit to not being loving enough ourselves or not having been loved enough in the past. While we judge someone, we also judge ourselves. When we love someone, we also love ourselves. The way we see the world reflects how we see ourselves. Therefore, when we criticize the mistakes our spouse, students, children or friends make, we are actually pointing out our own errors or lack of compassion. To see and mind someone else's faults requires a "faulty" vision, one that is based on the limitations and shortcomings of the ego. A person who chooses love as the principal force of dealing with and viewing the world's situation, sees no injustice done, only cause for forgiveness and room for improvement.

Judgment is self-directed just like everything else we do in life. It materializes when something within us is not sorted out, or is confused, dishonest and vague. Since we are often afraid to confront our unresolved issues or recognize them as our own weaknesses, we prefer to project them on others. When you feel the urge to judge or criticize someone, ask yourself what within you prevents you from being happy and satisfied. Every judgment stems from what we think we are, and represents the value that we give to ourselves. Could it be that we are critical of others who are wealthy, happy or in a better position than we are because they have something we cannot have or deny ourselves?

It is good to keep reminding ourselves that we send thought forms to everyone we think of. Even by reading about an incidence in the newspaper or watching someone on the television set, we are likely to direct either negative or positive thoughts towards that person. If the thoughts turn out to be negative, we link into the "personal library" of similar negative experiences from our past (including those of our previous lives), which may blow out of proportion the judgment we are passing on that particular person. Negative thought forms are deposited in our mental and emotional bodies and thereby drain our energy; you may verify this loss of energy through kinesiology (muscle testing).

Instead of you looking for what is wrong in others, you may be better off looking for something that deserves your approval. Every human being is spirit born into matter. The spirit part always remains pure, divine and full of love. Nevertheless, when the spirit or soul

194

enters a human body, the memory of his divine nature fades away and the laws of *Karma* begin to dominate his awareness. Whatever the person does because of his past actions is an attempt to work through *Karma* and thereby raise the level of planetary vibration. This is laudable in every respect. The soul essence remains pure even if *karmic* obligations and contracts force someone to do seemingly dreadful things. Every human soul is from Spirit and has volunteered to do this challenging work of accumulating and working through *Karma* for the betterment of all life forms in the universe and as such is worthy of our utmost love and admiration.

As long as there is something you like about yourself, there will always be something that you will appreciate in other people as well, for like attracts like. Try to focus on ways to uplift, enrich and support others rather then putting them down. Find out what you like in yourself and dwell on it. Soon you will see the same good quality reflected in others as well. Perception is always consistent, whether we see things positively or negatively. How you view things in your life reflects your thinking, but your thinking reflects your choice of what you want to see. So in order to change other people or even the world, you only need to change your choice. You can do this right now.

Opening the Sixth Gateway

I will open the gateway of non-judgment by increasing my well-being in every way I possibly can. I recognize that this is the only way I can see others in a more positive light and relinquish the need for judgment. I recognize that there is no pleasure in being against anyone or anything in my life for this would only weaken me. I am finally making peace with myself by giving up the desire to change others. I realize that each one of us has created a unique way of living in order to learn the lessons of patience, unconditional love, forgiveness, compassion, acceptance and service. I understand that the law "as you sow so shall you reap" is perfectly sufficient to correct people's mistakes in its own time and therefore does not need any judgment on my part. I want to make the increase of love the most important priority in my life

195

because love is also about letting go of the desire to change others. I accept myself as I am at this moment and this will help me to accept others as they are. Thus, I directly contribute to global peace and harmony.

7. The Gateway of the "Highest First"

"The Principle of the Highest First" can best be described by the following phrase: *"Strive first for the Kingdom of Heaven and you will be provided with everything you need and desire on Earth."* Don't seek small opportunities. Always make your goals bigger than yourself. Also, think big, not small, for what you think will manifest.

Restrictions and limitations have no part in the nature of consciousness. They belong to fearful thinking and fear prevents you from feeling free, successful and abundant. Your true inner nature is unbounded and infinitely resourceful. Our consciousness, being infinitely intelligent and creative, was able to mastermind the conception and construction of this uniquely designed body, which is at least as complex as the structure of the universe. You may think that it is your mother that made you in her womb, but it is the creative intelligence of your consciousness, your soul, that has magnetized the appropriate aspects of matter and energy to manifest first as an embryo, then as a child and finally as a grown-up person. Your unbounded awareness oversees and effects the replacement of all the trillions of cells in your body each year, a task that a limited mind and even the most powerful of computers could never accomplish. The very belief that we are limited and powerless, however, is enough to manifest as strong limitations and difficulties in our body. This misunderstanding contrived by our intellect is the origin of illness and misfortune.

Time demands to give up the false idea that you are not worthy or competent enough. It is you, the highest and only unbounded consciousness that pervades all life forms, animate and inanimate. Your are the "sap" of life that brings nourishment to all. You deserve the experience of heaven while here on Earth because your very nature is divine. It is your birthright always to have the best of everything. It is time to remember who you are.

The Kingdom of Heaven is not an esoteric, mystical or religious concept, but the perception of you as a pool of unconditional love and happiness. Once you recognize and live your own vast and gratifying potential, you will see this potential reflected in everything and in everyone. Heaven on Earth is the combined effect of the fourth or higher- dimensional experience, where love and spiritual light are the dominating force, with the third dimensional reality of down-to-earth matter. The new era will be blessed with the "descent" of the spiritual light into matter. This will enlighten our awareness and undo all the "wrong" that has occurred here on Earth for the past thousands of years.

We are all invited now to become the channels and guardians of this spiritual light, so it is best to not stand outside while all of Heaven waits for you within. Seek the ultimate truth in everything you do. Don't be satisfied with little truths or belief systems. The truth is abundant within you, so you don't need to search for it outside yourself. By accepting or being satisfied with a little knowledge or partial truth, you may harm yourself, as can be seen in the symptom-oriented approach of conventional medicine. By merely relieving the symptoms of a disease you may intensify its cause. Don't be satisfied with half-satisfying answers but look for complete knowledge instead. If you cannot find it today, try again tomorrow but make no compromises.

The principle of the highest first is so powerful that when applied it can create a problem-free life. Living by partial knowledge may impair the life force and drain our energy. The idea that the surgical removal of a tumor cures cancer is only related to the symptom of the disease whereas it leaves the root causes intact. The combined focus of the doctor and his patient on a particular symptom may energies it, which can drain both the doctor's and the patient's energy resources.

The idea that the removal of the symptom of a disease is its cure is a powerful thought that creates its own reality – a thought form. This thought form or belief might remain active in the mental body of a person throughout his life. The thought form repeatedly manifests physical problems that may lure a patient or a doctor into accepting a "quick fix" solution, until the thought form is eventually replaced by another that allows healing to take place on all levels of mind, body and spirit. In some people negative thought forms can create such a solid structure around them that, even though an alternative holistic cure may exist, they are not be able to let it into their space. It may be very difficult for some of us to see these rigid thought patterns in the mental body because we have identified with these belief systems for so long. Only when we "take a step back" and begin to be an observer of our thoughts and actions can we gradually change our old habits and beliefs.

To escape a false sense of reality, begin focusing on the highest ideal in yourself and you will see it reflected everywhere. By ignoring it you will see problems and difficulties everywhere. All that our soul wants us to experience in life is that everything is within us and that we *are* one with everything that exists. And since everything is connected to the same infinite source of intelligence, you need not struggle to achieve the very highest in life. This recognition alone will draw towards you everything you want and everything you need. It serves as one of the most powerful thought forms than can clear your mental body of negative thought forms, including those that are self-judging and derogatory.

To establish the *Gateway of the Highest First*, it is necessary to share with others whatever you have learnt yourself. The reason you have been gifted with certain skills or abilities, apart from serving yourself, is to benefit others. It is invaluable both for you and your surroundings to give freely whatever you have found to be useful in your own life since your environment is nothing but your extended self. By holding on to your things, money or knowledge, you cut the lifeline to your own unbounded nature. This creates a false identity, which leans on external power or material wealth to make you feel you are somebody. This also prevents you from "thinking big." However, by sharing with the world what you have gained for yourself, you open the gates of wealth, bringing you a flood of opportunities and the very best you can possibly gain. By looking out for the highest good or very best in everything and everyone you will appreciate and love yourself more than ever before; this will stop conflict in life. Since there is no use in knowing about the faults of others, try to discover their best qualities. This will spontaneously improve your self-esteem.

Whatever you want for yourself, first see and appreciate in others, and it will manifest in you, too. If you want to be loved and admired, love and admire others first, but do not try to seek to be loved or demand love from others for you will only become disappointed and angry. If you cannot fulfill your desires, it is because you have obstructed your own deserving ability by wanting for yourself what you don't want others to have. This is what thinking small means. You are what you see for there cannot be any other world for you than the one you wish onto others.

Your ideas of the world cannot leave their source, which is no other than your limited self, the ego. When you change your mind on what you want to see, the world changes accordingly. Whatever you are able to appreciate or acknowledge in others, you are also able to value in yourself, and whatever you share with others becomes stronger in you. So don't hold back. As you value yourself in the highest possible way, you will spontaneously begin to share all you have and this will change both yourself and your world exactly the way you want it to be.

Opening the Seventh Gateway

Having accepted that I am the creator of my own body and my own mind, I understand that I can change them in any way I want. In the same way as I can cause my own illness and difficulties, I can also create the best of health and opportunities in life. I am willing to accept responsibility for everything that happens to me, both positive and negative. The way others value me is exactly determined by how I value myself. By adopting the principle of the highest first, I will begin to value myself for what I really am – an unbounded field of creative power that is ready to be used for the purpose of enjoying Heaven on Earth. As I begin to see goodness and great potential in everything and everyone, I will witness problems and any lack disappear from wherever my attention goes. I can create a better world because I can create a better me. It is my choice whether I prefer to have the very best of life or settle for less. Heaven on Earth is but a recognition of my own potential. It is not necessary to seek enlightenment or to wait for better times, for all I need to do is open my eyes and see that I am already there. The Kingdom of Heaven is already within me. A spirit of infinite love is the highest perception I can have of myself, so from now on I will choose to see the highest good in others and myself. The rest are details that will be taken care of by the spiritual universe.

8. The Gateway of Silence

Power rests with silence and not as it appears to be, with activity. Activity by itself is weak, undirected and chaotic if silence has not been established first. The moment before an arrow is shot, the restful state of the arrow imbibes great dynamic power. Once let lose, the arrow hits its target with strong force.

Silence is the basis of activity. Everything that happens in the universe goes through cycles of rest and activity. There is always a resting phase, a period of silence, between the phases of activity. We are only able to breathe because there is a moment of breath suspension just before inhaling or right after exhaling. We can only hear sounds when we are silent ourselves. The silence of the night is alternated with the buzz of the day. Without the regular experience of restful sleep at night, our body is not able to function properly during the day. Apart from emotional and psychological stability and to remain undisturbed, the numerous biological rhythms are very dependent on the experience of rest and silence.

When there is not enough quietude in our lives, we begin to lose orientation. A high building requires a strong foundation; otherwise, it will sway and collapse at the onset of a strong storm. Likewise, our activity will be ineffective if we neglect to establish a strong foundation of peacefulness and silence first. Silence represents the resting phase of life which our fast paced world has no time for anymore. Yet by neglecting the quiet part of our life, we are cutting off the branch we are sitting on. Adequate restfulness and tranquility are vital to life and the basis of lasting success. Silence creates order in our brain cells and the rest of the body and serves as the most important communication link between people. If two people only want to talk, which is activity, and no one wants to listen, which is silence, there can only be confusion, misunderstanding and conflict. To stop conflicts in life, we need to master the lesson of silence first.

Whenever there is silence, there is also peace. A peaceful mind knows neither division nor impatience. The undivided and patient mind is attuned to the world and meets no obstacles, for it is too powerful to be stopped. It is easy to undermine or oppose somebody's actions, yet silence cannot be destroyed or otherwise manipulated. The noisy and scattered mind creates a big fuss, but accomplishes only little or nothing. The majority of the modern business community is "burnt out" because they don't make enough time for recharging their minds and bodies through the experience of silence. While walking, one leg moves while the other doesn't. Likewise, progress is composed of both an active phase and a resting phase. There cannot be real, problem-free progress based on only one of its phases. Both rest and activity make life possible; neglecting one of them destroys it.

So if you want to make major improvements in your life, whether they are related to your health, beauty, relationships, work, leisure or general well-being, make certain that you spend at least one hour a day in silence. Apart from the rest gained during sleep, you need to experience silence in a more conscious way, too.

For example, you can get in touch with your inner power of silence through meditation. Choose a form of meditation or relaxation that seems most suitable for you. The conscious breathing meditation described earlier is both very simple and very effective in establishing deep silence in the practitioner. Whatever method you may use, to bear good results, it should be simple, effortless and easy to practice for it would defeat the purpose of the practice if you needed to put energy or concentration into it. I suggest that you meditate both in the morning and in the evening for about 15 – 20 minutes, before eating food.

Everyone can practice the technique of conscious breathing because there is no way of doing it incorrectly. Whatever presents itself during one particular meditation is what we need at the time and may be completely different from what we will experience during the next meditation. The main thing is to take it easy and to take it as it comes.

Silence comes naturally when we stop being active. This includes giving up trying to be without thoughts.

Another method of saturating yourself with silence is to spend time in nature; sit somewhere where no one can disturb you. Close your eyes and listen to the sounds of the natural world without doing anything else. All natural sounds are alternated with moments of silence. By listening to the sounds, these silent moments can quickly recharge your "batteries."

Occasionally, you may want to spend an entire day in silence and not talk at all (provided this does not offend anyone). This can make you aware of how much energy you may be wasting by talking about "nothing." When you do this for the first time, you may find that your mind produces a flood of turbulent and chaotic thoughts. This is a good sign and shows that silence disperses existing nervous energy and removes stress and tension; old and stuck thought forms can get released from the mental body and karmic patterns be broken down. It also shows how gossiping can deplete our energy resources more than any other activity. Once you experience silence regularly, your mind will increasingly penetrate into the deeper realms of silent awareness and the need to spend your energy on "meaningless" words and thoughts will drastically lessen.

By learning to be comfortable during these periods of silence, you automatically become more acute in your thinking and clear-headed during activity because silence removes clutter from the mind. Your thoughts become like targeted arrows of silence, swiftly and spontaneously producing the desired results. The only real preparation you need to make in order to become more successful, efficient and happy in life is to spend enough time in silence. Everything else is secondary. Activity based on silence makes life easy and effortless. Activity without it causes stress, strain and hardship.

The law of least effort, which is so eloquently applied by nature in the growth of a plant or the movements of stars, is the same principle that guides an action based on silence. Flowers make no noise when they grow. Even though the world is so huge, it revolves around the sun in perfect silence. All activities accompanied by silence are perfect. By making this principle your own, you will witness your personal world transform into a paradise.

Opening the Eighth Gateway

I will open the gateway of silence by spending a considerable amount of time in silence every day. I recognize that whatever I do in life, to be rewarding and effective, it requires the support of silence. Since silence can be more powerful than activity, I understand that investing time in silence can create plenty of excellent opportunities for improving my life in every possible way. I can bring peace to my mind through meditation, Yoga, watching a sunset, sitting or walking in nature or by deciding not to speak for a given period of time. Also, soft and gentle music can take me into the realm of silence. Making time for silence in my life is one of the greatest priorities for me because without it I don't have time for real living. Silence is the dynamic power that propels all activity. It keeps my body sound and healthy and my mind clear and alert. Silence makes me face myself and sort out what doesn't belong in me. I owe my life to silence and honor it wherever I am. I feel no need to make a noise because noise creates chaos in my life. Silence transforms chaos into love and oneness. My natural commitment is to silence.

9. The Gateway of Body Awareness

The body is the most important tool we have to develop higher states of consciousness. It is also the most precious gift we have been given and deserves to be treated well. The body is a learning device for us and can teach us everything about personal and universal life.

The body never exists in isolation. Physically, it depends on a nearly infinite number of atoms that are securely fixed for short periods of time within the trillions of cells in our body, just to be "called away" again to "serve" other forms of matter somewhere else in the universe.

This makes our body a universal crossroads or meeting place for all the forms of matter, energy and information that are constantly engaged in constructing and sustaining the universe. There is indeed nothing outside us that cannot be found inside us.

Our physical body has developed to a point of awareness that can give us the realization of being significant. We are now also beginning to understand that there are external forces such as the ones produced by climate, constellations of stars, circadian rhythms and sun activities, which all can influence our body in many different ways. The quality of food, air and water is increasingly seen as being crucial to our physical well-being and survival.

We often hear ourselves say that one thing makes us feel good or another makes us feel uncomfortable. Now is the time to understand that both these experiences of the body hold opportunities to further our spiritual growth. Body awareness is not only about feeling good. It is more about noticing the signals sent to us by the cells of the body which tell us that they want to be treated as lovingly as we want to be treated ourselves. When you begin to love and appreciate your body, you come to certain conclusions about your purpose here on Earth.

Body awareness is rapidly increasing among large numbers of people today because the body is now meant to become host to a multidimensional self with infinitely greater potential than we are using at this point in time. The intensity of bliss that awaits us cannot be held or endured by a body that is polluted, emotionally distraught and low in vibration. If your body is free of toxins and congestion, and is nourished by foods and thoughts that are of high vibrational energy, the "love" signals from your cells will collectively magnetize new energies that will reveal and sustain your multidimensional self.

This makes body awareness to be one of the most important keys to create Heaven on Earth. Bliss, which is the dominating quality of divine perception, carries the highest frequency of human experience, i.e. love. We are meant to fully experience love in this body and in everything around us, from the highest, most powerful level of creation to the lowest, most diminished one. Yet this supreme form of love is not developed through an external focus, which can only make us vulnerable and dependent on how other people value and treat us. However, love as an internal focus projected outward generates increasing waves of self-worthiness and blissful feelings of unity and harmony with all of creation.

By becoming increasingly aware of the various signals our body is sending us and responding to them in a caring way, we will be able to refine our ability to perceive the finer structures of creation, which are divine in nature. The same three-dimensional image of a flower or tree of today will then present itself in its higher dimensional reality. The great splendor and different color and sound realities of the flower will trigger waves of bliss in the perceiver and the knowledge gained from the perceptual experience will be an "eye-opener" of unimaginable beauty and inspiration. The entire world will be seen in a fundamentally different light and unhappiness and conflict will vanish because of the overwhelming experience of all-comprehensive love. Body awareness opens the gate to the Kingdom of Heaven within us.

So whatever we can do to increase body awareness is precious and useful. Cleansing the liver and gallstones alone can help remove most toxins in the body within a short period of time. Body work, Chi Lel Chi Kung, Yoga, regular exercise, conscious breathing, following a natural diet according to body type and the rhythms of nature[14], and anything else that can create a purer and healthier body, are all suitable methods to improve body awareness. Especially drinking plenty of fresh water can increase intercellular communication and raise the frequency of body awareness. Cold showers help to cleanse the aura of stagnant energy, the influence of negative thought forms and other effects of external disruptive influences. By giving your body the attention and the love it deserves, it will become a *temple of God* – a field of all possibilities in life.

Opening the Ninth Gateway

I will open the gateway of body awareness by beginning to appreciate my body for what it is - a vehicle that can take me to the highest realm of spiritual existence and divine perception. As I learn to understand the significance of my body, I will be more and more willing to take care of it as I would take care of my best friend. I choose to give my body

---

[14] See my book *Timeless Secrets to Health and Rejuvenation*

the very best of everything in terms of food, environment, sensory exposure and loving thoughts. As the awareness of my body continues to become increasingly acute, I will learn the lessons of life more consciously than before. The body is but a learning device of the mind. This I understand is its true purpose. By getting in "touch" with the cells of my body, I receive their waves of blissful well-being which makes me feel loved, whole and healthy. In case the cells send me signals of "dis-ease" or discomfort – caused by my own negative emotions and misalignment of my purpose – I will patiently go through the difficult periods and see them as lessons to heal my soul. Whenever I suffer from an illness, I will first consult my body in order to find out where I have gone astray. Once I have understood the way my body works, I will be able to let go of my thoughts of fear, difficulties and sickness. I am ready to trust that my body always knows best what to do at what time and, as long as I don't succumb to fear, it will continue to serve me on my spiritual journey of awakening. All that I am required to do is to maintain body awareness. Since conscious breathing, cleansing procedures, conscious eating, regular routine etc. are direct means to create and maintain body awareness, I will set aside enough time to give my body the energy and attention it requires to function at its best.

10. The Gateway of Inner Guidance

Trust your inner guidance because it is one of the most important tools of self-discovery. Your inner guidance rarely presents itself to you in verbal form; it is more likely to be an inner feeling. This sense of inner feeling or knowing accompanies every thought and action. Some people call it "conscience" although they may associate it only with negative experiences. Your conscience is the language of your soul, just as thoughts are the language of your mind and emotions the language of your body.

Your inner guidance is always there, but it is noticed more when you put your attention on the region of the heart. The body always knows whether the influence of a sensory or mental experience is suitable for its growth or not. The brain translates the vibrational energy of our thoughts, actions or perceptions into chemicals that generate specific physiological changes. The body instantly recognizes both good and harmful influences, and transmits the corresponding signals to the heart, causing an emotion or physical sensation. From there, the messages spread to every part of the body.

This gateway teaches you to listen to the messages from your heart. The only requirement to use and benefit from your inner guidance is "listening." Listening is easier when the attention is brought to the heart. All one needs to do in order to do the right thing at any moment of one's life is trust one's inner guidance. The inner voice tells you when to eat, drink, or sleep, and not to put your hands in fire if they get cold. It also urges you to take a cold shower when you are hot, stretch your body when it is stiff, drive slowly when you reach a crossroads, tidy up your garden when it overgrows, meditate or listen to music when you need to relax, empty the dustbin when it is full, or ask forgiveness if you have hurt a close friend. Your inner guidance is always there as long as your heart beats.

Fearful thoughts, however, interfere with inner guidance. Fear and worry are rooted in past experiences, the memories of which become our present beliefs. Belief systems, rules and regulations have managed to keep us from listening to and following our inner voice, which is the only guidance that can truly be trusted. To act on these beliefs or the *do's* and *don'ts* dictated to us by society reinforces the fear, which in turn casts even more doubt on our inner knowing. However, we don't need crutches to walk through life. There *are* no boundaries other than those that have been superimposed on us by our own beliefs.

Instead of following the fear signals that arise from the past and are projected into the future, listen to your heart, which can only speak to you or be heard by you in the present moment. It will tell you that you are a free spirit and no longer restricted by anything or anyone, regardless of the disappointing experiences you may have encountered in the past. When you truly listen to your inner guidance and are willing to act on it, all your needs will be taken care of before you can even wish for them. You will be given everything you require in order to proceed on your journey of self-realization. Your inner guidance will never fail you because it comes from your Higher Self, which is an essential part of cosmic intelligence. Life will be free of complications and conflict if we keep this channel of inner dialogue open at all times.

The inner guidance is not something mystical at all. It expresses itself in very mundane ways. For example, you may suddenly have this feeling that you need to call your best friend. If you follow this impulse right away, you and your friend will greatly benefit from communicating with each other. If you ignore this desire, the energy supporting it will become dispersed. If you postpone calling your friend by a few hours or until the next day, your mind has to hold this desire for that period, which can weaken it. This also takes your mind out of the present moment and locks it into a future event that may or may not take place.

Similarly, if you feel angry because someone left rubbish in your favorite picnic area, follow up this impulse by picking up the rubbish and putting it in the nearest dustbin. This reduces your anger and even makes you feel good about yourself. If you feel unjustly treated by a civil servant in a government office, instead of trying to "keep the peace" and be upset for several days, express your discontent and tell him how you feel right there and then, regardless of the outcome. By following our inner guidance more and more, we are able to avoid accumulating stress, tension and resentment in life.

Inner guidance can come in many ways. These can be divided into two categories, i.e. "comfort" or "discomfort." Both types of signal make you aware of your quality of living. When you violate the laws of nature (lifestyle, diet, behavior etc.), your signal will be discomfort and when you abide by natural law, you will sense comfort and well-being. All these experiences taken together determine your level of consciousness. The more conscious you are each moment of your life, the clearer and purer will be your conscience or inner guidance. You can learn to live more consciously by *putting your attention on everything you do*. This simple technique of mindfulness will develop honesty, openness and purity of heart. There can be no higher value in life than having a pure conscience or unfailing inner guidance. It is a major gateway to Heaven on Earth.

Opening the Tenth Gateway

With the realization that my beliefs have kept me from living freely and spontaneously, I am now willing to entrust the organization of my life to my own unlimited potential. The infinite organizing power that governs the universe also controls my life. I therefore do not require man-made rules, regulations or belief systems to know what is right for me. In particular, I feel no longer bound by beliefs that generate fear or negativity. What I need to do in order to be in tune with the laws of nature is listen to my inner guidance or conscience, which I sense as subtle impulses of feeling within the region of my heart. It is the infinite wisdom of my Higher Self that generates this inner guidance and it always knows what is good for me in every moment. There are only two kinds of experience in life: one that makes me feel happy and another that makes me feel unhappy. Naturally, I will attempt to make only those decisions that make me feel good and desist from making decisions that make me feel uncomfortable. I use this simple technique to let myself be guided through all the thick and thin of living, knowing that this will open my infinite potential and secure the support of natural law in all my decisions, thoughts and actions. I trust my inner guidance because it is the only one that knows my unique wishes and personal needs.

11. The Gateway of Spiritual Wisdom

Life on Earth is largely controlled by the law of *"Karma"* or cause and effect. To develop spiritual wisdom and fulfill the purpose of our time here on Earth we need to understand, follow and fulfill the law of *Karma*.

The law of cause and effect teaches us that there cannot be anything within this universe that has not been caused by something else. Each cause produces an effect and each effect becomes a cause for something else. Your body is an effect and so is your mind. In fact, all our thoughts, feelings, emotions, desires, likes, dislikes etc., have an underlying cause. Even the Earth we live on, the sun that nourishes the Earth, the galaxy that sustains the sun, are all effects, they have been created by something else or are controlled by forces other than their own. All situations in our life are merely effects of previous situations. Every moment in time is preceded by another moment, which in turn was preceded by an infinite number of other moments.

To be truly knowledgeable about something, such as our own life or that of a particular person, society or nation, we would need to be fully aware of the nearly infinite number of factors that directly and indirectly contributed to being the person we are today or to making the population of a country so unique and different from any other population in the world. In fact anyone who claims to really know everything about his field knows very little about it. All we can know on an intellectual level is a tiny portion of the huge cake of knowledge that pertains to every object or field of study. When we take a photograph of somebody we catch only one moment out of the trillions times trillions moments of his life and still know nothing about his life. Such is the reality with everything we learn. The more we think we know about something, the less we have access to the true source of that knowledge. We may be so fascinated with one aspect that we lose sight of all the moments that occurred before and those that possibly come afterwards. We may even be so deluded to assume we are real experts in what we have learned.

To attain spiritual wisdom, however, which is complete inner knowingness, we do not need to know all the causes for all the effects. Spiritual wisdom is about knowing who or what is at the beginning and end of each cause and effect. The invisible connection that binds an effect to its cause is the timeless consciousness – the ultimate Self. Without the knowledge and experience of Self, the world of cause and effect can be most bewildering and confusing.

It might very well be that a particular event such as a person's involvement in a two-way car accident is related to a cause that he and the other party have created in another lifetime thousands of years ago. The "indiscriminate" intellect which is only concerned with the immediate cause(s) of the accident, i.e. drunkenness, fatigue, fog, ice on the road etc., is unable to determine the real reasons behind the accident. The "discriminative" intellect, on the other hand, knows the difference between the timeless, unbounded Self and the world of

Karma, i.e. action and its consequences. By fathoming this distinction, we can gain access to the knowledge of cause and effect, regardless of the limitations superimposed on us by the experience of time and space. We can become an unattached observer or witness to these events whether they took place hundreds of lifetimes ago or yesterday.

All past experiences are forever contained in the "Akashic Records", the eternal memory of our soul. The person who knows himself also knows the relationship between cause and effect and thereby stays in control of his thoughts and actions. He will naturally abide by the laws of nature because he no longer sees any benefits in creating new Karma. He also knows that he, being the ultimate cause of *Karma*, will remain unaffected by it; he has indeed attained *spiritual wisdom.*

The *Gateway of Spiritual Wisdom* helps you to increase the vibration of your body and mind by establishing in your intellect the law of cause and effect. It is a perfect law and it never fails. This knowledge will help you to trust that there cannot be injustice of any kind even if everything points in this direction. You will also begin to realize that diseases can never be caused by external factors other than the ones created by yourself, and that accidents don't just happen either. By consciously going through the experience of an effect, which means from beginning to end, you effectively put yourself in control of its cause. This also puts you in touch with your Higher Self. As you learn to patiently handle every effect in this way, even if it seems uncomfortable for a while, you will suddenly begin to see the dawn of a completely new and different reality of life.

The more familiar we become with our true Self, the more we begin to understand that most situations occur to help us evolve or learn important lessons. For example, a thief who steals money from us, may in fact turn out to be a friend in disguise who simply gives us the opportunity to return our debts from a previous lifetime. He only takes from us what we owe him. By defending ourselves or threatening him, we merely create another cause for a similar event in the future until finally one day or one lifetime we are willing to give him what he has been asking for. The same applies to societal groups, separatist movements and entire nations that seek compensation, political freedom or economic independence.

At this point, you may argue that it isn't right that someone robs us and insist that he be punished for such a crime. This is only so if you are not emotionally involved or upset. Yet if you feel hurt by someone it is important for you to know that what really hurts is your own inability to forgive yourself for having hurt that person before, during this or a previous life time, hence your anger or frustration. By forgiving a person who has done you wrong you pay your old debts to him. It is for this reason that Jesus Christ asked his followers to love their enemies. Those people around us with whom we have the most difficulties in life, are the ones that give us the best opportunity to undo the hard knots of our *Karma*. By letting go of our pride and forgiving those that have hurt us in life, we significantly increase our own vibrations and consequently feel better about them and ourselves.

If you find it difficult not to react negatively to a person who criticizes you, look at the place between his eyebrows (his Third Eye) instead of directly into his eyes. This will allow you to send him light, love or forgiving thoughts because in this way you will see beyond his dual character or superficial self. Instead of only seeing anger as the cause of his criticism you will see it as an effect of an underlying tremendous sadness or fear. Looking at his third eye allows you to transcend the superficiality of cause and effect and directly link into that part of his soul that reflects love and light. No longer will you be propelled to react in kind by reacting or defending yourself. When you feel compassion and forgiveness, you have no need to defend yourself any more. This will effectively cut asunder the vicious cycle of cause and effect. Spiritual wisdom is the spontaneous result of living from moment to moment, when whatever anyone has done to us in the past is not relevant any more and the need for forgiveness does no longer arise.

Opening the Eleventh Gateway

I will open the gateway of spiritual wisdom because it offers me the freedom from the bonds of Karma. I want to become aware of all the things, persons, situations etc., that upset me. I know that whatever upsets me is linked to me through the law of cause and effect, giving me the unique opportunity to undo what I have done wrong somewhere, some time ago in the past. This fills me with gratitude. I am responsible for everything that happens to me in my life and I feel therefore motivated to clear any outstanding debts. I welcome my enemies or adversaries because they come to me as friends. They help me understand myself better. By forgiving them, I forgive my own past deeds that may have hurt them in some way during a previous encounter. This will free the trapped life force within me and remove the causes of disease, misfortune and conflict in my life. I am willing to acknowledge, face and work through all my resistance against people, problems or situations, for they are only there to teach me the lesson of love and raise my consciousness to a level where spiritual wisdom can become my daily experience and reality.

12. The Gateway of Fulfilling Desires

The gateway of fulfilling all desires represents the most powerful tool we have to initiate even the greatest of changes in our life – it is the art of desiring. Desires are thoughts we have given form and direction through an inner drive for more happiness and satisfaction in life.

Everything we represent today is the result of the thoughts we had until this moment. Unless we have cleansed our thinking apparatus or mental body from negative thought forms, our thoughts, feelings and emotions do not harmonize with their source and can become a cause of misfortune in life. The human mind and intellect are subjected to the following laws or mechanisms which, when clearly understood, can help you master the ability of fulfilling your desires.

Each thought is a subtle force of creative energy that, though invisible to our physical eyes, has a powerful effect on your body and surroundings. Thoughts draw towards them equal thoughts, similar to a snowball that rolls down a mountain, gathering more and more snow until it turns into a powerful avalanche. Every thought you think instantly becomes a mental picture that has its own specific form, color and life. Its color and form depends on the content of the thought and its motive, whereas its life span is determined by the strength (or weakness) of the person's mind.

The mental impulse which develops into a mental being or thought form, plays an extraordinary role in determining human destiny. Some thought forms can rule for thousands of years over entire populations. They are continuously energized by the people who keep believing in them, thus becoming long-lasting ideas, doctrines, beliefs, philosophies etc. Every thought form continues to exist in the subconscious realms of the mental body of the thinker unless it has been cleared or transmuted altogether. In most cases, however, it has been suppressed or overpowered for a certain period and it re-emerges when it is time to deal with it.

Thus, your feelings and thoughts construct the very foundation of your subconscious and make you conform to a destiny that you have brought on yourself. Whenever you direct a happy or angry thought towards another person, a situation or a group of people, it returns to you sooner or later in one form or another; in truth it will never leave your mental body (unless you know how to neutralize it). The law of cause and effect controls this mechanism.

Each thought of yours, whether it is harmful and negative or nourishing and uplifting, generates lower or higher urges within you, the thinker. This happens regardless of whether you are aware of it or not. In a similar way, your thoughts connect to and influence other people whose minds are of the same kind of vibration as yours, according to the law *like attracts like*. This puts an enormous responsibility on you. The effects of your thoughts are in no way restricted to your own life but influence other human and non-human beings as well. Your little fearful thoughts can lead to an entire avalanche of fear and cause chaos and confusion all around you. Similarly, your sudden, clear understanding of a particular phenomenon can cause an upsurge of wisdom in millions of people at the same moment.

Do not underestimate the power of your thoughts. By believing that your thoughts are weak, you generate very strong thought forms within your mental body, which make certain that you remain weak. When you say "I don't have the will to give up smoking or to eat healthy food", you energize the very thought form in your mental body that keeps you from developing the strong and effective will necessary to make major changes in your life. This shows the enormous power you have over every given situation; you are powerful enough even to resist the powerful stream of natural law, at least for a while. It is a much greater "feat" to remain weak and powerless than to use the existing creative energies to fulfill your desires. Since there is nobody else but you to translate *your* thoughts into *your* reality, and since no thought can ever get lost, you are, along with all your good sides and not so good sides, a product of your own thought factory.

Thought forms can manifest in all kinds of physical shapes and forms. The neurotransmitters in your brain are nothing but the physical counterparts of your non-physical thought impulses. That your neurotransmitters can heal a tumor or create one is well known; they are in fact responsible for every function in your body. However, they can only come into your existence when *you,* the spirit or soul, is present in the body and when *you* produce the appropriate mental impulses such as thoughts, images, feelings or emotions etc. Many of these mental impulses "disappear" into the subconscious of your mental body, but they are not really gone or lost. They become the unconscious causes for problems, conflict and ill-health but also for happiness and success in life.

An unsuccessful marriage, a thriving business, unlawful behavior or accidents are the products of one's own thought forms and their influence on other people's minds with a similar vibration. Another person's "mistake" that causes you to hurt or have an accident is but triggered by your own thought forms. If this person suffers too, his thought forms are responsible for his share of the negative event. Anything that happens to you at this moment is the combined consequence of all the thoughts you are having right now and the ones you have had in this or previous lifetimes, although you may not be aware of the latter ones.

Also, by reading this book you create thought forms in your mental body, which, depending on your interpretation of this presentation, can correct any imbalances or misunderstandings that you may have acquired regarding various important issues in your life. If you resonate with these thought forms, you become thoroughly enriched by them, as they become part of your mental world.

To master the ability to fulfill our desires and make a difference in this world, we need to increase our own vibration of consciousness and then express the intent of what we want to change or improve in life. By using the suggestions made in this book, or any other useful methods of personal growth and self health care available to mankind today, you can significantly raise your mental vibrations. Cleansing the liver from gallstones can by itself bring about an unprecedented clarity of the mind, remove angry thought forms and depression, and trigger constant healing responses throughout the body.

Whenever your attention rests on yourself – whether you give yourself an oil massage, consciously eat a wholesome meal, sleep on time, meditate, exercise or practice Chi Lel, Yoga or conscious breathing – you generate new thought forms of love, appreciation and caring. They are the seeds laid in your mental body which gradually begin to sprout and raise the vibrations of your body, mind and spirit. The new thoughts, which you are going to produce, will be based on yourself rather than on other people's ideas, opinions, beliefs etc. This greatly increases your power of thought, so much so that you can literally create Heaven on Earth for yourself and others. All you need is to ask for it.

Also check your hopes, expectations and worries. If you expect something undesirable to happen in your life, you can be certain that it will happen in one form or another. This is because *you* are powerful. If you keep telling yourself "I really feel bad" or "I am depressed" you are likely to shape your reality in a way that will fulfill and support these thought forms. When you tell yourself out of fear that you should save money for the times of emergency, for sickness, or old age, your thought forms may materialize and draw rough times, disease and aging into your life.

Thoughts become negative and harmful for both yourself and your environment if they are predominantly used to gratify the experience of sensory pleasure or material wealth. There is nothing wrong with material wealth, quite the opposite. Material wealth can well be a means of increasing happiness and comfort in life. Yet acquiring wealth just for the sake of having it reduces the joy of living.

Your happiness begins to grow rapidly if you begin to cherish those desires that help and support your extended self – the human race, the animals and nature, the Earth, the sun, the universe. Focus on these aspects of your extended self and what you could do to be of service in whatever small or big way possible. This will create loving thought forms all around your mental body, and according to the law of "like attracts like", magnetize every possible support from your environment. Eventually, there won't be a single space left in your mental body to accommodate negative thoughts. The beneficial effect of generating loving thought forms in your life is that you will receive many more opportunities for growth, success and happiness than you have ever had before. Material wealth will come to you automatically, without much effort on your behalf.

By sowing the seeds of love in other people's minds, you can even improve your environment. If you don't have anything material to give, you still have loving and healing thoughts that you can share with others. They are free. Give them freely but do not give them with expectations in your mind. When you give something with the expectation that you will receive something in return, your motivation is ego-centered and will attract more egotistic thought forms into your life. One method of cultivating this "ego-less" attitude, is to give something even if it is just a prayer or a loving thought, a friendly gesture or an encouraging word to someone in need or someone who is not in the position to return your expression of love or care. Do this for the joy of doing it, which certainly is a far greater reward than receiving something else in return. This swiftly upgrades your vibrations and increases your deserving ability. You will attract new people and situations into your life that reflect your newly created thought forms of love and joy. You will spontaneously live in greater harmony with the laws of nature and receive their constant support. This will make the fulfillment of your desires easy and effortless.

Man is a spiritual being living in a physical body. His primary needs are of a spiritual nature and not of a physical one. It is therefore not human to look for physical gratification that does not enrich the spirit at the same time. The main purpose of the five senses of perception is to increase spiritual wisdom. Eating good food, love making and other forms of sensual pleasure are wonderful means of self-development if used for this purpose. Sensory pleasure without a spiritual meaning, on the other hand, only gratifies the ego and not the spirit and can, therefore, not serve to increase real happiness.

When you create a spiritual purpose in your life, then everything you do will soon become a means to enhance the vibrations of bliss in your life. If your body is sick, don't just try to fix it; learn to find out what kinds of thought forms such as fear, anger, jealousy etc. within you have led to this predicament. You may also discover that a cold, the flu, or other *cleansing disorders* and in fact most diseases are opportunities to quickly remove old *Karma* that otherwise would take much longer to resolve. Blocking the body's efforts of self-cleansing through drugs or other unnatural methods makes the Karma heavier and potentially more painful. If you need healing, it is good to generate a desire to help heal others. If you want to be forgiven for your mistakes, start to forgive other people's mistakes. If you wish to be happier than you currently are, look for ways to bring happiness to other people. Whatever you want in life, give it first to others. This will free the river of life and give you unlimited access to everything you need and want.

Opening the Twelfth Gateway

I open the gateway of fulfilling all desires by desiring a better world, a better understanding between people, the elimination of crime, terrorism and social unrest, as well as the dawn of love, harmony and togetherness of all mankind etc. I will look for opportunities where I can be of help or service, just for the joy of it. Regardless of whether I will be rewarded for my actions and contributions or not, I still have the satisfaction of greater love and self-appreciation. Every time I send out a good thought to someone, I feel better about myself. I am willing to give something to someone each day and not expect anything in return, even if it is just a well-wishing thought or gesture. This will help me get in touch with the deeper aspects of myself, all of which are part of the oneness. I realize that everything that I do for others I am actually doing for myself.

I recognize that in order to fulfill my desires and enjoy greater prosperity in my life I need to increase the thought forms of giving, sharing, loving, forgiving etc. By giving to others what I want for myself, I am no longer limited by my own ego because my motivation comes from my extended or

Higher Self. This puts me into the power needed to fulfill all my desires.

The Earth is my worldly home. I desire to create a better home for all. This helps towards ending all conflicts over territory or resources, money and possessions. I may be partially responsible for all the conflicts I see or know of because I have the power to either worsen or improve them through my thought forms. I am not powerless, a feature that is attributed only to my ego. My power is infinite because I am one with everything. I no longer want my power to be dispersed by allowing other people's beliefs and opinions to rule over my life. From now on, I will rely on my own knowledge and understanding but I am open to learning from everyone I meet and every situation that presents itself to me.

To fulfill my desires easily and effortlessly, I only need to create a thought form of what I want. Mere intent is enough to start the ball of desire to roll. My intent makes me get up in the morning, move my body, eat a meal, play an instrument, drive a car from A to B, perhaps conceive a baby, or go to sleep. I can use the same power of intent to fulfill all my desires, as long as they are in accord with the laws of nature.

To fulfill all my desires I only need to desire and let go and trust that my extended self – the Force of the Universe – takes care of the details. *Should a desire not become fulfilled then I know that I have either projected a doubt which is an equally powerful thought form as the desire, or that the desire does not harmonize with the greater purpose of my life or my surroundings. In that case, I will not blame others for my own failure or misfortune. I understand that doubting jeopardizes the fulfillment of my desires. "Luck" comes automatically when I have no doubt about my own* *power to achieve what I want and what I need. Unfulfilled desires may indicate that my motives are purely ego-centered and may have a detrimental effect on the happiness and well-being of others. This helps me to understand that only desires that spring from the heart are worthy of becoming fulfilled for they increase my ability to love myself and this world. There is no motivation on behalf of the spiritual universe to support desires that do not serve the whole. Verbalizing my intents and actually hearing me say them are a good method to dispel doubts and increase the power of desiring.*

CONCLUSION

I wish to conclude this chapter with "A Simple Prayer" by St. Francis of Assisi. It has the ability to realign the ego-self with the Higher Self and produce those thought forms that generate love and happiness while preventing harmful thought forms from arising. The prayer represents some of the most powerful thought forms we can generate and it contains the contents of the Twelve Gateways to Create Heaven on Earth in a nutshell. Once it has "settled" in your mental body, it can serve you as personal guide for your every day living.

A Simple Prayer
By St. Francis of Assisi

O Lord make me an instrument of Thy peace;
Where there is hatred, let me bring love,
Where there is resentment, let me bring forgiveness,
Were there is discord, let me bring unity,
Where there is doubt, let me bring faith,
Where there is error, let me bring truth,
Where there is despair, let me bring happiness,
Where there is sadness, let me bring joy.
Where there is darkness, let me bring light.
O Master grant that I may desire:
To console rather than to be consoled.
To understand rather than to be understood.
To love rather than to be loved.
Because
It is in giving that we receive;
In forgiving that we receive forgiveness;
In dying that we rise to eternal life.

ABOUT THE AUTHOR

Andreas Moritz is a medical intuitive, a practitioner of Ayurveda, Iridology, Shiatsu and Vibrational Medicine, a writer and artist. Born in Southwest Germany in 1954, Andreas had to deal with several severe illnesses from an early age, which compelled him to study diet, nutrition and various methods of natural healing while still a child.

By the age of 20, Andreas had completed his training in Iridology – the diagnostic science of eye interpretation – and Dietetics. In 1981, he began studying Ayurvedic Medicine in India and completed his training as a qualified practitioner of Ayurveda in New Zealand in 1991. Rather than being satisfied with merely treating the symptoms of illness, Andreas has dedicated his life's work to understanding and treating the root causes of illness. Because of this holistic approach, he has had astounding success with cases of terminal disease where conventional methods of healing proved futile.

Since 1988, he has been practicing the Japanese healing art of Shiatsu, which has given him profound insights into the energy system of the body. In addition, he devoted eight years of active research into consciousness and its important role in the field of mind/body medicine.

Andreas Moritz is the author of *The Amazing Liver & Gallbladder Flush, Timeless Secrets of Health and Rejuvenation, Lifting the Veil of Duality, Cancer is Not a Disease, It's Time to Come Alive,* and *The Art of Self-Healing* (mid-2006).

During his extensive travels throughout the world, he has consulted with heads of state and members of government in Europe, Asia, and Africa, and has lectured widely on the subject of health, mind/body medicine and spirituality. His popular *Timeless Secrets of Health and Rejuvenation* workshops assist people in taking responsibility for their own health and well-being. Andreas runs a free forum "Ask Andreas Moritz" on the popular health website Curezone.com (5 million readers and increasing).

After taking up residency in the United States in 1998, Andreas has been involved in developing a new innovative system of healing – *Ener-Chi Art* – which targets the root causes of many chronic illnesses. Ener-Chi Art consists of a series of light ray-encoded oil paintings that can instantly restore vital energy flow (Chi) in the organs and systems of the body.

Andreas is also the founder of *Sacred Santèmony – Divine Chanting for Every Occasion,* a powerful system of specially generated sound frequencies that can transform deep-seated fears, allergies, traumas and mental/emotional blocks into useful opportunities of growth and inspiration within a matter of moments. Andreas's latest system "Art of Self-Healing" (as Book/CD or DVD), to be released during 2006, is comprised of his Ener-chi Art and specific Sacred Santémony sounds.

Other Books. Products
and Services by the Author

The Amazing Liver & Gallbladder Flush
A Powerful Do-It-Yourself Tool to Optimize
Your Health and Well-Being

In this revised edition of his best-selling book, *The Amazing Liver Cleanse,* Andreas Moritz addresses the most common but rarely recognized cause of illness – gallstones congesting the liver. Twenty million Americans suffer from attacks of gallstones every year. In many cases, treatment merely consists of removing the gallbladder, at the cost of $5 billion a year. But this purely symptom-oriented approach does not eliminate the cause of the illness, and in many cases, sets the stage for even more serious conditions. Most adults living in the industrialized world, and especially those suffering a chronic illness such as heart disease, arthritis, MS, cancer, or diabetes, have hundreds if not thousands of gallstones (mainly clumps of hardened bile) blocking the bile ducts of their liver.

This book provides a thorough understanding of what causes gallstones in the liver and gallbladder and why these stones can be held responsible for the most common diseases so prevalent in the world today. It provides the reader with the knowledge needed to recognize the stones and gives the necessary, do-it-yourself instructions to painlessly remove them in the comfort of one's home. It also gives practical guidelines on how to prevent new gallstones from being formed. The widespread success of *The Amazing Liver & Gallbladder Flush* is a testimony to the power and effectiveness of the cleanse itself. The liver cleanse has led to extraordinary improvements in health and wellness among thousands of people who have already given themselves the precious gift of a strong, clean, revitalized liver.

Timeless Secrets of Health and Rejuvenation –
Breakthrough Medicine for the 21ˢᵗ Century (488 pages)

This book meets the increasing demand for a clear and comprehensive guide that can help make people self-sufficient regarding their health and well-being. It answers some of the most pressing questions of our time: How does illness arise? Who heals, who doesn't? Are we destined to be sick? What causes aging? Is it reversible? What are the major causes of disease and how can we eliminate them?

Topics include: The placebo and the mind/body mystery; the laws of illness and health; the four most common risk factors of disease; digestive disorders and their effects on the rest of the body; wonders of our biological rhythms and how to restore them if disrupted; how to create a life of balance; why to choose a vegetarian diet; cleansing the liver, gallbladder, kidneys and colon; removing allergies; giving up smoking naturally; Using sunlight as medicine; the 'new' causes of heart disease, cancer and AIDS; and antibiotics, blood transfusions, ultrasounds scans, immunization programs under scrutiny.

Timeless Secrets of Health and Rejuvenation sheds light on all the major issues of health care and reveals that most medical treatments, including surgery, blood transfusions, pharmaceutical drugs, etc., are avoidable when certain key functions in the body are restored through the natural methods described in the book. The reader also learns about the potential dangers of medical diagnosis and treatment as well as the reasons vitamin supplements, 'health' foods, light products, 'wholesome' breakfast cereals, diet foods and diet programs may have contributed to the current health crisis rather than helped resolve it. The book includes a complete program of health care, which is primarily based on the ancient medical system of Ayurveda and the vast amount of experience Andreas Moritz has gained in the field of health during the past 30 years.

Lifting the Veil of Duality –
Your Guide to Living without Judgment

"Do you know that there is a place inside you – hidden beneath the appearance of thoughts, feelings and emotions – that does not know the difference between good and evil, right and wrong, light and dark? From this place, you naturally embrace the opposite values of life as *One*. In this sacred place you are at peace with yourself and at peace with your world." *Andreas Moritz*

In *Lifting the Veil of Duality,* Andreas Moritz poignantly exposes the illusion of duality. He outlines a simple way to remove every limitation that you have imposed upon yourself during the course of living duality. You will be prompted to see yourself and the world through a new lens – the lens of clarity, discernment and non-judgment. And you will find out that mistakes, accidents, coincidences, negativity, deception, injustice, wars, crime and terrorism all have a deeper purpose and meaning in the larger scheme of things. So naturally, much of what you will read may conflict with the beliefs you currently hold. Yet you are not asked to change your beliefs or opinions. Instead, you are asked to have *an open mind,* for only an open mind can enjoy freedom from judgment.

Our personal views and worldviews are currently challenged by a crisis of identity. Some are being shattered altogether. The collapse of our current World Order forces humanity to deal with the most basic issues of existence. You can no longer avoid taking responsibility for the things that happen to you. When you *do* accept responsibility, you also empower and heal yourself.

Lifting the Veil of Duality shows you how you create or subdue your ability to fulfill your desires. Furthermore, you will find intriguing explanations about the mystery of time, the truth and illusion of reincarnation, the misleading value of prayer, what makes relationships work and why so often they don't. Find out why injustice is an illusion that has managed to haunt us throughout the ages. Learn about our original separation from the Source of life and what this means with regard to the current waves of instability and fear so many of us are experiencing.

Discover how to identify the angels living amongst us and why we all have light-bodies. You will have the opportunity to find the ultimate

God within you and discover why a God seen as separate from yourself keeps you from being in your Divine Power and happiness. In addition, you can find out how to heal yourself at a moment's notice. Read all about the "New Medicine" and the destiny of the old medicine, the old economy, the old religion and the old world.

Cancer is Not a Disease!
Discover the Hidden Purpose of Cancer, Heal its Underlying Causes, and Let Your Body Take Care of the Rest

This latest book by Andreas Moritz may rock or even dismantle the very foundation of your beliefs about the body, health and healing. It offers the open-minded reader concerned about cancer a radically different understanding of what cancer really is. According to Andreas Moritz, cancer is a desperate and final attempt by the body to stay alive for as long as circumstances permit – circumstances that are, in fact, in your control.

Today's conventional approaches of killing, cutting or burning cancerous cells offer a mere 7% "success" rate for cancer remission, and the majority of the few survivors are "cured" for just a period of five years or less. In this book, you will discover what actually causes cancer and why it is so important to heal the whole person, not just the symptoms of cancer. You will also learn that cancer occurs only after all other defense mechanisms in the body have failed, for obvious reasons. A malignant tumor is not a vicious monster that is out to kill us in retaliation for our sins or abuse of our body. As you will find out, cancer does not attempt to kill the body; to the contrary, it tries to save it. However, unless we change our perception of what cancer really is, it will continue to threaten the life of one out of every two people. This book opens a door to those who wish to become whole again, in body, mind and spirit.

Topics of the book include:
- Reasons that coerce the body to develop cancer cells
- How to identify and remove the causes of cancer
- Why most cancers disappear by themselves, without medical intervention

- Why radiation, chemotherapy and surgery never cure cancer
- Why some people survive cancer *despite* undergoing dangerously radical treatments
- The roles of fear, frustration, low self-worth and repressed anger in the origination of cancer
- How to turn self-destructive emotions into energies that promote health and vitality
- Spiritual lessons behind cancer

Art of Self-Healing
Instantly Access The Power
To Heal Your Body, Mind and Emotions!
(To be released mid-2006)

At this time of great challenge and confusion in all areas of life – individual, social, national and international – we are also blessed with powerful solutions to our most pressing problems. Something we least expected, art and sound are now emerging to become the leading healing methods of our time.

Art of Self-Healing by bestselling author and health practitioner, Andreas Moritz, is a unique approach that gives a person instant access to his/her own healing powers. The approach consists of a series of 32 light-ray-imbued pictures (Ener-Chi Art) created by the author, and specific healing sounds (Sacred Santémony) that he has recorded on CD for the purpose of removing any obstacles to healing one's body and mind and emotions. The supplied CD is synchronized with viewing the pictures for about half a minute each.

All books are available as paperback copies and electronic books through the Ener-Chi Wellness Center.
Website: http://www.ener-chi.com
Email: andmor@ener-chi.com
Phone: (864) 848 6410 Evoice: (615) 676-9961

Sacred Santémony – for Emotional Healing

Sacred Santémony is a unique healing system that uses sounds from specific words to balance deep emotional/spiritual imbalances. The powerful words produced in Sacred Santémony are made from whole-brain use of the letters of the *ancient language* – language that is comprised of the basic sounds that underlie and bring forth all physical manifestation. The letters of the ancient language vibrate at a much higher level than our modern languages, and when combined to form whole words, they generate feelings of peace and harmony (Santémony) to calm the storms of unrest, violence and turmoil, both internal and external.

In April 2002, I spontaneously began to chant sounds that are meant to improve certain health conditions. These sounds resembled chants by Native Americans, Tibetan monks, Vedic pundits (Sanskrit) and languages from other star systems (not known on planet Earth). Within two weeks, I was able to bring forth sounds that would instantly remove emotional blocks and resistance or aversion to certain situations and people, foods, chemicals, thought forms, beliefs, etc. The following are but a few examples of what Sacred Santémony is able to assist you with:

- Reducing or removing fear that is related to death, disease, the body, foods, harmful chemicals, parents and other people, lack of abundance, impoverishment, phobias, environmental threats, the future and the past, unstable economic trends, political unrest, etc.

- Clearing or reducing a recent or current hurt, disappointment or anger resulting from past emotional trauma or negative experiences in life.

- Cleansing of the *Akashic Records* (a recording of all experiences the soul has gathered throughout all life streams) from persistent fearful elements, including the idea and concept that we are separate from and not one with Spirit, God or our Higher Self.

- Setting the preconditions for you to resolve your karmic issues not through pain and suffering, but through creativity and joy.

229

- Improving or clearing up allergies and intolerances to foods, chemical substances, pesticides, herbicides, air pollutants, radiation, medical drugs, pharmaceutical byproducts, etc.
- Undoing the psycho-emotional root causes of any chronic illness, including cancer, heart disease, MS, diabetes, arthritis, brain disorders, depression, etc.
- Resolving other difficulties or barriers in life by "converting" them into the useful blessings that they really are.

To arrange for a personal Sacred Santémony session with Andreas Moritz, please follow the same directions as given for Telephone Consultations.
(As per 2005, the fee for a half hour is $85)

Ener-Chi Art

Andreas Moritz has developed a new system of healing and rejuvenation designed to restore the basic life energy (Chi) of an organ or a system in the body within a matter of seconds. Simultaneously, it also helps balance the emotional causes of illness.

Eastern approaches to healing, such as Acupuncture and Shiatsu, are intended to enhance well-being by stimulating and balancing the flow of Chi to the various organs and systems of the body. In a similar manner, the energetics of Ener-Chi Art is designed to restore a balanced flow of Chi throughout the body.

According to most ancient systems of health and healing, the balanced flow of Chi is the key determinant for a healthy body and mind. When Chi flows through the body unhindered, health and vitality are maintained. By contrast, if the flow of Chi is disrupted or reduced, health and vitality tend to decline.

A person can determine the degree to which the flow of Chi is balanced in the body's organs and systems by using a simple muscle testing procedure. To reveal the effectiveness of Ener-Chi Art, it is important to apply this test both before and after viewing each Ener-Chi Art picture.

To allow for easy application of this system, Andreas has created a number of healing paintings that have been "activated" through a unique procedure that imbues each work of art with specific color rays (derived from the higher dimensions). To receive the full benefit of an Ener-Chi Art picture all that is necessary is to look at it for less than a minute. During this time, the flow of Chi within the organ or system becomes fully restored. When applied to all the organs and systems of the body, Ener-Chi Art sets the precondition for the whole body to heal and rejuvenate itself.

Ener-Chi Ionized Stones

Ener-Chi Ionized Stones are stones and crystals that have been energized, activated, and imbued with life force through a special activation process introduced by Andreas Moritz – the founder of Ener-Chi Art.

Stone ionization has not been attempted before because stones and rocks have rarely been considered useful in the field of healing. Yet, stones have the inherent power to hold and release vast amounts of information and energy. Once ionized, they exert a balancing influence on everything with which they come into contact. The ionization of stones may be one of our keys to survival in a world that is experiencing high-level pollution and destruction of its eco-balancing systems.

In the early evolutionary stages of Earth, every particle of matter within the mantle of the planet contained within it the blueprint of the entire planet, just as every cell of our body contains within its DNA structure the blueprint of our entire body. The blueprint information within every particle of matter is still there – it has simply fallen into a dormant state. The ionization process "reawakens" this original blueprint information, and enables the associated energies to be released. In this sense, Ener-Chi Ionized Stones are alive and conscious, and are able to energize, purify and balance any natural substance with which they come into contact.

By placing an Ionized Stone next to a glass of water or plate of food, the water or food becomes energized, thereby increasing digestibility and nutrient absorption. Ionized stones can also be used effectively in conjunction with Ener-Chi Art – simply place an Ionized Stone on the corresponding area of the body while viewing an Ener-Chi Art picture. For more potential uses please check out the web site given below.

Telephone Consultations

For a Personal Telephone Consultation with Andreas Moritz, please

1. Call or send an email with your name, phone number, address, digital picture (if you have one) of your face and any other relevant info to:
E-mail: andmor@ener-chi.com
Telephone: (864) 848-6410 **Evoice:** (615) 676-9961 (USA)

2. Set up an appointment for the length of time you choose to spend with him. A comprehensive consultation lasts 2 hours or more. Shorter consultations deal with all the questions you may have and the information that is relevant to your specific health issue(s).

Fees (2005): $85 for 1/2 hour, $170 for one hour, $255 for 1 1/2 hours, and $340 for 2 hours

Note: Shorter consultations deal with all the questions you may have and the information that is relevant to your specific health issue(s). For a comprehensive consultation, (if you have a digital camera) please take a snapshot of your face (preferably without makeup) and email it to Andreas before your appointment with him. This can greatly assist Andreas in assisting you in your quest for better health.

To order Ener-chi Art pictures, Ionized Stones,
And other products
please contact:
Eener-Chi Wellness Center, LLC
Web Site: http://www.ener-chi.com
E-mail: andmor@ener-chi.com

Phone: or (864) 848-6410 **E-voice**: (615) 676-9961 (USA)

Lightning Source UK Ltd.
Milton Keynes UK
04 January 2010

148143UK00002B/68/A